CW01494346

Bernhard Reitsma masterfully frames questio the church and Islam in a biblical theology of of God. Through his biblical theological mo as well as missiological questions. His treatment of Israel and the land – both biblical and political – and of contextualization at the nexus of theology and missiology, as well as his treatment of the question of religious persecution and suffering, all benefit from his thoroughly biblical approach in a way that is creative, innovative, and insightful. His decidedly and comprehensively biblical approach gives a powerful thrust to his argument that Christians and Muslims share more commonalities than differences, and that this shared space, if approached by the church with humility, can be the foundation of constructive relations that will allow them to live and partner together in mutual witness for the common good of their shared societies everywhere.

Martin Accad, PhD
Director, Institute of Middle East Studies
Chief Academic Officer, Arab Baptist Theological Seminary, Beirut, Lebanon
Associate Professor of Islamic Studies,
ABTS and Fuller Theological Seminary, Pasadena, California, USA

This volume nurtures tolerance and dialogue between religions in the Middle East. Bernhard Reitsma offers us a contextualized and enlightening reading of burning issues such as election, revelation, and mission as they are understood in ancient and contemporary Christianity and Islam. Based on a solid interpretive work of the Bible, *Vulnerable Love* offers theological insight in search of a plausible practical coexistence between both religions – in the Middle East, in Europe and the entire world. Mercy and forgiveness are two foundational elements in Christ's message, and Reitsma proposes them as interpretive keys to understand religion in this postcolonial era and to envisage a world where religions not only practice dialogue with engagement but also work together to build peace among the nations.

Daniel Alberto Ayuch, PhD
Professor of New Testament,
St. John of Damascus Institute of Theology,
University of Balamand, Tripoli, Lebanon

Here is a thoroughly biblical and theological approach to Christian engagement with Muslims and Islam. Having lived and worked in the Netherlands and Lebanon, Reitsma has shared very honestly how, as a Christian theologian, he has wrestled for many years with all the vital questions about Christian approaches to Islam.

Rev Colin Chapman
Former Lecturer in Islamic Studies,
Near East School of Theology, Beirut, Lebanon
Visiting Lecturer, Arab Baptist Theological Seminary, Beirut, Lebanon

Springing from his own experience of living for a number of years in the highly volatile situation of the Middle East, Bernhard Reitsma engages courageously with the always problematic challenge of relating his Christian convictions to the many questions raised by the history and present realities of Islam. Although this is his main purpose, what shines throughout the book is his call to the Christian community to rediscover its true nature and mission in the light of the crucified Messiah, by which it is named. The book covers much ground, using both his own personal knowledge of Islam and a wide variety of sources. I commend it as a book that brings many new, penetrating dimensions into the long, turbulent relationship between the two faiths. There is much to learn here.

Rev J. Andrew Kirk, PhD
Former Director, Centre for Missiology and World Christianity,
University of Birmingham, UK

Bernhard Reitsma reminds us that far more than one billion Muslims cannot be put in one box, but that we need a contextual approach with a lot of willingness to invest time to study their situation and our own history. Between strictly distancing oneself from Muslims on the one side, and white-washing the situation on the other side, he calls for a Christ-like "merciful humanity." His approach has been lived out in Muslim countries and practices over decades and combines a lot of biblical insights with practical experience. I hope Reitsma finds many followers!

Bishop Thomas Schirrmacher, PhD
Professor, Sociology of Religion,
University of the West in Timisoara, Romania
Associate Secretary General, Theological Concerns, World Evangelical Alliance

Amid the so-called *clash of civilizations* that all too often pits Christianity against Islam, Bernhard Reitsma writes as one rooted in historical orthodoxy but open to reimagining contemporary Christian approaches to Muslims. His posture of vulnerable love is not borne out of a politically correct toleration but flows forth from a biblically grounded understanding of the church as part of the wider people of God that points beyond the present status quo to the divine salvation that is coming. Evangelical Christians, not only in North America where such labels are fraught and contentious, but also those around the world who trust the Langham imprint, will benefit from this prophetic call to engage the diversity of Muslims everywhere with the gracious and expansive hospitality of Triune love.

Amos Yong, PhD
Professor of Theology and Mission,
Dean, School of Theology and School of Intercultural Studies,
Fuller Theological Seminary, Pasadena, California, USA

Vulnerable Love

Langham

GLOBAL LIBRARY

Vulnerable Love

Islam, the Church and the Triune God

Bernhard J. G. Reitsma

© 2020 Bernhard J. G. Reitsma

Published 2020 by Langham Global Library
An imprint of Langham Publishing
www.langhampublishing.org

Langham Publishing and its imprints are a ministry of Langham Partnership

Langham Partnership
PO Box 296, Carlisle, Cumbria, CA3 9WZ, UK
www.langham.org

ISBNs:
978-1-83973-000-9 Print
978-1-83973-001-6 ePub
978-1-83973-002-3 Mobi
978-1-83973-003-0 PDF

Bernhard J. G. Reitsma has asserted his right under the Copyright, Designs and Patents Act, 1988 to be identified as the Author of this work.

All rights reserved. No part of this publication may be reproduced, stored in a retrieval system or transmitted, in any form or by any means, electronic, mechanical, photocopying, recording or otherwise, without the prior written permission of the publisher or the Copyright Licensing Agency.

Requests to reuse content from Langham Publishing are processed through PLSclear. Please visit www.plsclear.com to complete your request.

Unless otherwise stated, Scripture quotations are from The Holy Bible, English Standard Version˚ (ESV˚), copyright © 2001 by Crossway, a publishing ministry of Good News Publishers. Used by permission. All rights reserved.

Scripture quotations marked (NASB) taken from the New American Standard Bible°, Copyright © 1960, 1962, 1963, 1968, 1971, 1972, 1973, 1975, 1977, 1995 by The Lockman Foundation. Used by permission.

Scripture quotations marked (CEV) are from the Contemporary English Version. Copyright © 1991, 1992, 1995 by American Bible Society. Used by Permission.

Scripture quotations marked (NIV) are taken from the Holy Bible, New International Version°, NIV°. Copyright © 1973, 1978, 1984, 2011 by Biblica, Inc.™ Used by permission of Zondervan.

British Library Cataloguing-in-Publication Data
A catalogue record for this book is available from the British Library

ISBN: 978-1-83973-000-9

Cover & Book Design: projectluz.com

Langham Partnership actively supports theological dialogue and an author's right to publish but does not necessarily endorse the views and opinions set forth here or in works referenced within this publication, nor can we guarantee technical and grammatical correctness. Langham Partnership does not accept any responsibility or liability to persons or property as a consequence of the reading, use or interpretation of its published content.

Contents

Foreword

This is an important book related to the relationships between Christians and Muslims today. We know that Islam and Christianity represent two of the largest religious perspectives in the world. In this new century, on every continent it is imperative that we learn to understand each other and live together in positive ways that are deeper than merely tolerating each other. If we want to avoid violence and conflict, Christians and Muslims need to listen to, and learn from, one another. At the same time, the Christian community is shaped around the confession that God has revealed himself in Jesus Christ. So, what is the calling of the church in relation to Islam?

This is a complex topic. There is huge internal diversity within both Muslim and Christian viewpoints not only in terms of theory and theology but also in terms of the lived-out practices of folk Islam and folk Christianity. In this book, my friend and colleague Professor Bernhard Reitsma has done a superb job of showing us pathways through the complexity, summarizing foundational issues that Christians face in conversation with our Muslim neighbors. He challenges us to self-examination as an essential step in the process if Christians are to experience fruitful dialogue with Muslims.

An important aspect of Muslim-Christian conversation involves challenging ourselves as Christians to examine our own theology, based on what we can learn from Islam. For example, Islam is radically monotheist. Christians claim to be. Reitsma draws from Christian trinitarian theology as he affirms a Christian understanding of the one true God. He does this creatively and constructively by beginning the conversation with discussions about creation. By beginning with creation rather than issues of soteriology, brother Bernhard offers a way for Christians and Muslims to consider their common humanity, their common understanding of the nature of God and God's creation, and their common recognition that something has gone wrong in creation. But Reitsma emphasizes that it is in Christ alone, and specifically in his death and resurrection, that God's original intention for the world has been restored.

Professor Reitsma's work has helped and inspired me. He builds on a line of thought that one can trace from Samuel Zwemer through Hendrik Kraemer, Johannes Verkuyl, Kenneth Cragg, David Bosch, and Dudley Woodberry. An essential element of that tradition is a challenge to Christians to examine the way we understand and live out being the church. As Christians called to converse in Christlike ways with Muslims today, it is important that we take to heart Jesus's words:

> Do not judge, so that you may not be judged. For with the judgement you make you will be judged, and the measure you give will be the measure you get. Why do you see the speck in your neighbor's eye, but do not notice the log in your own eye? . . . You hypocrite, first take the log out of your own eye, and then you will see clearly to take the speck out of your neighbor's eye. (Matt 7:1–5 NRSV)

Christians are called to be clear and forthright – transparent – about our gospel proclamation in word and deed, and yet we are also called to demonstrate kindness, love, compassion, respect, and grace in our conversations with Islam and Muslims.

Brother Reitsma is committed to expressing love, concern, and compassion for the followers of Islam. This does not mean that he is unwilling to disagree. He remains solidly grounded on the Bible, clear in his understanding of the gospel of grace in Jesus Christ, and forthright in expressing where he disagrees with Islamic thought. Yet, his attitude toward Islam and Muslims is always grace-filled, polite, humble, respectful, and loving. This work arose from Dr Reitsma's own searching question: "What does the coming of God in Jesus Christ through the Holy Spirit mean for the encounter between Christians and Muslims?" In this book, fruit of his reflection over many years, brother Bernhard "offers a biblical-theological framework that can stimulate Christians in very different situations to think about their attitude towards Muslims" (p. xvii). The self-giving unconditional love of Christ on the cross is the basic foundation for his call to *Vulnerable Love*.

Professor Reitsma has included a helpful discussion concerning gospel contextualization as it incarnates in a variety of cultures. In *Transforming Mission Theology*, I outlined five broad paradigms or perspectives of contextualization: communication, indigenization, translatability, local theologies, and epistemology. I would place this work in the fifth paradigm of contextualization that I called epistemology. In this paradigm, Christians are challenged to rethink and reconsider their own understanding of God, drawing from what they have learned in their new context: "An epistemological approach emphasizes the sense that in each new context, in each new cultural setting, followers of Jesus Christ have an opportunity to learn something about God they had not previously known. Christian knowledge about God is seen as cumulative, enhanced, deepened, broadened and expanded as the gospel takes new shape in each new culture."[1] Professor Reitsma challenges us to reread the Bible with care and rethink our understanding of God in Jesus Christ as the Holy Spirit enables us.

It is important for Christians to remember that our witness in word and deed has almost always been carried out by the Christian church in religiously plural contexts. This fact is as true today as it was in the first century. In the West, for several centuries, we forgot this element of Christian witness. But in today's contexts everywhere in the world Christian witness happens in the midst of a multiplicity of competing religious viewpoints, including in the Netherlands, where this book was first published in Dutch. Happily, with access to this English translation, we can all be taught, helped, and challenged by Dr Reitsma's writing.

This book is written for Christians. It also offers creative pathways for Christians and Muslims to think, listen, and talk together. This work is not only written for Christian cross-cultural missionaries, mission executives, or mission mobilizers. This book is essential reading for all pastors, church leaders, and members of Christian churches who are willing to consider carefully how they may "give an answer to everyone who asks you to give the reason for the hope that you have" and to do so "with gentleness and respect" (1 Pet 3:15 NIV). This work will make an excellent resource for adult Bible study groups in local churches as well as in university and seminary courses in Christian theology.

Rev Charles E. Van Engen, PhD
Holland, Michigan, USA
Spring 2020

---

1. Charles Van Engen, *Transforming Mission Theology* (Littleton, CO: WCL, 2017), 163.

Preface

In 1998 I traveled with my wife and two children to the Middle East. I was going to be teaching at the Near East School of Theology in Beirut and walking alongside the students of Lebanon InterVarsity Fellowship, a student movement. My wife did social work and was engaged in the medical field. We went with a lot of enthusiasm but also some trepidation. What were we going to experience in a context where Muslims are in the majority? Would we be able to share what was important to us or would they not be open to it? Isn't Islam unfavorable towards Christians? We were prepared to experience culture shock, had studied Islam somewhat, and had finished a few months of language-learning. Still, we knew very little about life in the Middle East.

Our time in Lebanon changed our lives. It was an intense as well as enriching experience to interact with Christians who sought to stand tall in an ocean of Muslims. What I experienced was not at all what I had expected. Let me mention three things that struck me during that time that still preoccupy my mind to this day.

To start, I was confronted with a big tension. Muslims treated me with more respect in the Middle East than I had ever experienced by people in the West. Whether it was going to the bakery to buy bread, waiting for hours on a visa, or visiting people in a refugee camp, the Muslims that I encountered showed admiration for people who believed in God. The fact that I was a theologian and pastor intensified this. However, this respectful treatment also had another side. I met countless local Christians who were treated with far less dignity. Some of them were discriminated against, bullied, or persecuted. Christians with a Muslim background, especially, experienced a lot of difficulties. This strange contradiction confused me and has continued to consume me. Apparently, Islam is not as simple to explain as I thought when I left the Netherlands.

The second thing that struck me was the fact that there was a lack of missionary interest among local Christian fellowships. Many Christians lived in worry and fear even before ISIS came onto the scene. They wondered if there would be a future for them in the Middle East. The Christian communities were shrinking as they left the region for economic and political reasons. The pressure from extremist Muslims hurried that process. The only mission Christians were on was one of "survival." They did not have any message for Muslims. They could no longer see that they were entrusted with a treasure, even though it was found in jars of clay (2 Cor 4:7). They would pull back in isolation, and Christ disappeared with them behind the doors of the church. This, too, consumes my mind and that of countless Christians in Islamic countries. What is the mission of the church among Muslims, and how do we keep the missionary calling alive?

The third thing that shocked me was the fact that Christianity is known as something negative among Muslims. I had never encountered that in this way. To me, the gospel is breathtaking. It is so wonderful that God would love this world and embrace it through Christ. Many Muslims have a different experience. To them, Christians are colonialists and crusaders, people with godless morals who are continuously seeking to undermine Islam: "You have to be careful with Christians." If you turn a "cross" upside down, it looks like a sword. It is a symbol of a history of oppression. Because of that, countless Muslims are hurt and hardened against the gospel. That really affected me. Christendom has veiled the gospel. People are no longer able to see who Christ is. They can no longer experience how great his grace and love are.

All this made me think and forced me to go back to the biblical basics in order to see what God's objective and calling is when I meet Muslims. I have had the privilege to read the Bible with Arab Christians and talk about their questions and concerns. Together we asked ourselves what our mission should be in the context of Islam. Additionally, I was constantly questioned about my own religious tradition and my roots in Western culture. Students were critical of "my" colonial history and of the lack of sensitivity of many mission organizations today. From armed crusades to missionary conquests, Arab Christians, too, have suffered due to Western Christendom.

Upon my return to the Netherlands, these questions continued to consume my mind. It was and is, however, not very easy to find biblical-theological answers. There is a lot of discussion about Islam and whether Muslims form a threat for Western society, but there is very little interest to dive deeper into the questions that the presence of Islam is asking. The debate is continuously fed with one-liners without any nuance. It would be wonderful if all answers could fit in a 280-character tweet. Thus, the Bible is often only used in a superficial way when dealing with these questions. We are much better at picking and choosing loose verses here and there than doing a thorough study of what the one God in Jesus Christ has to say through his Spirit. In the meantime, Christians in the West wrestle with the same questions in a secular, multireligious context as Christians in the Middle East. How do we survive, how do we continue to be witnesses of Christ when our numbers are decreasing? And how will things go if Islam's presence continues to increase? What will happen to us?

From that confusion, *my* confusion, this book was born. It is a representation of my thinking from the last few years as I've pushed the pause button for a moment. It is the kind of pausing moment that is meant to allow you to stop and reorient yourself. Where are we, how did we get here, and where do we need to go? Are we going in the right direction? The central question with this reorientation is: What does the coming of God in Jesus Christ through the Holy Spirit mean for the encounter between Christians and Muslims? This is not only important for Muslims – how will they hear of the gospel if the church of Christ is failing? – but it is equally important for the church. The encounter with Islam is a test case for the Christian church from which it needs to become evident whether or not we truly give representation of who God is in our walk and talk. Are we truly a reflection of God's great deeds in Christ and through his Spirit? Or have we received the grace of God in vain, and have we become a stumbling block for the gospel (2 Cor 6:1, 3)? The nature of the church is perhaps even more at risk in relation to Islam than it is in its confrontation with secularization. The conclusions are therefore relevant in every context where Islam is present both in the West and elsewhere for it concerns how the church relates to Islam, whether Islam is found in the majority or not.

This book offers a biblical-theological framework that can stimulate Christians in very different situations to think about their attitude towards Muslims. In that way, I hope to start a thorough study of the Bible regarding Islam and to find out what the gospel of Jesus Christ has to do with Muslims today. After an exploration of the questions, in part I, I will set out the framework that will form the basis for thinking along biblical-theological lines about the attitude of the church towards Islam. In part II, I will focus first on an interpretation of Islam in light of this biblical framework, and then, in part III, I will look at the nature of the church. Both the nature of Islam as well as that of the church will then determine how the church should relate to Islam as discussed in part IV. It is important to note that I use the term "God" in this book to denote both the God of Christianity and the God of Islam without drawing any conclusions about the identity and essence of God. Allah means "God" in Arabic, just like the terms "El" and "Elohim" in the Hebrew tradition. However, the question of how the God of the Bible and how God in the Islamic tradition relate to each other will definitely be discussed.

The primary focus of this book is on Christians who are concerned with the mission of the church in the world – those in the church and in higher education. The encounters with Muslims are part of my theological development, and this is reflected in my theologizing. I will only partly have a conversation with Islam, but I warmly encourage Muslims to read this book and start a dialogue about it. Also, if there are readers who up till now have had little interest in God, I hope that through this study they will discover something about God and God's purpose for this world and all of creation.

Diverse people have read and given their commentary on this text. They have helped me say what I had in mind in a more robust way. I thank Ad van der Dussen, Bert de Ruiter, Rik Lubbers, Rienk van Velzen, Anneke Verhoeven, Koos van Noppen, and all those that have been in discussion with me or have asked me questions and given feedback. The board of "Stichting Leerstoel: De kerk in de context van de islam" has made this research possible.[1] The hospitality that I experienced at the monastery of the Norbertines in Hierden was heartwarming. I often found an oasis of rest there that helped me order and write out my thoughts. I was always welcome.

It has been a great privilege to work with the team from Langham Publishers. It is an honor for me to have Langham publish this book and I pray that it will contribute to the mission of Langham to equip pastors and leaders with God's word and – in line with John Stott's vision – to raise up a new generation of biblical leaders for growth with depth in the global church. I am tremendously grateful for the publishing team at Langham who have definitely improved this edition. Whatever is imperfect in this book is on my account only.

Finally, I would like to thank my wife Heleen and my kids for their patience, their inspiration, their interest, and sometimes their impatience. This combination gave the push I needed to finish this book. I pray that they will continuously be touched by the vulnerable love of God in Jesus Christ and that they will share this love with every person that he brings to their path.

We are created to worship God with our lives, including through the books we write. It is therefore my longing that this book will also glorify him.

---

1. Foundation Chair: The church in the context of Islam.

Abbreviations

AB	Anchor Bible
BKAT	Biblischer Kommentar, Altes Testament
EI	*Encyclopedia of Islam*
EKKNT	Evangelisch-Katholischer Kommentar zum Neuen Testament
EMQ	*Evangelical Missions Quarterly*
ESV	English Standard Version
HThKNT	Herders Theologischer Kokmmentar zum Neuten Testament
IBMR	*International Bulletin of Mission Research*
KD	Karl Barth, *Kirliche Dogmatik*
LSJ	H. G. Liddell and R. Scott, *A Greek-English Lexicon: With a Revised Supplement*
NCB	New Century Bible
ND	Nederlands Dagblad
NICNT	New International Commentary on the New Testament
SBB	Stutgarter Biblische Beiträge
THAT	*Theologisches Handwörterbuch zum Alten Testament*
THKNT	Theologischer Handkommentar zum Neuen Testament
TWNT	*Theologisches Wörterbuch zum Neuen Testament*
WA	M. Luther, *Weimar Ausgaben,* 1883–1929
WUNT	Wissenschaftliche Untersuchungen zum Neuen Testament

1

Exploration

"Here, then, we have a missionary religion that would like to convert the world; and while the Christian church seems to be contracting in the West, Islam seems to be expanding."[1]

"The Christian Church is in a state of confusion as to the attitude she should adopt towards this other major world faith, seemingly sharing so much doctrine in common with Christianity and yet so very different in manifestation."[2]

1.1 Preface

Is there a Christian response to Islam? Volf suggests it is possible. His book *Allah* carries the subtitle "A Christian Response."[3] The diversity of Christian views of Islam (see below) seems to suggest otherwise. There is certainly a need for a Christian response to Islam. There is a lot of confusion and anxiety among Christians. Confusion, because Christians wonder how they should interpret the presence of Islam. They are often not sure what to expect of Islam in society today. They wonder if what Muslims believe is similar to Christianity or completely different. For example, do Muslims and Christians worship the same God or different gods? And isn't it true that the presence of Islam has a negative effect on the freedom of the church in society? These concerns are fed by extremist attacks in the name of "Islam," which have made the world feel unsafe since 9/11, and by the position of Christians in Muslim-majority countries. For example, it seems significant that in seven of the top-ten

---

1. Chapman, *Cross and Crescent*, 12.
2. Sookhdeo, *Islam*, 9.
3. Volf, *Allah*.

countries where Christians are persecuted, Muslims are in the majority.[4] The fate of Muslims who choose to follow Jesus Christ is especially precarious.[5] The question is if this is due to Islam itself or just a specific *type* of Islam. Christians, as well as Muslims, emphatically differ in opinion on this.

Inversely, it is equally true that Muslims today are worried about the aspirations of modern Christendom. The history of colonization and the missionary expansion of Christianity and Western culture are of great concern to many Muslims. The anxiety of many Christians towards Islam is mirrored by a similar anxiety many Muslims have towards Christianity. Isn't the Christian faith expansive by definition and thus a threat to Islam? Does the Christian West not inherently assume a crusader mentality?

The history of Christianity and Islam, however, also has a different face. Although it is easy to find dozens of examples where Christianity and Islam have clashed with each other, there are equally as many examples of Muslims and Christians living at peace with each other, seeking to learn from each other, and making positive contributions to society together.[6]

This ambivalent history somehow reflects what Muslims and Christians believe. On the one hand, Islam and Christianity have many things in common. For example, they share the belief in one God, in life after death, and in a final judgement where each person has to account for his or her life on earth to the Almighty God. The obedience to and belief in God impacts all facets of life for both. On the other hand, however, there are fundamental differences between Muslims and Christians. For example, they have different thoughts about the nature of the one true God, the way in which he reveals himself, what he expects of human beings, and how he intervenes for the restoration of his creation and the salvation of humankind. These beliefs, too, impact all facets of life.

This book is about the challenge Islam poses to the church. How should Christians and Christian communities respond to Islam? What does that have to do with the nature of the church? What does the ambivalent or paradoxical relationship between Muslims and Christians mean for the calling of the church in engaging Muslims?

---

4. See http://opendoorsanalytical.org/world-watch-list-documentation/. Password: "freedom." See chapter 9 below for more detailed discussion.

5. Meral, *No Place to Call Home.*

6. The memorandum of the Protestant Church in the Netherlands on Islam names a range of positive and negative examples that could easily be added onto. Reitsma, *Integrity and Respect: Islam Memorandum.* See also Koffeman and Reitsma, *Vervolgnota Integriteit en respect.*

There are many different approaches to the study of the relationship between the church and Islam: historical, political, psychological, etc. For this research, I chose the biblical-theological approach: can we draw some basic principles from the Bible for the Christian church that can help determine its attitude towards the Islamic community? To find the answer to this question there are at least three complicating factors: the many different Christian views on Islam, the unprecedented diversity of Islam, and the hermeneutical tension between the biblical tradition and a religion that emerged much later.

1.2 Christian Diversity

Christians give very different answers to how the church should relate to Islam. That is caused, in part, by context. Christians who form a minority in an Islamic country are naturally faced with a different set of questions compared to people in the West. However, it has a large part also to do with the great diversity of Christian traditions. Exclusivism, inclusivism, and pluralism are the most commonly referenced Christian views towards other religions.[7] Because I concern myself in this book with the theology of a Christian response to Islam and not just a *theologia religionum*, I will use another classification – namely, (1) the antithetical approach, (2) the synthetic approach, and (3) the contextual approach.[8] This is a generalized classification; each viewpoint contains a great amount of nuance, and the dividing line between these three approaches is fluid. Nonetheless, it helps us to address the most important issues.[9]

1.2.1 The Antithetical Approach

This view emphasizes the contrast between Islam and Christianity. The key point here is the fact that Islam rejects the core creed of the Christian church, namely that God became man in Jesus Christ. For Muslims, God is not triune, and Christ is not seen as a savior who died on the cross to reconcile the world

---

7. See Kärkkäinen, *Introduction*, 23–25.

8. This is close to the distinction that Bijlefeld makes with respect to the radical rejection and positive appreciation of Islam. See Bijlefeld, *Islam*, chs. 4–5, who chooses a different approach. Kärkkäinen, *Introduction*, 25–26, chooses a grouping according to the lines of exclusivism, inclusivism, and pluralism, but complements it with ecclesiocentrism, christocentrism, and theocentrism/"reality"-centrism.

9. For an extended overview of the Christian views of Islam, see among others: Bijlefeld, *Islam*; Bennett, *Understanding Christian-Muslim Relations*; Poorthuis and Salemink, *Van harem tot fitna*; Tolan, *Medieval Christian Perceptions*; Zebiri, *Muslims and Christians*.

to God. Commonalities between Christianity and Islam are not denied in this approach, but the conviction that both religions are principally and fundamentally opposite to each other dominates. Islam is a "false" or even "anti-Christian" religion and is no way of salvation.

The origin of Islam is sought in human beings. Because of that, it is seen as a variation of paganism: human beings have made an idol of God (i.e. Isa 44:14–17).[10] Islam is a human aberration of the true faith and therefore fits a "heresy" or "cult" categorization.[11] In extreme versions of this antithetical approach, Islam is explicitly linked to the work of the antichrist or the evil one and is seen as the "stronghold of the devil."[12] According to Kraemer, Islam originated with Satan, although he does not imply that Islam as a religion is itself satanic.[13] For others, however, this is the case, and the origination qualifies the essence of Islam.[14] Muhammad is a false prophet who was inspired by Satan.[15]

The logical consequence of the antithetical approach is that Islam should be combatted. Sometimes this has taken a very literal form as a political or even military battle, like the Crusades, when cross and sword were bound together. Other times, the focus was more on "spiritual battle," like with prayer, fasting, and humbling one's self. This view of Islam as a "spiritual power" is prominent in pentecostal and charismatic circles.[16] At times the connection is made with "end-time prophecies" found in apocalyptical literature in which

---

10. See Bijlefeld, *Islam*, 64, which refers to A. T. van Leeuwen, "Islam en Jodendom," *Wending* 11 (1956-1957), 288.

11. According to John of Damascus, *De Haeresibus*, ch. 100, cited in Damascenus and Abū Qurra, *De eerste christelijke polemiek met de islam*, 31. It still is an antithetical approach. See also Petrus Venerabilis in Bijlefeld, *Islam*, 83. Bijlefeld also refers to Zwemer who speaks of a corporate sin against the Holy Spirit, Bijlefeld, 70. Verkuyl, *Inleiding*, 479, also mentions the influence of human responding and projecting, seeking and tasting, as one of the aspects of Islam.

12. Martin Luther is an example of this perspective. Initially, the antichrist and Satan were distinguished from each other, but especially in the seventeenth century, the two characterizations get used interchangeably more and more. See Bijlefeld, *Islam*, 52, 56–58.

13. Kraemer, *De islam als godsdienstig en als zendingsprobleem*, 10.

14. Bijlefeld, *Islam*, 58, 62.

15. Ricoldo da Monte Croce (d. 1320), for example, typifies Muhammad as "the instrument Satan used to spread Satanic temptation throughout the world." Bijlefeld, *Islam*, 49.

16. Cimino, "No God in Common," 168.

Israel also plays a crucial role. Islam is seen as the great opposer and threat to the people of God.[17]

It is clear from this approach that the God of Christianity and the God of Islam have very little in common.[18] Some identify Allah in Islam with the pre-Islamic moon god. For others, the God of Islam is Satan himself.[19] The Qur'an will not get much appreciation. The book is argued to have been concocted from the fantasies of Muhammad or inspired by the evil one or both.[20]

The antithetical approach offers little room for Christian communities to treat Muslims in a positive way. The emphasis is more on the fact that one needs to turn away from the threat of Islamic peril than on sharing the love of Christ. The uniqueness of Christ as Son of God and Savior takes centerstage. The primary mission of the church is to conquer the temptation of Islam.

1.2.2 The Synthetic Approach

The synthetic approach seeks to find the connection between Christianity and Islam. The apparent differences between both religions are of course not denied, but they are subordinate to the similarities and do not take away from the commonalities in any substantial way. Connectedness takes priority. With this, the exclusivity of both Christianity and Islam is discarded. Both religions contain ways to salvation. The God of Christianity is deep down the same as the God of Islam. The prophet Muhammad is recognized as a prophet as he

---

17. Cimino refers, among others, to Lindsey's *Everlasting Hatred*, Hitchcock's *Coming Islamic Invasion*, and Jeffrey's *War on Terror*. Cimino, "No God in Common," 167. One specific aspect of these "spiritual warfare" theories is the idea that P. Wagner introduced and conceptualized, which is that there are "spirits" and "powers" that have control over a certain region, group of people, or authorities. Regions where Islam is dominant could be the areas where specific demonic and satanic powers are dominant. As Wagner has stated, "one billion Muslims worship a high-ranking demon, who has gone by the name of 'Allah' since long before Mohammed was born." Cited in Cimino, "No God in Common," 168.

18. Cimino, 168.

19. Luther has said, for example – as kind of an afterthought – that the God of the Turks is none other than the devil himself, quoted in Bijlefeld, *Islam*, 50; Luther, *WA* 30 II, 116. The question here is whether Luther meant the same thing in his time as how we interpret this today, namely through the lens of spiritual warfare that is influenced by demons. My impression is that Luther was speaking in more of a general theological way, in light of his strong emphasis on the centrality of Christ. For him, anyone who denies or rejects the justification through faith in Christ and grace alone was the Satan-inspired antichrist. That's why he put the Roman Catholic Pope, the Jews, and also "the Turks" (Muslims) in that category.

20. Revisionism – which is, by the way, not Christian but pretends to be a neutral academic view – does not discard the fact that the Qur'an could have been a product of a much later time. See Van Koningsveld, *Revisionisme en Moderne Islamitische Theologie*, who views it as an academic fallacy. For an overview, see Mulder and Milo, *De omstreden bronnen van de islam*.

has experienced and passed on something from God.[21] That does not mean that Muhammad was always entirely right; he is not a *Christian* prophet. The Qur'an, in this view, is a "book from God," meaning that the reader is "in some way confronted with the Word of God."[22] The Qur'an, too, is not always right. Eventually it is about the fact that all religions contain some truth and follow parallel roads to God.[23] Muslims and Christians can therefore help each other get to know the one God better. The truth lies not in either religious tradition but beyond them. God transcends the different interpretations of both religions.[24]

It speaks for itself that the synthetic model is heavily focused on meeting each other. The dialogue with others is used to discover more about the divine secrets behind both religions. That's the primary missionary drive. It distinguishes itself in this way from the classic missional paradigm where the uniqueness and exclusivity of Christ plays a decisive role.

1.2.3 The Contextual Approach

Where the antithetical approach emphasizes its own unique identity at the cost of an openness towards Islam, the synthetic approach threatens to give up its individuality for the sake of connectedness to Islam. The approach that I call contextual tries to bring both sides together. This approach is above all Christocentric: God's unique revelation in Jesus Christ takes centerstage, thereby connecting to the antithetical approach. The focus on this uniqueness, however, does not exclude the fact that traces of God are found throughout creation. This includes the diversity of religions – and that's where the synthetic approach comes in. Islam may not offer salvation, but it can contain kernels of truth.

---

21. Wessels, *De moslimse naaste*, 134, 136, and more recently, Wessels, *Thora, Evangelie en Koran*.

22. Wessels adds to that that he would explain the Qur'an in certain parts differently, namely where it goes against his own religious tradition. Wessels, *Moslimse naaste*, 136.

23. Raimundo Panikkar calls this "parallelism": all religions run parallel like train tracks and meet each other at the end of time in the ultimate intra-religious dialogue. Panikkar, *Intra-Religious Dialogue*, as cited in Kärkkäinen, *Theology of Religions*, 24–25.

24. Steenbrink sees Islam, for example, as an Arab contextualization of the Christian faith, Steenbrink, *De Jezusverzen in de Koran*, 164. See also Kärkkäinen, *Theology of Religions*, 291; Knitter, *No Other Name?*; Hick, *God Has Many Names*; Hick, *Christian Theology of Religions*; Hick and Knitter, *Myth of Christians Uniqueness*; and Panikkar, *Unknown Christ of Hinduism*. In the pluralistic model it is less about a God or gods and more about an ultimate reality whatever name is given to it. See Kärkkäinen, *Theology of Religions*, 25–26.

Both religions confess that there is only one God, the Creator of all things. In this approach, the God of Islam and the God of Christianity are seen as the same being. At the same time, both religions think very differently about the nature and actions of this Creator. All of that has to do with the interpretation of the personhood of Jesus/'Isa.

The prophet Muhammad is seen in this approach as someone who had sincere intentions. Although it may go too far to call him a prophet in the Christian sense, it does need to be recognized that he turned against polytheism and stood up for the God of the Jews and Christians. Chapman compares Muhammad in this context with Gideon, who, as a judge for God, started out right but eventually turned the people of God to idolatry (Judg 8:24–27).[25] According to the Nestorian Patriarch Timothy I (d. AD 823), if a prophet is someone that turns people from serving demons to serving and worshipping one God then Muhammad walked on the path of the prophets.[26] Cragg recognizes Muhammad as a prophet but only in the Islamic sense. From a Christian perspective, however, he poses the question to Islam if there is not something more needed than this prophethood.[27] Those who advocate the contextual approach do not all share the same opinion on this point. There are some that do not recognize Muhammad in any way as a prophet of God.[28]

What counts for Muhammad in this approach is similarly applicable to the Qur'an. The book does not have the status of being God-inspired, but there are differing opinions on the extent to which God-inspired truth and wisdom can be found in the Qur'an. There are also differing opinions on whether or not the Qur'an can be used by Christians when sharing the gospel with Muslims.[29]

Throughout history, prominent Christians have interpreted Islam in light of God's judgement. Baumann shows a popular but interesting study of how widespread this interpretation is in both older Eastern/Oriental and modern Western Christianity.[30] The Reformers saw Islam as a judgement of God on the disobedient form of Christianity that existed in their day.[31] Cragg doesn't call Islam a direct "judgement" from God but a challenge to Christianity to

---

25. Chapman, *Cross and Crescent*, 303–304.

26. Timotheüs was Patriarch from AD 780–823. See Bijlefeld, *Islam*, 80–81.

27. Cragg cannot exclude a certain "divine cause" but questions the way in which Muhammad shaped this "divine cause." Cragg, *Muhammad and the Christian*. See Zebiri, *Face to Face*, 201.

28. Moucarry, *Faith to Faith*, 264.

29. Accad, *Building Bridges*.

30. Baumann, *Der Islam*.

31. Baumann, 41–48.

investigate itself. Has Christianity succeeded in showing the true Christ to Muslims? And if not, why is that? The Islamic call to prayer from the minaret is an appeal to the Christian church to revival.[32] This appeal is strengthened in the Western world due to the fact that Christianity's center of gravity is moving to the southern hemisphere. The majority of Christians are no longer living in Europe and North America but in Africa, Asia, and South America.[33] What barriers and opportunities can be found in these developments in the relationship towards Islam?

1.3 The Diversity of Islam

Islam has many "faces" and versions. In Indonesia, Islam has a different character compared to Iraq or Egypt, and an everyday Muslim in Saudi-Arabia looks very different from his Dutch counterpart. The African American "Nation of Islam" in North America cannot be compared with the Islamic Uyghurs of China. This isn't just a question of culture and context, and this difference is determined just as much by the contents of the faith. Liberal Muslims who pursue democratic reform relate differently to their sources than radical Muslims who want to establish an Islamic caliphate through violence. Salafis hold to a different form of Islam than Sufis.[34]

Even just a very general sketch of some of the differences shows the complexity of the phenomenon of Islam today.[35]

1.3.1 Sunnis and Shi'ites

The main division within Islam is between Sunni and Shi'a Islam. The majority of Muslims (85–90 percent) belongs to the first group, the rest to the second.[36] According to Nasr, the "confrontation of Sunni Islam with Shiism has shaped

---

32. Cragg, *Call of the Minaret*, 220.

33. Tennent, *Invitation to World Missions*, 33–37; Jenkins, *Next Christendom*. For statistics, check Johnson et al., "Christianity 2016," 22–29.

34. For an overview of the diversity among Muslims, see Rippin, *Muslims*; Esposito, *Islam*; Waardenburg, *Islam*.

35. It is impossible to give a complete overview of all the different branches of Islam and the different views that are present in a variety of movements. Just a few thoughts are presented here by way of illustration.

36. Pew Forum, "Mapping the Global Muslim Population," 1. The Pew Forum estimates the respective percentages to be in the range between 87–90 and 10–13 because, in many countries, there are only estimates, no hard numbers. The expectation is that the ratio will remain the same in the near future. See Pew Forum, *The Future of the Global Muslim Population*, 18.

the history of Islam more than its confrontation with Christianity. The extremist Sunni's demonization of Shiism regards the faith as a heresy and a bigger threat to 'true' Islam than Christianity and Judaism."[37] This schism has been present since the first century of Islam and is partially caused by a different view on the succession of the prophet Muhammad and therefore on the leadership of the "Umma," the Islamic community. Sunnis consider the successor only as a worldly leader and call him caliph; the Shi'ites see him also as a spiritual leader and call him imam.[38]

The word Sunna means "a way or manner of acting." Yet it soon came to stand for "the generally approved standard or practice introduced by the prophet as well as the pious Muslims of olden days."[39] In this way it became the second root of the Islamic law and from there "came to stand for the all encompassing concept of orthodoxy."[40] The example of the Prophet Muhammed, the Sunna, was passed on through stories (*Aḥādīth*; plural of *al-ḥadīth*) that eventually were brought together in different, more or less reliable, *ḥadīth* collections. The Ahl al-Sunna, the people of the tradition, came to be seen as orthodox Islam,[41] while the shī'at 'Alī, the Ali-group or Shi'ites, were (from a Sunni perspective) seen as heterodox. Shi'a Muslims believe the opposite, of course.[42] Shi'a Islam considers 'Alī b. Abū Ṭālib, Muhammad's cousin, the rightful successor to the prophet. However, not Ali but Abū Bakr became the first caliph. When Ali was eventually chosen as the fourth caliph, after 'Umar b. al-Khaṭṭāb and Uthmān b. 'Affān, his followers expected that succession would now follow his family line. However, after the short-lived leadership of Ali's son Hassan, his second son, Hussein, was brutally killed at Karbala (Iraq) by the Ummayads. His martyrdom has permanently marked the history and faith experience of the Shi'ite community. The reality and presence of Shi'a Islam has somehow

---

37. Nasr, *Shia Revival*, 54. In the developments in the Middle East since the so called Arab Spring – the civil war in Syria (since 2011) and the rise and fall of IS (ISIS/ISIL) – the opposition between Shi'ites (Alawites in Syria and Shi'ites in Iraq, Iran, Lebanon, and parts of the Gulf region) and Sunnis (the opposition in Syria, the old regime in Iraq, Saudi Arabia, and other Gulf states) is still a decisive factor. That conflict has been present in this region since the beginning of Islam for more than fourteen centuries. The long history of strife, conflict, and war, together with the political aspirations of different countries and Western interference, highly complicates any peace negotiations.

38. According to the Sunni tradition the successor of Muhammad did not have to be a relative but was chosen on the basis of the principles of tribal succession. According to the Shi'ites, the successor of the prophet needed to come forth from Muhammad's bloodline.

39. Juynboll and Brown, "Sunna," §1.

40. Juynboll and Brown, §1.

41. Juynboll and Brown, §1.

42. See Juynboll and Brown, "Sunna."

continued to challenge the legitimacy of a Sunni Caliphate. This is one of the reasons that Sunnis have always considered Shi'ites as heretics and treated them as fake Muslims. It has often resulted in persecution of Shi'ites by Sunnis. Every year, therefore, Shi'ites "celebrate" the festival of *Āshūrā* in commemoration of Hussein's martyrdom. There is a well-known expression that one tear shed for Hussein will wash away one hundred sins.[43]

Shi'a Islam distinguishes itself from Sunni Islam in a number of ways. According to Shi'ites, the "truth" is not located in the community of believers, as the Sunnis believe, but in the leadership of the prophet and his successors. For Sunni Muslims, the message is more important, and every human being is able to understand religious truth. According to the Shi'ites, the vehicle of the message takes center stage.[44] Human beings need spiritual direction in order to live according to the principles of Islam. They need special guides, holy people who are appointed by God. Only the prophet and the imams are blessed with special knowledge to interpret both the explicit and the implicit secret and truth of the Qur'an. Philosophy and theology therefore are more important in Shi'a Islam than in Sunni Islam. The same is true for holy places. Shi'ites see these as places of grace where God is present and will listen more promptly to the prayers of faithful believers. Shi'ites have different collections of stories concerning the life and example (Sunna) of the prophet. Finally, the Caliphate is primarily a Sunni ideal.[45]

1.3.2 Other Developments within Islam

Second, within this major division of Islam, we must distinguish between a great variety of groups and movements. An important mark of classical

---

43. See Nasr, *Shia Revival*, 57; Madelung, "Shi'a."

44. See Nasr, 38; Madelung.

45. There is a lot of discussion on the meaning of so-called *taqiyya*. It has even come up in discussions in the Dutch Parliament. The far-right leader Geert Wilders emphasizes the issue that Muslims are supposedly allowed to lie about their real intentions for society; they hide their objective of transforming the Netherlands into an Islamic State. The concept of *taqiyya*, however, is originally a Shi'ite concept. Brown describes two Shi'ite responses to losing the Caliphate to the Sunni majority, the quietist and the rebellious. The majority chose the first approach, in which it is required to conceal one's true beliefs if that is necessary to preserve the Shiite community in a hostile environment, Brown, *New Introduction to Islam*, 157–158. On a more personal level believers were allowed to hide their Shi'ite identity if their lives would be in danger. That of course does not exclude the use of *taqiyya* in a wider sense or in a Sunni context. See Strothmann and Djebli, "Taḳiyya," and Howarth, "Taqiyya (Dissimulation) and Integrity," 218–236.

orthodox Sunni Islam is the link to one of the current four schools of law.[46] In due time the emphasis has come to fall primarily, although not exclusively, on Fiḫh, or jurisprudence. The interpretation of the Islamic law, Shari'a, is the ultimate goal of interpreting the Qur'an and the tradition. There are strict rules on how to interpret these sources of Islam and how to apply Islamic law.[47] There are even rules about how to change the rules. Every school of law has its own juridical tradition and differs in several ways from other schools of law. The primary sources for Fiqh are the Qur'an and the Sunna. Apart from the consensus of the Ulama, the Islamic scholars, the principle of analogy (*qiyas*) is crucial for the right interpretation of the law.[48]

Within Islam there are many different movements and positions. There is, for instance, (Sunni) Salafism, which can be seen as a renewal movement intent on reforming Islam in line with the so-called golden age of Islam, the first century of Islamic history. The Rightly Guided Caliphs, the first four successors of the prophet Muhammad, represent exemplary Islam.[49] Salafis, therefore, reject the later theological and juridical interpretations and developments and only want to follow the Qur'an and the Sunna, the example of the Prophet Muhammed. In this, many (but not all) within this movement are inspired by several radical Muslim scholars, such as Taḳī al-Dīn Aḥmad Ibn Taymiyyah (1263–1328) and Muḥammad b. ʿAbd al-Wahhāb (1703–1792).

There is also a movement within Islam that wants to go back beyond the tradition of the prophet to the Qur'an only, as a guide for life. This so-called "purism" is attractive to many women, since the Qur'an is seen as more positive about women than the Sunna.

---

46. Rippin, *Muslims*, 90–91; Goldziher et al. "Fiḫh." Nasr emphasizes that, in Shi'ism, piety comes before the law. Before there was Shi'a law there was Shi'a piety, and therefore it seems that the role of law schools is different within Shi'ism than in Sunni Islam. If Sunni Islam is about law and the "thou shalls" and "thou shall nots" of Islam, Shi'ism is about rituals, passion, and drama. Nasr, *Shia Revival*, 58. Rippin points to an interpretation in which Shi'ism seems to be "little more than another legal school, parallel to the four major Sunni schools." Rippin, *Muslims*, 132. However, within Shi'a Islam there are also different schools of interpreting the law, e.g. the Ja'fari and the Zaidiyyah. These ways of interpretation are largely identical to the various branches of Shi'a Islam, the Ja'faris (twelvers), Ismā'īlis (seveners), Zaidi (fivers), and Alawites. Twelvers and Seveners are named after the last imam in the line of Muhammad, who has disappeared and is believed to return at the end of history.

47. See Accad, *Sacred Misinterpretation*, 34–74.

48. See Accad, 44; Rippin, *Muslims*, 94.

49. See Shinar and Ende, "Salafiyya." Salafis want to return to the tradition of the "pious forefathers," al-salaf al-ṣāliḥ.

A very old trend within Islam is Sufism, the mystical form of Islam. Sufism is focused on experiencing God more deeply and, for some, even unification with him through different forms of meditation, study, music, and dance.[50]

In the West, we see the development of a so-called European or Western form of Islam. The condition in which Sunni Muslims are a minority amidst a more or less secular majority is relatively new. According to Ramadan, the classical opposition in Fiqh between the Dar-al-Islam (the house/abode of Islam) on the one hand and the Dar Al-Harb (the house/abode of war) on the other, as excluding realities, is no longer applicable in the modern world. Reality has changed. Whenever Muslims are free to celebrate all their Islamic festivals and to live out their faith, then that is enough. Then the world is no longer at war with Islam but can be considered the house/abode of peace or of the covenant.[51]

Finally, there is the academically hard to map phenomenon of what is often called "folk" Islam. We could define folk Islam as the linking of several forms of traditional beliefs with the elements of official Islamic faith. It can contain a great diversity of phenomena, such as divination, witchcraft, visiting traditional healers, the use of amulets, belief in spirits, visiting holy places, adoration of saints, etc. Folk Islam is not a specific system that can be studied on the basis of written or oral sources. It is a question whether folk Islam even exists, or if we should speak about a collection of quite diverse forms of folk beliefs.[52] Many of these practices are considered unorthodox and "un-Islamic" by the leaders of classical orthodox (Sunni and Shi'a) Islam. Nevertheless, in the ordinary life of many Muslims, these practices are very important and widespread.

All these differences are, of course, also related to many contextual factors, such as culture, ethnicity, historical developments, etc. Muslims therefore differ greatly on all kinds of issues, such as the position of women, dress code, the meaning of Jihad, whether or not to strive for an Islamic state or caliphate, apostasy, relationships with non-Muslims, etc.

---

50. A Sufi is first of all someone who wears woolen clothes (ṣūf), "the rough garb of ascetics and mystics." Massington et al., "Taṣawwuf."

51. See Ramadan, *Western Muslims*; cf. McRoy, *From Rushdie to 7/7*, 97–99.

52. Folk Islam is difficult to define. It can hardly be called a movement within Islam; it is a collection of many different kinds of beliefs, rituals, and practices that differ substantially in different regions. Nevertheless, it is characterized by the mixing of elements of Islam with all kinds of folk belief. The following texts try to describe some of the phenomena that can be seen as part of folk Islam: Parshall, *Bridges to Islam*; Love, *Muslims, Magic and the Kingdom of God*; and Musk, *Unseen Face of Islam*.

1.3.3 Shared Views

From this brief sketch, it is clear that Islam is a very diverse phenomenon. Biblical-theological reflection on the calling of the church in the context of Islam will have to take this diversity into account. That does not mean there is no unity in Islam at all. There are a number of central ideas and practices that the majority of Muslims share, even if they use or interpret them differently.

First of all, there is the concept of *Tawhid* (oneness), the belief that there is no other God than God. This is not just the foundation of Islam; it also establishes the Islamic "worldview" that in all of creation everything is connected with everything else. The one God is absolutely transcendent and ultimately supreme over everything. The whole world is subjected to him. The law of God applies to everything in life, from the life of faith to responsibility in the world.[53]

Second, for every Muslim the Qur'an is the primary point of reference. For Muslims in the classical orthodox tradition it is the direct and literal revelation of God, which Muhammad received in oral form; liberal Muslims use the Qur'an more freely as a source of inspiration for their modern interpretation of Islam.

Third, all Muslims recognize the value of the Sunna. The example of the prophet operates as indicated above more or less as a second source of interpretation for Islamic law. Only the purists refrain from using the Sunna in this way, although even then it can be inspirational.

Fourth, most Muslims value the interpretation of the scholars of Islam in order to understand God's will for everyday life. Muslims differ in answering the question of who is allowed to interpret the Qur'an and the Sunna and regarding the authority and scope of that interpretation.

The Islamic law – the Shari'a – is essential to all Muslims, although the interpretations of what the law requires differ quite substantially. To be a Muslim means to surrender to God and his will for humankind. In that sense, Shari'a belongs to the essence of Islam. The idea of Shari'a is often met with opposition among non-Muslims, because it calls to mind all kinds of negative realities. The Shari'a is thought to call for the oppression of women and minorities, requiring horrible sentences to punish criminals, calling for holy war, and forbidding religious freedom. Muslims often do not recognize this criticism, since the Shari'a is not a written document, like a manuscript you can simply pick up in any library. It is basically a virtual collection of many rules and regulations that try to point a Muslim to the way of faithfulness to God.

---

53. See Rippin, *Muslims*, 88–89.

The Shari'a is hidden in the Qur'an, hidden to be found by human beings.[54] Just as committed Christians want to obey the law of God, so Muslims desire the same. They think primarily here of simple regulations for every part of life.

Finally, there are the five pillars of faith that are shared by most Muslims, although different movements and groups deal with them differently. Islam is built on these pillars: faith (*imaan*), prayer (*salat*), fasting during the month of Ramadan (*sawm*), tax for the poor (*zakat*), and the pilgrimage to Mecca once a lifetime, if possible (*hajj*).

1.3.4 Understanding Islamic Diversity

Globally speaking, there are two ways in which the multicolored nature of Islam is interpreted:

1. *It is about a single Islam that different Muslims interpret in very different ways.* This first view suggests that there is an ideal reality hiding behind the religious environment of Muslims which would be the real or true Islam. Even though many Muslims do not practice it, there is such a thing as a "primal Islam." For some, this true Islam is very positive, a religion of peace. For others it is actually negative; it is in its deepest essence a religion of violence and extremism. The question, then, is what does this primal Islam look like? It does not really exist. It is a virtual reality, an abstract. It cannot be studied scientifically because Islam only exists in its "flawed" form and in the way in which people have given expression to it. Even the age-old Islamic tradition as a faith system is an interpretation by Islamic scholars and spiritual leaders. This interpretation has developed throughout history as well, so how do we know which is the true version? The only tangible reality behind the faith of Muslims that we can witness are the sources of Islam: the Qur'an and the Sunna, the example of the prophet. The problem here is that these sources are explained and applied differently by each tradition. Thus, sources alone do not form a finalized religious system.

2. *Islam is a collective name for what all Muslims believe. "The" Islam does not really exist as a system.* This second approach acts on the premise that Islam is simply a collection of loose forms and thoughts without a clear consistent unity. This, too, is an inadequate picture

---

54. See Berger, *Klassieke sharia*, 13, 17, 19.

of reality. Even with its many varieties, Islam transcends a merely accidental contextual expression of faith; it clearly differentiates itself from other religions. Muslims share the beliefs in "oneness" (*Tawhid*), the five pillars of the faith, the sacredness of the Qur'an, the prophethood of Muhammad, and the decree of God as a guide for life. The fact that these core tenets can be interacted with in different ways does not take away from them. Additionally, there is a historical continuity. Categorically rejecting that Islam has an "essence" would lead to a form of relativism that does not do justice to Muslims.

How do we find the right balance between unity and diversity? I distinguish between three viewpoints:

1. *The "objective" perspective of religious studies.* This describes the diversity of Islam with its many varieties as objectively as possible. The focus is on the "phenomenon" of Islam. It is about the kind of Islam that is presented to us in the world around us. This is the diversity of Islam, of which I have sketched a very general picture above.

2. *The "subjective" perspective of practicing Muslims.* This is about internal religious conversations and it is not surprising that each movement cherishes its own interpretation of what does and does not belong to true Islam. Sunnis have trouble accepting Shi'as as true Muslims, so-called "folk" Islam is rejected by orthodox Muslims as heresy and unbelief, and the most classical or orthodox Muslims do not recognize ISIS as true Islam.[55] Extremist groups like ISIS, in turn, see regular Islam as practiced today as a rejection of the principles of Muhammad. It is exceptionally hard for an outsider to distill principled expressions of "the true Islam" from this subjective debate. At the end of the day, only among each other can Muslims figure out how they want to define Islam.

3. *The normative outsider's perspective.* This is about figuring out Islam from a non-Islamic tradition. Within the Christian tradition it is about a *theologia religionum*, a Christian view of Islam. How does the phenomenon of Islam relate to the revelation of God in Christ?

---

55. See an open letter written by 126 scholars to the leader of ISIS: "Open Letter to Dr Ibrahim Awwad Al-Badri."

In this book we will concentrate on this third perspective – a Christian interpretation of Islam – with a focus on the question of how the church should relate to Islam.

1.4 Hermeneutic Confusion

In addition to the enormous diversity within Islam,[56] the many nuances of the Christian interpretations of Islam is also a complicating factor in formulating a biblical-theological view on the attitude the church takes towards Islam. There are different hermeneutical decisions at play.

Each of the three aforementioned approaches – the antithetical, synthetic, and contextual – has its own biblical interpretation at its foundation. Which Bible verses should be applied to Islam? On the basis of what criteria do we select these verses? Can we even apply Bible passages to the relationship of the church and Islam at all today?

Take for example the story of Elijah who engaged in a battle with the prophets of Baal (1 Kgs 18). It has to become clear who the real God is in order for Israel to fully dedicate themselves to this one true God (1 Kgs 18:21). At first glance this looks like the relationship between Christians and Muslims. Christians are worshipping the true God and Muslims an idol like Baal. The prophet Muhammad could be compared to the Baal priests, calling Muslims to worship a different God than YHWH.

But it is not that simple. First of all, those worshipping Baal were not from a different nation with another religion. This was about the people of Israel itself, the covenant people, who besides YHWH also worshipped Baal. This is an internal conflict within "the church of God." This would only be comparable to the relationship between Christianity and Islam if Islam were to be seen as a Christian denomination. In other words, this comparison does not apply. In addition, we could compare the prophet Muhammad to Elijah as well as to the Baal priests. Muhammad, after all, railed against the worship of (many) idols, just like Elijah. He called the Arab people to the worship of the one God. Just like Israel eventually declared that there was no God but YHWH (1 Kgs 18:39), in the same way Muhammad preached that there was no God but God. That his understanding of God was different from the God of the Old, and especially the New, Testament does not take away from that.

---

56. Therefore, each time we talk about Islam, we mean the complexity of the various forms of Islam.

There are many more examples like this. Therefore, we have to be very careful in the hermeneutical decisions we make and upon which we base our view of how the church should relate to Islam.

1.5 Structure

We have a complex question before us. There is a diverse group of Christian traditions and an even greater diversity of streams within Islam. We bump into a complicated hermeneutical process of explaining the Bible in such a great variety of contexts. Islam is not only a challenge to Christians in countries where Muslims are in the majority, like the Middle East and parts of Asia and Africa, but just as much in the West where Muslims are in the minority. All this makes it impossible to come up with one biblical theology that describes how the church should relate to Islam that would always be applicable. In each situation, we would need to again take the time to think through how the church should relate to Islam. This requires a constant exercise in listening, interpreting, and reconsidering. That's why I'm not looking for one answer that would always apply but a biblical-theological framework that would be helpful for defining the calling of the Christian church in relation to Muslim communities in different contexts.[57] The principles of this framework should then be processed and applied in each separate situation. In this way we demarcate a space in which Christian theology can do its work.

This design has a few *methodological consequences*. First of all, I do not select one single model from the given Christian approaches to Islam. Doing that would fail to appreciate the diversity of the Christian tradition and too easily disqualify elements of other models as lesser-than or even un-Christian. The Christian tradition is not that one-sided. That is not to say that all models are equal. Not only does the context determine how the church relates to Islam, but it also determines the history of Christian tradition. Throughout history the Christian community has drawn boundaries. Even in Christianity, the religious studies perspective of Christianity (perspective 1, p. 15) is not identical to the subjective perspective of practicing Christians (perspective 2, p. 15). The tension between the two should always be felt.

Second, I will not be choosing from a select few verses that say something about serving God and idols. I will be painting a biblical framework that helps understand how God and the world relate to each other (part I). This framework will shine a light on the question about the nature of Islam (part

---

57. Glaser, "Thinking Biblically about Islam," 14–34, 15.

II) and the nature of the church (part III). This will then lead to the design of a model on how the church could and should relate to Islam (part IV).

To get a precise view on the framework we will first focus on the beginning of the Torah, the "law." This is not specifically about a set of rules but a portrait of life in the way that God intended. The first chapters of Genesis describe the foundational framework. I read this prologue as a prophetic-theological text, not as a journalistic report or a scientific account of creation. It is a confession of who God is and how he intends the world to be. In that, we also discover the essence of human beings and their relation to the Creator and creation.[58] This creation story from Genesis was explicitly taken up by John in his gospel. In a variety of ways, this gospel takes up the theme of creation and offers a revision or reworking of the history of God, the world, and Israel in light of the coming of Jesus Christ. This is apparent in a few different passages. First of all, John starts his gospel in the same way as Genesis by starting at the beginning: with God and the creation of the world (John 1:1–3). The Word that created everything calls into memory the speaking-into-being that God does in Genesis 1.[59] The coming of the Word into the world (John 1:14) is not only related to Israel (John 1:11, 17) but also to all of creation. Jesus's cry on the cross that "It is finished" (John 19:30; cf. 19:28) likewise refers to the Genesis story. It echoes back to the conclusion of the creation story in which it says that God finished his work (Gen 2:1–2).[60] In Christ, God is again working on finalizing his creation.

In both Genesis and John, the seventh day, the Sabbath, takes a key position. The day of rest gives structure to life: after six days there is a day that is holy, set apart. In the Gospel of John, Jesus is seen regularly bringing annoyance to the Jewish leaders by doing work on this sacred day. That is not without reason as we'll see later on. It is on the sixth day that Jesus calls out "It is finished" and on the seventh day he rests. It is therefore very interesting to see the connection between the first day of rest in Genesis and the Sabbath on which Jesus healed a man that had been sick for thirty-eight years (John

---

58. As seen in Van Wolde, *Terug near het begin*, it does not matter here if this part is about the "creatio ex nihilo" or not. Even if Genesis 1 does not provide a scientific account of creation, it is not therefore "untrue." Karl Barth calls Genesis, in that respect, a "unhistorische (of prä-historische) Geschichte." It is "unhistoric" because it a unique and one-off happening of its own nature and, in that way, precedes history, but it is "History" nonetheless. Barth, *Die Kirchliche Dogmatic*, 3.1, 84–87.

59. See Ps 33[LXX 32]:9.

60. Both the usage of *sun-teleō* (συντελέω) in the Septuagint and John's *teleō* (τελέω) show that it is almost undeniable that there is a connection between the words of Jesus and Genesis 2.

5:1–9). If we understand the meaning of the Sabbath, we will also understand the connection between God, human beings, and the world (chs. 2 and 3).[61]

In using this framework to address Islam, we will repeatedly bump into the question of whether "God and Allah" are the same or if Allah has something to do with the evil one. This issue will be addressed when looking at 1 Corinthians 8–10 where Paul emphasizes the confession of Israel that there is only one God (Deut 6:4) through whom everything is made (ch. 4). We will then also look more closely at how the religious experiences of Muslims relate to the work of the Spirit of the one God through Jesus Christ. What are Muslims experiencing when they experience God/god (ch. 5)?

To discover the nature of the church, we will subsequently look at the nature of the kingdom of Christ, which Jesus himself says is "not of this world" (John 18:36) (ch. 6). That concept will be developed into three themes that play a role in the attitude towards Islam: the undeniable bond between the church and the people of Israel (ch. 7), the issue of how the church should relate to the culture in which it finds itself (ch. 8), and the question of the suffering of the church in the Islamic world (ch. 9).

Once we have an overview of the nature of Islam and of the church, we will then cover how the Christian community should relate to Islam in part IV.

1.6 The Triune God

Now that we are starting on the journey that I just outlined, I want to make one more important remark. In the classical Christian tradition, it is confessed that God is three-in-one (the Trinity). In the classical Islamic tradition this is seen as *shirk*; ascribing partners to the one God is "polytheistic." This is a strong judgement. It is even a sin in Islam that cannot be forgiven. This is where Islam and Christianity are divided. In the Islamic tradition it is emphasized repeatedly that God "does not have a son."[62] When speaking of the church, Islam, and the triune God in this research, it needs to be noted that I do not imply any dogmatic presuppositions that immediately put Muslims and Christians on edge. I am of the opinion that the conversation between Muslims and Christians about God being triune has developed a caricature-like character. It almost sounds as if Muslims believe there is only one God and

---

61. This framework is also a hermeneutical choice, but it is one that is fundamentally important for the attitude of the church in the context of Islam. At the same time, it leaves enough room to be in dialogue with other structures.

62. For example, Surah 34:91 (sūrat al-Mu'minūn).

that Christians believe there are three gods. Even though Christians may create the impression that they believe in three gods, they are and will continue to be monotheists. For Christians, there is only one God and this God is one in the absolute sense.[63] I, therefore, wonder if Muslims can really accuse Christians of this unforgivable sin. Shabbir Akthar, a Muslim who is well-informed on the Christian tradition, suggests that Christians are "errant monotheists" according to Islam[64] and thus aren't guilty of committing the sin of *shirk*. The discussion, therefore, should be focused on the nature of the oneness of God.

I am not discussing the relationship between the church and Islam based on a dogmatic formula of the Trinity. It is not possible to create a simple division where one part is the Father, one part the Son, and another part the Holy Spirit.[65] That doesn't do justice to the complexity of the work of the one God. When I expound upon what God has meant for the world to be and what he is asking of human beings, then we naturally deal with the multicolored nature and complexity of the one living God. When I try to explain how the One is at work in the world, then I need to speak multiple words at the same time. I can only discover the nature of the work of the one God in the person and actions of Jesus Christ, and I see and experience the reality of God's presence only in and through the Spirit. The multiplicity of God is a way of saying that God is love. This love is visible in the foundation of existence and active in the history of God's interaction with this world. This love is also vulnerable. This is seen in the self-sacrificing love of Jesus Christ on the cross. There we find in its deepest essence also the secret of the calling of the church of Christ in relation to Islam.

---

63. See Turner, "Christians, Muslims," 18–26, 27. Cragg, *Call of the Minaret*, 278–279. The teaching of the Trinity is an attempt at describing the "oneness" of God.

64. Akthar, *Islam as Political Religion*, 7.

65. As seen in Tennent, who does do that in relation to missions. See for example parts 2, 3, and 4 of *Trinitarian Missiology*. This is somewhat artificial.

Part I

Framework for Thinking Biblically about the Church and Islam

The Triune God and His Plan

2

The Triune God and the Secret of Creation

"You stir man to take pleasure in praising you, because you have made us for yourself. . . ."[1]

2.1 Introduction

Genesis 1 describes how God created the world in six days. Creationists take this time span more or less literally, while God-believing evolutionists mostly interpret this symbolically. Either way, in Genesis 1 the first six days are crucial for creation, and the seventh day, seemingly, is separate from that. The day of rest is not part of the creative activity of God but follows it (Gen 2:1–3). Elsewhere in the Torah that fact is used as an argument for the command to have a Sabbath: because God created the heavens and earth in six days and rested on the seventh, human beings also should not do any work on the seventh day (Exod 20:11; 31:17). However, when we read Genesis 1 and 2 more closely, we see that something else is going on. The Sabbath is not separate from the creation process of the first six days but is inexplicably connected to it. The description of creation in the book of Genesis does not end on the sixth day (Gen 1:31) but continues to include the seventh day (2:3). This is apparent in several ways.

First of all, there is a transition between 2:3 and 2:4. In Hebrew, the story is built from Genesis 1:1 onwards, until (and including) 2:3, through the repeated usage of the word "and" in the narrative.[2] After a "breathing space," the narrator starts a new storyline in verse 4. This is supported by a change in the use of

---

1. Augustine, *Confessions*, Book 1.1, as translated by Henry Chadwick.
2. The so-called *waw consecutivum*.

God's name. In Genesis 1:1–2:3 the more general term *Elohim* is used, but from 2:4 onwards the covenant name YHWH is employed.[3] From Genesis 2:4 onwards there is also a shift in the content. It is now no longer about creation but about the "history" of the (created) heaven and (created) earth. The Hebrew word *tôlĕdôt*, which is translated as "history" here, always points ahead in the book of Genesis, always referring to the future, to that which will continue from what has preceded it.[4] It introduces what is to follow. The *tôlĕdôt* of Adam (Gen 5:1) describes the children of Adam, not the history of Adam himself (Gen 5:3–32); the *tôlĕdôt* of Noah (Gen 6:9; cf. 10:1, 32) paints a picture of the significance of Noah and his descendants for the salvation of humanity; and the *tôlĕdôt* of Jacob (Gen 37:2) focuses on the life of Joseph and his brothers. In this way, the *tôlĕdôt* of heaven and earth in Genesis 2:4 refers to what the act of creation itself has produced. It describes what happened next and what has become of creation since (Gen 1:1–2:3). Genesis 2:4 is therefore not an ending of what was before – as the NRSV wrongly suggests in its section headers – but the beginning of what is to come.[5]

In Genesis 2:2 the seventh day is explicitly connected to the preceding part. It says that God finished his creation *on the seventh day* – not on the sixth – and rested from the work that he did. In other words, the completion of creation is taking place *on* the day of rest. This has puzzled interpreters from the very beginning. How can God rest if he is also finishing the work? The text has therefore often been interpreted in a way that would explain that the finishing of the creation was on the sixth day. The latter requires that "finishing" would need to be separated from "resting" as taking place on the seventh day. But the text gives no reason for this – they are described here as two aspects of one act.[6]

Thus, the seventh day does not *follow* the creation but *is an essential part of it*. Without the seventh day, creation is not finished. It is the climax of the

---

3. Even if the change has to do with the fact that the author/editor was using two different sources – P (Gen 1:1–3:3) and J (from 2:4 onward) – there would still be a difference between 2:3 and 2:4.

4. *Tôlĕdôt* (תּוֹלְדֹת) comes from the root *jalad* (יָלַד): to procreate or produce offspring. It is almost exclusively used in the Pentateuch to mean "history" (NBV) or "generations." Brown, Driver, and Briggs, *Hebrew-Aramaic and English Lexicon of the Old Testament*.

5. See Wenham, *Genesis 1–15*, 49, 55.

6. See Wenham, *Genesis 1–15*, 35: "It doesn't mean that God was still working on the seventh day before finalizing." That tension has led to a secondary textual variation in the LXX that reads "sixth" instead of the seventh day. Westermann, *Genesis*, 233–234 emphasizes the declarative nature of this verse: God declares that his creation is complete. The *pual impf.* form of *kala* in 2:1 ("were being completed") and the *piel impf.* form in 2:2 ("he completed") seem to say something here about what happened on the seventh, not the sixth, day.

creation process. That's why, in the Jewish tradition, the Sabbath is called the queen of creation. The Sabbath – not the human being – is the crown of God's creation work. In a sense, this day is therefore the key to the secret of creation.

2.2 The Seventh Day
2.2.1 God Works on the Seventh Day

The seventh day is the day that God finished his creation and upon which he rested. What does that mean for the totality of creation? Finishing in Genesis 2:1–2 (*kala*)[7] could indicate the formal ending of an act: God is ready with his work and is "clocking out."[8] However, when *kala* is used elsewhere in the Torah, it is not only about the finishing of an act in the past, but it, at the same time, points forward to that for which the act was meant. When Isaac finished the blessing of Jacob, it means that the entire blessing has been poured out upon Jacob and that he can from now on experience the fruit of that blessing. The blessing has changed something in the status of Jacob (Gen 27:30). The same is seen with the finishing (ending) of the work of the tabernacle (Exod 39:32). It is not the factual announcement that the technical work is finished, but it shows that the tabernacle is now ready to be used. With the tabernacle, God meant to create a place where he would live and where human beings would be able to serve him.[9] We can say something similar about the completion of creation. It is more than just a moment in which "creating" becomes "no more creating." It is about how creation was completed and ready for all that God had in mind with it. The creation is ready to be activated. Genesis 1:1–2:3 is the prologue to the real story that is about to start, the history (the *tôlĕdôt*) of heaven and earth (Gen 2:4). It is for that history that (the completion of) creation was meant.

The Septuagint has been able to capture this purpose-driven focus by translating the Hebrew *kala* with the term *sunteleo* (συντελέω; Gen 2:1–2). This verb is related to the term *telos*, which points to something at the end, in the sense of "purpose" or "aim."[10] *Sunteleo* is well-represented as finalizing and completing in order to realize the purpose that was aimed for. The completed creation is very good (1:31) because it is completely available for what God had intended it.

---

7. בלה; Gen 2:1 passive (*pual*) and 2:2 active (*piel*).

8. See, for example, Gen 24:15, 19, 22, 45; Exod 5:13–14; Deut 20:9; 32:45.

9. See also Exod 40:33; Num 7:1; Deut 31:24; Ruth 3:18; Job 36:11.

10. See Liddell and Scott, *Greek-English Lexicon*; see also Reitsma, *God of My Enemy*, 74–76.

The meaning of the word "rest" in Hebrew is close to *kala*, completing, although various translations can easily mislead us. The root *šbt* (שׁבת; Gen 2:2) puts the emphasis on *ceasing* to do or be. It is not about "resting" in the sense of passive inactivity but the ceasing of activity.[11] Ceasing to work of course also leads to a certain "rest," but in Genesis 2 it does not mean that God is pulling out of creation to let it fend for itself like the clockmaker does in deism. The continuation of the book of Genesis shows that God continues to work after the seventh day and is actively involved with creation. "Resting" or "ceasing to create" means that God starts working in *another* way.

On the seventh day, God finalizes his creating activity. But that is not the full story. Without taking away from what was mentioned above, the seventh day does have a separate position in the creation process. The day is described differently from the first six. For example, the recurring structural elements are missing. The oft repeated "and God said" (Gen 1:3, 6, 9, 11, 14, 20, 24, 26, 29) and "there was evening and there was morning" (Gen 1:5, 8, 13, 19, 23, 31) are not used on the seventh day. There are also no new material things added to the creation on this day; nothing new is created. That's also why it is said in Exodus that God created everything in six days and rested on the seventh day (Exod 20:11; 31:17). God explicitly set this day apart from the others; he blessed and made the seventh day sacred (Gen 2:3). In the Old Testament, blessings are primarily connected to living things (Gen 1:22, 28). It is a promise of "fruitfulness." God set this day apart from the others as a day on which all that was created on the first six days can bloom. It is on this day that God gives meaning to creation and everything starts functioning as he meant it to.[12]

The six preceding days function in a similar way to the preparations for a wedding. Everything is focused to make this day a special day of celebration. The preparations are done as soon as the wedding day starts. That's what it was all about. Once the couple is married and the party is over, then everything is completed. However, that does not mean the end of the marriage but the start of it. Two people do not marry to then say goodbye to each other after the wedding but to go through life together. The wedding day is the crown of the

---

11. See also Exod 5:5; 16:30; 20:11; 23:13; Lev 26:34; Josh 5:12; Job 32:1; Jer 31 [LXX 38]:36. As seen, there is no order showing that the finishing needs to happen first before resting can take place. It is about the two sides of the same coin that both happen on the seventh day. Resting, in the sense of relaxing and recuperating, is used in other passages in a complementary way. For example, in Exod 31:17 the root *npš* (נפשׁ) is used next to, and almost synonymously with, *šbt* (שׁבת). See also Exod 20:11; 23:13: *nwḥ* (נוח); Josh 1:13, 15; Josh 21:44.

12. Moltmann, *Gott in der Schöpfung*, 283. He connects his eternal presence with the creation, and it is pursuant to his rest in and with his creation. Everything is created with an eye on the resting day. Moltmann, 280.

preparations, and at the same time, the start of everything that is about to take place. In this way, the seventh day of creation is the climax to the preparations and the beginning of what God had intended all of it to be about.[13] Philo calls the seventh day the party of the earth, the birthday of the world.[14]

2.2.2 Human Beings Rest on the Seventh Day

Whatever is true for creation as a whole is specifically true for human beings as well. If God completes and sets his creation in motion on the seventh day, that would also apply for human beings. The seventh day is making it clear that human beings, in close relationship with the Creator, are made to carry responsibility for everything that God has created. That is where their destiny lies; that's what human beings were designed for.

With that framework in mind, it can be seen why it is not accidental that the first day the created human beings experience on earth is a day of rest. Before they take on their dominion over creation and become fruitful and multiply (Gen 1:26, 28), there is first the seventh day. It is not human beings with their mandate and activity that are at the center of life, but God and the history that he has called into being. People are not created for themselves, for their labor, or for the riches of creation, but for life with God in the world. Thus, from the very first page the Bible is opposed to every form of divine glorification of the human being; humans are to glorify God by taking care of the world. It is through this that God's purpose is fulfilled. The seventh day is holy for human beings in order to continuously remind them of this.

This is closely related to the portrayal of human beings as created "towards" or "in" (בְּ) the image of God and in correspondence (כְּ) to his likeness (Gen 1:26–27). There are various opinions as to the exact meaning of this expression.[15] However, the details of this discussion are not relevant for our purposes here. Whether human beings are created *in* or *towards* the image of God,[16] both expressions make it clear that human beings take up their own

---

13. It is interesting that the Sabbath in the Jewish tradition is often compared to a bride. Israel is looking forward to its beloved, the bride, the entire week; see, for instance, Heschel, *Sabbath*, 48, 53.

14. Philo, *De Opificio Mundi*, xxx, 89.

15. Wenham, *Genesis 1–15*, 29–31, mentions five interpretations: (1) image and likeness referring to different aspects of the human nature, natural and supernatural; (2) the image of God referring to the mental and spiritual capabilities of human beings; (3) physical likeness; (4) the "representation" (of God); and (5) the capability of having a relationship with God. Towner, "Clones of God," 343–344, identifies eleven opinions.

16. See Wenham, *Genesis*, 32.

unique place in creation in relation to God. That makes them separate from the rest of creation. The focus of "the image of God" is not on external appearance as if to say that human beings look like God.[17] The word "image" (*tzèlèm*; צֶלֶם) is mostly used in the Old Testament for tangible images (idols) that represent the divine. It is more about giving expression to the qualities of character traits than the exact likeness. The golden calf in the desert would not have been thought of as an exact replica of the Almighty.[18] If human beings are called "the image of God," they mediate the presence of God like the statues in the Roman Empire symbolize the presence of the emperor. The same goes for the term "likeness" (*demoet*; דְּמוּת). The word is primarily found in the book of Ezekiel when the visions and glory of God are depicted. What the prophet sees can only be described approximately with certain earthly realities and cannot be contained by words or images. He sees something that "looks like . . ." and is not more than "a likeness of. . . ."[19] Although there may be some comparison between what Ezekiel sees and that which he compares it to, the visions are so different that a literal copy can in no way be made.[20]

Thus, when human beings are described as being the image and likeness of God, what is meant is that human beings mediate God's presence and represent him in some way. We cannot point to "something" in human beings specifically that makes them the image of God.[21] The "image of God" in Genesis defines human beings in the totality of who they are. The meaning is closely connected to the command to rule over "the fish in the sea and the birds in the sky, over the livestock and all the wild animals, and over all the creatures that move along the ground" (Gen 1:26).[22] Adam is created to live with God in the garden, to work it and take care of it (Gen 2:15), to give all animals names (Gen 2:19), and to walk with God in the garden in the cool breeze of the evening (Gen 3:8). Being the "image of God" is a sort of ambassadorship: human beings have a responsibility to take care of creation on behalf of God. They are not kings

---

17. See Vriezen, *Hoofdlijnen der theologie van het Oude Testament*, 187–188. The ancient Eastern idea about physical relation to divinity is not found in the Old Testament. God is entirely different. The father-child relationship description is, although implied, largely avoided.

18. It is used seventeen times and (with the exception of Gen 1:26–27; 5:9; 9:6) it is about idols.

19. Ezra 1:5, 10, 13, 16, 22, 26, 28; 8:2; 10:1, 10, 21–22; 23:15. See also Gen 5:1, 3; 2 Kgs 16:10; 2 Chr 4:3; Ps 58[LXX 57]:5; Isa 13:4; 40:18; Dan 10:16.

20. See for example Isa 13:4; 40:18.

21. What comes to mind is the external, physical likeness, rationality, self-awareness, feeling, consciousness, or simply that which distinguishes human beings from animals.

22. The term "ruling" (*rada*; רדה) is sparingly used in the Old Testament and denotes that something has a higher position compared to the other; see Lev 25:43; Pss 72:8; 110[LXX 109]:2.

but viceroys. Due to all this, the "image of God" indicates not only the special relationship between humans and God, and human beings and creation, but also the unique position of humans in relation to both.[23]

2.3 Conclusion

The seventh day shows what purpose there is to creation. On this day creation is completed and taken into use. Everything is created for the history that God is entering into with human beings in the world. The seventh day is a hinge: it finalizes the creation process and, at the same time, starts history. That is especially true for humanity. The seventh day is the start for the special relationship between God and human beings and is, at the same time, the verification point for it. Humans are created in the image of God to guard and take care of the garden on behalf of God.

It can be compared to the building of a large country house on an estate. Formally speaking, the house is finished once the walls are there, the roof has been attached, the windows and doors are installed, and the premise has been hooked up to gas, water, and light. Yet, it is not a "home" until people move into it. That's what the house was made and designed for. It is not meant to simply "exist." In the Middle East, estates are seen as the center of the family bond, or the clan. The extended family that has spread out to different places always returns there to meet with each other. It determines the identity of the family; it binds them together and materializes the family history.[24] Without this history, the estate loses its meaning, and without the estate, the family loses its honor. In the same way you can argue that our physical reality is meant for the "family" history of God and the world, God and humanity. On the seventh day they move into the home (Gen 2:15) and the *tôlĕdôt* of heaven and earth – the life of God, human beings and the rest of creation – starts. Everything is made to glorify the Creator. In this way God is continuously connected to his creation and actively involved in the world. This is how he, in his creation, is making himself known.

Karl Barth beautifully expressed this thought under the denominator of creation and covenant.[25] Creation is the external basis of this covenant ("außere

---

23. Barth strongly emphasizes the rational aspect; see *Die Kirchliche Dogmatic*, 3.1: human beings as opposed to God and human among each other (male/female); see Towner, "Clones," 343.

24. See Reitsma, *God of My Enemy*, 130–131.

25. Barth, *Die Kirchliche Dogmatic*, 3.1.41.

Grund des Bundes"), and the covenant is the internal basis of creation ("innere Grund der Schöpfung"). The covenant between humanity and the world is made possible by creation which gives it concreteness (external basis); the covenant is the deepest reason (internal basis) for creation. All of creation is meant to make the relationship between God, humanity, and all that is created viable, and this relationship is the driving power – the purpose – behind creation. The so-called first creation story (Gen 1:1–2:3) describes the external basis of the covenant; the second part (Gen 2:4–3:24), the internal basis of creation. The first finds its meaning and destination in the second.[26] That's why the covenantal name of God, YHWH instead of Elohim, is used in the "second" creation story. That was also the name with which God made himself known to Moses when he was making a covenant with Israel.

---

26. Barth calls the second the history of creation from within. He is inclining towards seeing Gen 1 as the prophetic approach towards creation and Gen 2 as the more sacramental approach. I personally would rather pick "theological" and "relational" as qualifying terms. This also explains the difference between the so-called "two creation stories." It is one story from two different angles.

3

The Triune God and the Secret of the New Creation

". . . and our heart is restless until it rests in you."[1]

3.1 Introduction

The created reality is unfortunately not as beautiful as the ideal that is presented in Genesis. The reality around us shows a very different picture, and relations between Christians and Muslims are under a lot of tension. We, therefore, cannot accurately paint a biblical-theological picture without taking this into account. What does the brokenness of creation mean for our question of how the church should relate to Islam? To find answers, we will focus again on the seventh day, now as described in the Gospel according to John.

3.2 The Seventh Day
3.2.1 There Is Something Wrong

As seen earlier, the story of God, his creation, and the people of Israel having received the Torah is taken up again by John. The God who created in the beginning by speaking his Word (Gen 1) is doing so again (John 1). This Word has come to live among people and has itself become "human" (flesh) (John 1:14). The story of Jesus is not only the realization of the story of Israel but also of all of creation. In the same way that Moses brought the Torah, Jesus brings the reality to which the Torah refers – that is, grace and truth and life according to the covenant. What that specifically means becomes clear when Jesus performs a miracle on the Sabbath (John 5). By doing so, Jesus provokes

---

1. Augustine, *Confessions*, Book 1.1, as translated by Henry Chadwick.

irritation from the Jewish leaders. However, that can hardly be the reason why he does this miracle precisely on the Sabbath.

When comparing the Sabbath in John 5 to the seventh day in Genesis, something has fundamentally changed. We read in the gospel that Jesus met a man on the Sabbath who had been sick for thirty-eight years. He was lying among a big group of sick people near the edge of the water of the pool called Bethesda. That is not the kind of life that God had in mind in the beginning. On the very first Sabbath, creation was very good. It was functioning as it should, in line with the covenant that God had made with human beings and the world. In John 5 that is no longer the case. There is illness, suffering, and discord. Human beings are not created to be lying on a mat for thirty-eight years. The paralyzed man does not even have anyone to help him to the water once it moves (John 5:7) even though God had said, "It is not good for the man to be alone" (Gen 2:18). Between Genesis 1:1–2:3 and John 5 something has clearly gone very wrong.

This is already seen in Genesis 3. Cracks are appearing in the edifice. Instead of peace there is shame and fear (3:8b). Being pregnant and having children is becoming a great pain for women. Yet, she will still desire her husband who will rule over her (Gen 3:16). The man must continuously toil and sweat to be able to continue to eat from the land where thorns and thistles grow. Eventually, human beings will return to dust (Gen 3:17–19). Creation will become a threat to humankind and human beings will become a threat to each other (Gen 4:8). Reality is not good anymore; it is not serving the purpose the Creator had for it.

According to Genesis 3, the disruption of creation is caused by the disobedience of human beings who were not content with taking their position as the "image of God" – as viceroys and ambassadors of the Creator. Human beings wanted to be like God himself. Upon the urging of the snake, they think they can determine for themselves what is good and evil (Gen 3:1). Human beings do what God had forbidden (Gen 3:11). Placing themselves at the center, they are no longer keeping the covenant with God. That is in essence the creation without the Sabbath, a history without the Creator. This is what derails life and makes all of creation share in the curse that has been spoken out over the snake (Gen 3:14, 17). This is the new history that is being written. It is not the day of rest and the relationship with God that are at the center but human beings and what they are creating. Genesis 11 illustrates this very clearly with the building of the tower of Babel. People wanted to "create a name" for themselves (Gen 11:4). In the Old Testament, this is something that is reserved only for God. God is the one who is creating a name for himself (Neh 9:10; Isa 63:12, 14; Jer 32:20) and for the patriarchs of Israel: Abraham and David (Gen 12:2; 2 Sam 7:9).[2] Human beings, on the contrary, are looking for "honor" for themselves rather than for God. In this way, they have become competitors with God, who do not accept their earthly position. By building a tower that reaches into the heavens, they show their desire to be like God (Gen 3:5) and secure their own future (Gen 11:4), just like Adam and Eve after the fall (Gen 3:24). Hence the fact that human beings are moving further and further away from paradise.

3.2.2 A Sign

In John 5 it does not only become clear that something has gone horribly wrong, but also that Jesus is going to do something about it. It is precisely on the Sabbath that he heals the man that has been sick for thirty-eight years.[3] For the religious context of his day, that was rather controversial. For the Pharisees, these types of incidents proved that Jesus could not have come from God (John 9:16). Why would Jesus heal this man on the Sabbath of all days? He must have had a purpose for it because, for the man to have been sick for that long, one day would have made very little difference; Jesus could have healed him the day before or after. It can hardly be a coincidence that Jesus chose the Sabbath.

Miracles in John always have a deeper meaning; they tell something about who Jesus is and they require faith.[4] This is why the evangelist talks about "signs" (John 2:11).[5] The conversations that follow a particular miracle explain its meaning.[6] This instance is no different. Jesus first talks with the healed man and after that with the Jewish leaders. From the conversations in this story, it is evident that the Sabbath is not a coincidental side issue.

3.2.3 A New Time

Jesus encourages the healed man to no longer sin so that nothing worse may happen to him (John 5:14). With this utterance, Jesus seems to suggest that

---

2. Wenham, *Genesis 1–15*, 239. These two are also mentioned as key figures in the genealogy of Jesus in Matt 1:1–17.

3. Jesus performs several other miracles on the Sabbath (Matt 12:10–15; Luke 13:11–17; 14:2–6). This passage in John is chosen due to the explicit reference that John makes in his gospel to the creation story.

4. Keener, *Gospel of John*, 275.

5. John 2:11; 2:23; 3:2; 4:48, 54; 6:2, 14, 26, 30; 7:31; 9:16; 10:41; 11:47; 12:18, 37; 20:30.

6. Every miracle shows a specific aspect of Jesus's identity. This explains also why John incorporated relatively few miracles into his gospel.

the sickness of the man is connected to his personal sin. But in John 9:3, Jesus resolutely rejects that kind of reasoning; the man born blind does not owe his disability to himself nor to the sins of his parents. There is no direct link between specific sins and brokenness. That will be no different in John 5 because, besides John 9, that is the only place in the Gospel of John where the notion of sinning comes up.[7] By saying "sin no more," Jesus wants to encourage the man to head in a new direction. How sin and illness are connected exactly, Jesus does not say. However, he makes it clear here that there is something that supersedes sickness and health.[8] Jesus calls this "something worse" (John 5:14) and that is what he wants to talk about. It could of course be an illness that is even worse. However, in the context of John 5 it is more obvious to think of the (definitive) judgement of God, the decision over (eternal) life and death. That is the most important part of the discussion with the Jews in the rest of chapter 5.[9] At the end of time, the dead will rise and have to give account of their lives (John 5:24). Those who have done well will rise in order to live, and those who have done evil will rise to be condemned (5:29).

The judgement of God and the resurrection of the dead are two fundamental, interconnected themes in the Judaism of the Second Temple period. Even though this Judaism is far from uniform, there was a broadly shared expectation that, based on the Torah, God – sooner or later – would intervene in history in a decisive way.[10] At the end of times, God would return to his people in order to reign as king (see for example Isaiah 40:10–11; 52:6, 7). The Jews were deeply aware that Israel was in some way still "in exile."[11] The people may have physically returned from Babylon, but the land was still ruled by foreign powers, and the greatest promises in the prophets concerning the new covenant had not yet been fulfilled. The expectation was that once that happened, the dead would rise and God would judge over them and the world, and that he would liberate his people. That would mean a definitive

---

7. Cf. Keener, *Gospel of John*, 643. John 8:1 is potentially a later addition.

8. Disobedience and brokenness are generally connected. See above §3.2.1, "There Is Something Wrong." This can even be in a personal sense: stealing will lead, for example, to jail time. Here, Jesus is not going into that connection, and it is about something different.

9. John 5:22, 24, 27, 29–30. Of all the times that John uses the term *krisis* and *krinein*, we find almost half of them in chapter 5.

10. Wright, *Jesus and the Victory of God*, 615–624.

11. Wright, *New Testament and the People of God*, 268–270, 299–301; Brunson, *Psalm 118*, 175.

return from exile, a new exodus.[12] Pain, death, illness, and injustice would then make way for joy, life, health, and justice.[13]

If Jesus heals a man on the Sabbath and talks about "something worse" than illness, it needs to be seen in light of this expectation of the future. The healing is a sign that the new time of salvation has started. Provisionally perhaps, but it has. Worse than sickness, however, is missing the new life God offers. Whoever listens to what Jesus says and believes in him who has sent Jesus has that life and will not be condemned by God. John calls this "eternal" life (John 3:18; 5:24). For this man, being healed physically does not mean that he is free from condemnation as well. That's why Jesus encourages the man to no longer sin and to change his direction in life by listening to him (John 5:24).

In the debate that follows with the Jews, Jesus takes it a step further, for he claims to be the one in whom the time of salvation has arrived. In the person of Jesus, God has returned to his people.[14] He says, "as my Father works, I work too" (5:17). He does only what he sees the Father do, and whatever the Father does, the Son does in the same manner (5:19). Like the Father raised people from the dead, the Son does too (5:21), because Jesus himself *is* the resurrection and the life (John 11:25). The Father has entrusted all judgement to Jesus (5:22, 27). Whoever honors the Son also honors the Father (5:23). Like the Father has life in himself, so, too, the Son has life in himself (5:26). In short, he and the Father are one (John 10:30).

For the Jews that is blasphemous language. By healing the sick man Jesus not only undermines the Sabbath, he also equates himself with God, the Father. That's why they attempt to kill him (John 5:18). Even though they study "the Scriptures" and pride themselves on knowing Moses, they show they are not accepting of the Word of God. Otherwise they would have acknowledged and believed Jesus. It is after all the Torah that testifies to him (John 5:37–46).

John writes his gospel in order to encourage the church to have faith that Jesus is the Anointed One of God and through that faith to participate in the "real" life (John 20:31). The Word has become "flesh" and has dwelt among

---

12. Wright, *Victory*, 477; see also Brunson, *Psalm 118*, 380. The expectation of a new exodus has three elements: (1) the return from exile, (2) the victory over evil and the enemies of Israel, and (3) the return of YHWH (as King) to Zion to live among his people and rule over them.

13. A comparable contrast is seen in the apocalyptic writings of Judaism from this Second Temple period between the *olam hazè* and the *olam haba*, between "this world (*aeon*)" and "the coming world (*aeon*)"; see Reitsma, *Geest en schepping*, 70, 71. It is very possible that John in his gospel, in speaking about "*this* world," is indirectly referring to this dualism (see 8:23; 9:39; 12:25, 31) even though he does not explicitly take on this schema. See Ashton, *Understanding the Fourth Gospel*, 208.

14. Wright, *Victory*, 651–653.

us.[15] He is God who comes to his people as king (John 18:36–38) in order to save them.[16] This salvation is the new, eschatological life that is seen through the signs that Jesus does.[17] It is a life full of joy (John 2); it is seeing light in the darkness (John 9); it is the healing of sickness (John 4:46–54); and it is enough to eat for the hungry (John 6). This is what God had in mind from the beginning. The Torah provides a sketch-like drawing of what that life looks like. Jesus is the one who actually realizes that life. He brings grace and truth (John 1:14, 17). This refers to the interconnected Old Testament terms *chèsèd* and *èmèt*. Together these terms describe God's covenantal love and faithfulness.[18] Even though *chèsèd* in the Septuagint is usually translated as *eleos* and not as *charis*, it is virtually impossible that John would not understand *charis* and *alètheia* in connection to the covenant (Exod 20:6; 34:6). The fact that the link with Moses is made (John 1:17) and that the Logos is spoken about as having come to "live" among us as a tent or tabernacle (John 1:14; cf. Exod 25:8) allows for no other explanation. The new time of salvation that has arrived with Jesus is nothing less than the realization of the new covenant that has been announced by the prophets. In contrast to the old covenant, this covenant will actually function. Israel will again, after all, live up to the principles and rules of the covenant and everyone will know the LORD. All injustice and every disruption of the covenant will be forgiven and restored (Jer 31[LXX 38]:34; Ezek 36:27). In this way, Jesus restores the covenantal community which was the purpose of the first creation. Jesus liberates people from each disruption of the creation and the covenant (John 8:36). That is a new exodus, the end of exile.[19]

It should not be forgotten that this story also demonstrates that the new time of salvation has not come into its full glory yet. Jesus heals only one person from a great group of sick people surrounding the pool of Bethesda. Moreover, Jesus even withdraws from the great crowds (John 5:13), possibly to not draw all the attention to the miracle itself. It is only a sign that points to more than

---

15. Literally: as a tent or a tabernacle. This is reminiscent of the time that the people of Israel spent in the wilderness when God lived among them in a tabernacle (Exod 25:8). The Father is present in the Son, and the Son represents the Father.

16. For "coming to," see John 3:19; 5:43; 6:14, 17, 19, 25; 7:28; 8:14, 42; 9:33, 39; 10:10. The concepts of "coming" and "sending" are used interchangeably in such a way that the reader recognizes the "sent one" in the "arrived one"; cf. Brunson, *Psalm 118*, 263.

17. See John 1:4; 3:15–16, 36; 4:14, 36; 5:24, 26, 29, 39–40; 6:27, 33, 35, 40, 47–48, 51, 53–54, 63, 68; 8:12; 10:10, 28; 11:25; 12:25, 50; 14:6; 17:2–3; 20:31.

18. Morris, *Gospel According to John*, 259–260; see also Quell, "Alētheia (Ἀλήθεια)," 233–237; Wildberger, "אמן ('mn)," 202–209.

19. Brunson, *Psalm 118*, 177–179; see Wright, *Victory*, 481.

physical healing. So the miracle both shows that the time of salvation has come, and at the same time, it points ahead to the full breakthrough of that time that is to come.

3.2.4 God Works on the Sabbath

Against this backdrop, it becomes clear why Jesus heals the man precisely on the Sabbath. After all, the Sabbath is a day of salvation. It is the day upon which God had set his good creation in motion and entered into a covenant with human beings and the world. How God meant for his creation to be is seen on the seventh day: a place where God and human beings could live and work together; a place where everything would be all right, *shalom* would prevail, and pain and sorrow would not exist. Jesus's healing of a man on this day explicitly recalls that first day of rest and God's purpose for life, including for this man. That's why this healing work suits the Sabbath eminently. The Sabbath serves to remind human beings that they are created for God. Life is about the Creator and the covenant with him. On this Sabbath, Jesus restores life as it was realized on the first Sabbath. He restores the covenantal community with God in all respects. This is how life was meant to be, and this is how it will one day be again. This healing is the start of the new Sabbath.

This is also captured in Jesus's statement that his Father is working *until now* and that he himself also works (John 5:17). The "until now" (ἕως ἄρτι) phrase emphasizes that God has been working *up until and including* this very day. God has always been working, since the beginning of creation and thus also on the Sabbath. Jesus is using this unusual time indication for a reason. All the emphasis lies on "until *now*" and that is something different from saying "always at his work" (NIV) or "non-stop at work."[20] Jesus really wants to emphasize that God, just like Jesus, works on the Sabbath up until and including the sign of the healing of the man in Bethesda. Does that then imply that God is not keeping his own commandments? Isn't it the case that no work is allowed on the Sabbath?[21] We have seen that God did stop creating

---

20. It is about the connection of the work that Jesus just did on the Sabbath with the work of the Father, so it is not about the general maintenance of creation. Bauckham, *Testimony of the Beloved Disciple*, 242. That is also God's work, but the focus is here specifically on the restorative and healing work of the Father and of Jesus.

21. The term that is used here (ἐργάζομαι) in Exodus and Deuteronomy (LXX) shows exactly that which human beings are not allowed to do on God's Sabbath: six days they are allowed to work, but on the seventh day they need to desist. Exod 20:9; 34:21; Deut 5:13. In the LXX it is a translation both from the root *abd* (עבד), to work or serve, and *p'al* (פעל), to do or

on the Sabbath but that he did not stop working. He switched into another way of working. He entered into the home of his creation in order to dwell in it together with human beings and bring it to its completion that way. That did not change after creation derailed. Since then, evil is also present on the day of rest and demands action. The work that Jesus has done by healing the sick man is the work that God does as well. From the beginning of creation, God has been at work to realize the purpose he had for creation. Since the derailment of creation, he has worked on recovery and healing. That is exactly what comes to light in the miraculous sign of Jesus. Jesus has come in order to restore the covenant of grace and truth. That is typical Sabbath work. As life came into force on the seventh day in Genesis, in the same way life is restored on the seventh day in John.

This Sabbath points forward to the Sabbath day on which Jesus rested in the grave. On that day the *new* creation begins to function. In the same way that God finished the first creation on the seventh day, Jesus finishes the restoration of that creation on the seventh day. It was on the cross, on the sixth day, that everything "material" was finished, just as in Genesis as well. Jesus calls out that it "is finished" or "completed" (John 19:28, 30; Gen 2:1–2). The day of rest is the transition to the beginning of the new history of heaven and earth. This starts on the first day when Jesus rises from the dead. Now the Spirit is again hovering over creation. Jesus gives his Spirit to those who belong to him, and then the peace, the shalom, of the first creation becomes reality again (John 20:19–23). Everything will once more become the way God had intended it. Therefore, in order to correctly understand the meaning of the seventh day, the work of the Spirit cannot be left out.

3.3 The Spirit
3.3.1 The Spirit of Truth

In the Gospel of John, the Holy Spirit is before everything else the Spirit of Truth.[22] This, too, correlates to the expectations of Judaism in those days. John frequently speaks about truth.[23] As was seen, this needs to be understood against

---

create. The term is used in Genesis for human beings who get to work in God's creation and may till and cultivate the earth, Gen 2:5, 15; 3:23; 4:2, 12.

22. John 14:17; 15:26; 16:13. The Holy Spirit is mentioned in one breath with the truth in 4:23–24. Besides that, the Spirit is also called the paraclete (14:16, 26; 15:26; 16:7). The term *pneuma* is used seventeen times in total in John.

23. See Morris, *John*, 259–262; the term truth (ἀλήθεια) is used twenty-five times in the gospel and twenty times in the three letters.

the background of God's covenant. The way in which John connects "truth" with "grace" or "kindness" (John 1:17 CEV) makes a Hellenistic background less likely.[24] The promise of the Old Testament is that when the new time of salvation arrives, God will pour out his Spirit not only on Israel but on all the nations (Joel 3:1–5; cf. Isa 11:2; 32:15; 44:3; 61:1; Ezek 36:26–27). The Spirit is the sign that the last days have arrived. In the Anointed One, God himself comes to Israel; he gives his Holy Spirit (John 1:33; 14:26) and redemption breaks through.[25] The whole world may share in it. The Spirit is the inaugurator of the new time of salvation, the new covenant (Isa 32:15). The "real" life that John speaks of so emphatically is life through the Spirit (see §3.2.3).

The same is also implied in what Jesus says in John about "water and Spirit." Only those who are born of water and Spirit can enter the kingdom (John 3:5). Even though this is sometimes seen as a reference to baptism,[26] it more obviously fits to understand "water and Spirit" as symbols of the new covenant.[27] In the new time of salvation when the exile will really come to an end, God will sprinkle clean water on his people, and he will give them a new spirit, his Spirit (Ezek 36:25–27; cf. Isa 32:15; 44:3). Being born of water and Spirit means receiving the life of the new covenant.

The Spirit is thus the sign that the eschatological time of salvation has arrived. The Spirit conceives life in the way God had already in mind at creation. That implies that the Spirit unmasks the old life as a disruption of God's good creation. This is also what is meant when Jesus calls the Spirit the helper (παράκλητος, John 14:16, 26; 15:26; 16:7). There is much discussion about the meaning of this term.[28] In John, the paraclete is the one who will take care of the believers when Jesus is no longer there. He is the "other" paraclete (John 14:16). He stands up for the believers against a world that hates them. He testifies of Jesus, and in this way helps the believers to testify

---

24. As Bultmann, "Alētheia (Ἀλήθεια)," 239–242, thinks. When Pilate asks what truth is in John 18:38, he is thinking in a Hellenistic framework, of course.

25. Jesus is the carrier of the Spirit (John 1:32–33). That connects to the expectation of the Old Testament that the Servant of the Lord is the carrier of the Spirit and will save his people as such (Isa 11:2; 61:1). Also, in the community of Qumran, the expectation was present that a spirit of holiness or a Holy Spirit would be given to three eschatological figures at the dawn of the eschatological time of salvation. See Notley, *Concept of the Holy Spirit*.

26. Compare to, for example, Schnackenburg, *Das Johannesevangelium*, 383. See also Bernard and McNeile, *Critical and Exegetical Commentary*, 164, 165. It would then have to be a later coloring of the words of Jesus by John. Blomberg, *Historical Reliability of John's Gospel*, 92–93.

27. See for example Wengst, *Das Johannesevangelium*, 123. For a comprehensive analysis of possible backgrounds to John 3:5, see Keener, *Gospel of John*, 537–544.

28. See Keener, *Gospel of John*, 953–963.

as well (John 15:18–19, 26–27). He will vindicate them and convict the world of sin, righteousness, and judgement (John 16:8). The Spirit of truth stands up like an attorney for the principles of God's good creation and unmasks the injustice of a creation that has been corrupted.

3.3.2 The Spirit and the New Life[29]

In Romans 8, Paul writes in a different but comparable way about the Spirit as the gift of the new time of salvation.[30] He does so in a letter in which he explicitly refers back to Genesis 3.[31] Creation is disrupted because, through Adam, not only sin but also death has come into the world (Rom 5:12–13). Sin and death are inseparably linked (Rom 6:23). Because each human being follows in the footsteps of Adam, death reigns over all since Adam (Rom 5:12–14).[32] This manifests itself in many different forms of suffering. Large ruptures permeate the world. All of creation is subjected to frustration or fruitlessness (Rom 8:20)[33] and is in bondage to decay (Rom 8:21).[34] This applies to human beings too. The human body is "dead" (Rom 8:10 ESV)[35] and "mortal" (Rom 8:11).[36] Because everything results in death, life is futile; it does not bear fruit and does not fulfill God's purpose. In this world, all kinds of things happen that are directly opposite to the life that God had in mind in Genesis (Rom 8:18, 35). All of creation, including the believer, groans and suffers the pains of childbirth (Rom 8:22–23). In Christ, however, a decisive turning point in time has taken place (Rom 6; 7:1–6; 8:1). God has intervened in history by

---

29. Paul says much more about the Spirit in his other letters. See for example Fee, *God's Empowering Presence*. Romans 8 gives several guiding principles in the context of creation and covenant and is, thus, relevant in this context.

30. See this detailed in Reitsma, "Power of the Spirit," 3–26, and Reitsma, *Geest en schepping*, 68–120.

31. See Reitsma, *Geest en schepping*, 100.

32. Human beings are not judged because Adam sinned but because they follow in the footsteps of Adam. Those that followed Adam do not act different from Adam and are in that sense his descendants. If by "original sin" we mean that we inherit the sin of Adam without any responsibility, then that term is not chosen correctly. Every human being is accountable for their own behavior.

33. The term *mataiotès* (ματαιότης) is in the NT only used in Eph 4:17 and 2 Pet 2:18. The Septuagint uses it in the book of Ecclesiastes to reflect the Hebrew word *hèbèl* (air, wind) through which the author relativizes life. See also Isa 59:4.

34. *Ftora* (φθορά) is also used in 1 Cor 15:42 and 50 and is the characteristic of earthly life: it is mortal and fleeting.

35. *Nekros* (νεκρός) means dead. It is different from "subjected to death" (NIV) or "mortal."

36. See this detailed in Reitsma, *Geest en schepping*, 80–82.

sending his Son and, in him, overcoming the power of sin (Rom 8:2–3). The powers of the old age, sin and death, that have entered the world with Adam (Rom 5:12–14, 17) now have to make way for the power of the Spirit. The Spirit is life (8:2, 4) and lives in the Christian community (Rom 8:9, 11). That does not mean that the sin and brokenness of the old creation are now gone entirely. Still, the Spirit is the first gift of glory (Rom 8:23).[37] Glory implies a total transformation of creation, a liberation out of the bondage to decay (Rom 8:21). Then, creation will answer to God's original purpose again. Since the very first Sabbath, God has been working towards that goal. Thanks to the cross and the resurrection of Christ, the suffering of this world is no longer the pain of death but the pain of childbirth (Rom 8:18, 23). The Spirit stands in the middle of the tension between corrupted creation, the new beginning through Christ, and the full revelation of God's glory. He is currently the presence of what is still to come. In the Spirit and through the Spirit, we can taste something of how God will one day restore his creation to full glory. In this we also see a glimpse of what God had in mind from the very beginning. At the same time, the Spirit unmasks the parts of creation that are opposite to God's original intention. Just like the projection of the renovation of a villa can reveal how far the decline is removed from the original beauty, so, too, does new life through the Spirit bring to light what has been corrupted in creation.

3.4 Excursus: Natural Knowledge of God?

In order to come to a Christian interpretation of Islam, it is important to briefly touch upon the implications of the close connection between God, human beings, and creation. Does this mean that the existence and essence of God can be read from creation? Is there something in human beings or in creation from which we can get to know God? This conclusion is drawn, in part, based on what Paul writes in Romans 1:20. In this passage, Paul states that that which is invisible of God – his eternal power and divine nature – can be seen and understood[38] from God's work in the creation of the world; it is clearly distinguishable.[39] In

---

37. *Genitivus subjectivus* not *partitivus*. Reitsma, *Geest en schepping*, 107.

38. The verb νοέω means to look through/understand with νοῦς, the mind or the intellect, but not in a rationalizing way. See *LSJ*.

39. See *LSJ*. Because καθορᾶται is singular, it is very possible that it refers back to τὸ γνωστὸν (Rom 1:19), unless it wants to focus on the concept of τὰ ἀόρατα. Because νοούμενα is plural, it seems more plausible that this term relates to τὰ ἀόρατα, and καθορᾶται is focused on τὸ γνωστὸν in the preceding verse. The reasoning is as follows: that which God has made available to be known is very clear because it has been clearly displayed since creation in God's work.

verse 19, Paul emphasizes that "what can be known about God is plain to them."
This is about the people who did know God but did not want to acknowledge
him (Rom 1:21). All this could indicate the idea of natural knowledge of God,
suggesting that human beings have some sort of innate knowledge of God or
that the existence of God can be deduced from the natural world. Sometimes
this goes together with references to the Stoa,[40] which assumes a natural affinity
between the divine and the natural in human beings. There is an immanent
presence of a godly spark (the *logos*) in every human being and in all of the
cosmos. People can learn to discover and live according to its deepest godly
nature through the instrument of reason (the *nous*).

The question is if this is what Paul means. First of all, he is talking about
the things that God has revealed (ἐφανέρωσεν; Rom 1:19). It is not inborn, and
thus passively present, but can only be known through direct relationship with
the Creator.[41] Second, it is about the things that can be known through the *acts*
of God, not through creation. The acts of God are about his work in all of the
cosmos. In the LXX and the New Testament, the word *poièmata* – in the NIV
translated as "what has been made" – can refer to both God's acts in creation
and in history.[42] Barely any distinction is made between the different aspects
of the acts of God. The *poièmata* are the deeds of God, from creation, to the
exodus from Egypt, to the calling of Abraham, to the laws revealed at Sinai,
to the exile and return to the land. From the acts of God in the cosmos (Rom
1:20), what is invisible of God is manifested and becomes knowable. The whole
world has after all been witness to what God has done: the Egyptians during the
exodus, the people who lived in the desert during the journey to the promised
land, the Canaanites during the entering of the land, later the Babylonians,
and now the Romans.[43] These acts of God have been there *since* the creation
of the cosmos (1:20), which means from the starting point of God's acts in
time. There is no reason to exclude creation itself from these acts of God.[44]

---

40. Greek philosophy is being thought of because Romans 1 uses terminology that is hardly
used in the Old and New Testament and seems to belong more to Hellenistic thinking. See Dunn,
Romans 1–8, 71. Although ποιήμα(τα) is used only here and in Eph 2:10 in the New Testament
and rarely in the LXX, the verb form of it is regularly used to refer to the work of God.

41. Dunn, *Romans 1–8*, 57: "God's knowability . . . was willed and effected by God."

42. See for example Gen 1:1, 7, 25–27 and Exod 8:9, 20.

43. According to Josh 2:9–11, Rahab tells the spies that the inhabitants of Jericho have
heard that God led them from Egypt, including the miracles of bringing them through the Red
Sea and defeating the enemies of Israel.

44. *Ktisis* (κτίσις) can indicate both the act and the result of creation. Since this passage
is about the activity of God, the first meaning is the most obvious. "From (ἀπό) the creation of
the worlds" does not have to mean "from the end of the act of creation" but could also refer to

Knowledge of God is therefore not something people are born with. Additionally, the reality and essence of God cannot logically be deducted from reality. There is knowledge of God because he was creatively and actively present in the real world from the very first moment. God has permanently bound himself with the world. If we want to speak of a creation that testifies to its Creator at all, then that would be in the same way that a work of art refers to its artist. In that sense there are traces of God in all of creation, but it requires revelation in order to recognize it. That is also due to the fact of what has gone wrong in history (see 3.2).

3.5 Conclusion

Creation is no longer the way God had intended it to be in Genesis. Because the relationship between human beings and God got distorted, all of creation is out of joint. Human beings were created for a relationship with the Creator, the covenant, of which the seventh day was the secret. However, human beings have, in a way, removed this day from their lives. That's why there are great ruptures throughout lived reality. There is suffering and pain. Death reigns everywhere. Jesus has come to restore creation. The climax of this is found on the cross where Jesus conquered sin. He subsequently restored the seventh day to its honor by resting in the grave on that day. On the first day, the new history of God with the world started when Jesus rose from the dead: a new creation in which the original intent of the Creator has been restored. In that sense, Noordmans is able to say that creation is visible as a place of light around the cross.[45] Human beings do not have direct knowledge of the pristine creation before the fall but only know the world as it has become. Creation coincides empirically with sin.[46] Only at the cross do we see elements of what creation is and one day will be in its fullness. Of this fullness, the Spirit is the first gift; the Spirit of the new covenant is the Spirit of life. Whoever lives from this Spirit, regains God's purpose.

---

the start of that activity. Creating is part of and included in God's acting.

45. Noordmans, *Verzamelde Werken*, 245.

46. Noordmans, 145. Creation belief starts right at the foot of the cross. Outside of Christ, creation is a mystery and merely brings dismay. Noordmans, 250–251. See Reitsma, *Geest en schepping*, 54–56.

Part II

Islam

A Challenging Community

4

God or Allah?

"Are Islam and Christianity talking about the same God? Those who say 'yes' to this too quickly will have to explain the meaning of the fundamental differences in the understanding of who God is in Islam compared to Christianity. These differences are so great that people may wonder if we are indeed talking about the same God. But those who answer the question too quickly with 'no,' find themselves getting stuck as well. This is because Christians are monotheists and can thus only believe in one God and that's why Muslims cannot be worshipping another God"[1]

"Allah has actually come to us in the wonderful glorious reality of Jesus the Messiah. . . .
    He is worth following, because this Jesus, He is El. He is Allah with us."[2]

4.1 Introduction

Even when we take all comments made about the great diversity among Muslims into consideration, it is not possible to escape a certain sense of generalization when we want to interpret reality in relation to the Creator. The biblical-theological framework of how God and human beings relate has been outlined in previous chapters. How do we now evaluate Islam, as a religion, in light of this knowledge (4.2)? And how does the God of Islam relate to the God of Christianity (4.3)?

---

1. Koffeman and Reitsma, *Vervolgnota*, 14.
2. Goldsmith, "Immanuel," 5.

4.2 Passion and Resistance: Islam in Light of the Cross

In light of the biblical-theological framework, we have to view Islam in two different ways at the same time. On the one hand, Islam can be seen as a specific expression of the relationship between human beings and God: people are created for a relationship with God. Reality in general, and human beings in particular, can only be understood in light of that relationship with God. Without God, human beings do not function in the way that God intended; the existence of creation remains a mystery. That enigma inspires human beings to contemplate their own existence – who are we and why are we here? Or, to recall the picture painted in chapter 2, an abandoned estate always begs the question of the origin and meaning of the home. It calls for the owner and the architect who can reveal the purpose. The phenomenon of religion can be typified as an attempt to understand the "internal basis" of creation. This is true of Islam as well. It is a human response to implicit and explicit references to God that are found in this world. In the analogy that Paul uses for Israel (Rom 10:2), we could say that Muslims have a "zeal" for God. Like every devout Israelite is seeking to completely obey God and live according to the Torah,[3] in the same way every devout Muslim is focused on surrendering entirely to God and living according to Shari'a. Sincere Muslims have a passion for God.

It is undeniable that Islam can also be an expression of the fact that human beings are prone to compete with God. The opposite side of "traces of God" in creation is "resistence" towards God among people. Muslims, too, are not by definition focused on God. Religion can also be a way to assert oneself against God or to resist him.[4] If God, in Jesus, realizes the deepest purposes for creation, then the rejection of Jesus signifies a rebellion against God. When someone has a passion or drive for God the way Paul describes, it does not mean that he or she necessarily knows God from experience (Rom 10:2). Religious involvement is not the same as a connection with the Most High. Therefore, it cannot be assumed that Muslims automatically participate in the fullness of life that God had in mind from the start and that is realized in Christ.

Those employing the synthetic approach seem, at times, to suggest that every religion per definition has something to do with the Most High. There is, after all, only one divine being to which both Islam and Christianity are referring, whatever we call it.[5] That human beings are estranged from God and

---

3. See Reitsma, *God of My Enemy*, 70–72, for an exegesis of Romans 9:30–10:3.

4. Verkuyl, *Zijn alle godsdiensten gelijk*, 122. In *Inleiding*, 479, Verkuyl calls this "human repression."

5. Kärkkäinen, *Theology of Religions*, 25.

that creation is profoundly out of joint is barely given any attention. However, that is something that should get equal weight. God may make himself known through the medium of religions, but religions themselves are not by definition the vehicle of the Most High simply and only because they are focused on the transcendent. How God can potentially allow himself to be known through Islam requires interpretation. Speaking from a biblical-theological framework, we must emphasize that the key to that interpretation can only be found in Christ. He has realized a new creation through his death and resurrection. The place of light around the cross shows us insight into the deepest essence of God.

4.3 God or Allah?

To discover how zeal *for* and resistance *against* God relate to each other, we will now take up the relationship between the God of Christianity and the God of Islam. Do Muslims and Christians, in essence, serve the same God? When Muslims display a passion for God; which God are we talking about? It is in this context that the question of whether God and Allah are the same is constantly asked, even though it hardly plays a role when Muslims and Christians meet. Apparently this question touches a sensitive nerve. That could be due to the fear of syncretism which says that it ultimately does not matter what you believe or what sacrifices you make for those beliefs. For others, it stems from their conviction that Islam is the work of the evil one. It could come from psychological factors, namely the fear of losing one's identity. People are inclined to divide the world into "us" and "them," "established ones" and "outsiders."[6] Whatever the reason, reflecting on the question of how the God of the Bible relates to the God of Islamic tradition can help us better understand Islam in light of biblical revelation.

I purposely speak about the God of the Bible and the God of Islamic tradition because Allah is the Arabic word for God. In line with all Arabic Bible translations, Christians in the Middle East, North Africa, and Asia use the word "Allah" for the God of the Bible. That means that the question of whether God is the same as Allah in itself is pointless: is God/Allah the same as God/Allah? Even the usage of phrases like "the God of the Bible" and "the God of Islamic tradition"[7] does not guard against potential confusion of tongues

---

6. See Elias and Scotson, *Established and the Outsiders.*

7. The God of the Bible also cannot just be compared to the God of the Qur'an because the Bible and the Qur'an are understood differently in Christianity and Islam. The Qur'an, as the ultimate revelation of God in Islam, is to be compared with the position of Jesus as the

because several Muslims in the Western world continue to use the Arabic word "Allah" to refer to the God of Islam even when "local" equivalents are available. This is in part due to the fact that according to the majority of Muslims the Qur'an – and thus also the word "Allah" – is untranslatable. It also coheres with the search for their own Islamic identity in a non-Islamic context.[8]

In order to avoid confusion, it is important here to distinguish accurately between the "images" that Muslims and Christians have of God and God as an entity, a "being." An example can illustrate this. When two former classmates talk about a former professor it can be that both of them experienced this professor in very different ways. One might have thought the professor was incredible, the other utterly annoying. This can be about one and the same person: both have a very different view of that person. It can, however, also be that they are, in fact, speaking about two different professors. That would explain why their memories are so different. When focusing on the God of the Bible and the God of the Islamic tradition, the question therefore arises if the difference is about having a different view of the "same" being or if it is about two different beings. The latter is possible even when our images of God have a lot in common. Figures 4.1 and 4.2 show these two options in a systematic, and thus simplified, manner.

As mentioned in the foreword the term "God" is used both for the God of Islam and the God of Christianity without drawing any conclusions in advance to the identity or nature of God. The latter we shall now explore further by looking at the meaning of 1 Corinthians 8:6 where Paul states that there is only one God, the Creator, and one Lord, the Savior. He does so with regard to the multicultural and multireligious context of the Greco-Roman empire. How should followers of Jesus position themselves in a society that is completely saturated with Hellenistic religiosity? Are they supposed to withdraw themselves from it or can they stay and participate?

Word of God in Christianity, as seen earlier. Additionally, the Bible has a similar meaning in Christianity as Muhammad in Islam, being the inspired witness of God's Word. This also means that Muhammad and Jesus cannot be compared. Lastly, it is not about the God of Christendom and the God of Islam, because the images of God in these two religions are not identical to who God is.

8. In 2007 the Malaysian government forbid a Catholic newspaper and an evangelical church from using "Allah" in order to refer to the God of the Bible. According to the government, it would be confusing for Muslims and this usage of Allah could be used to convert Muslims to the Christian faith. That prohibition provisionally got confirmed in 2014 by the supreme court. It did not apply to all Christians.

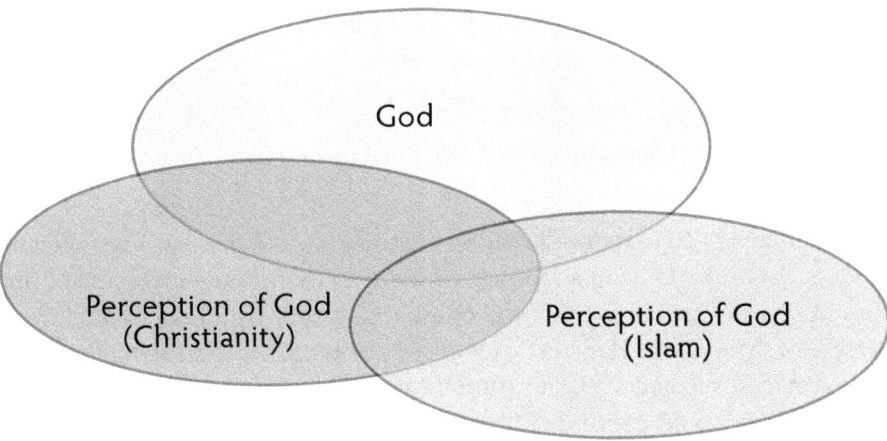

Figure 4.1

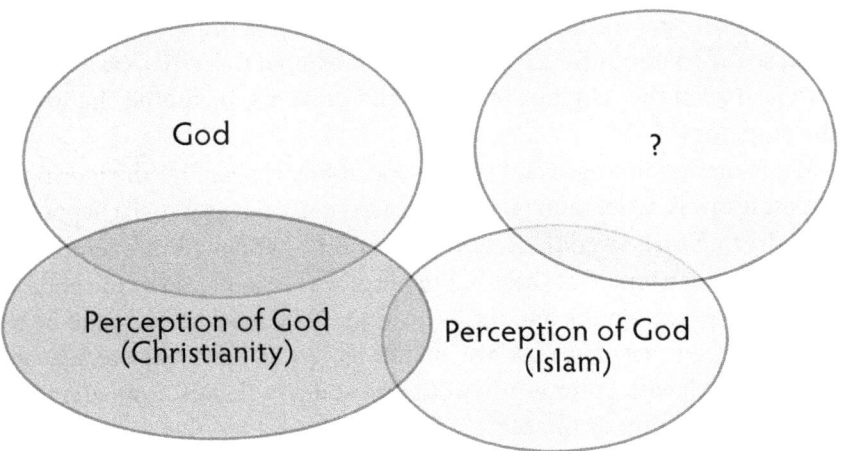

Figure 4.2

This passage can only be understood by taking the context of chapters 8 through 10, which forms a thematic unit, into account.[9] In chapter 10 the theme found in chapter 8, about food and the worship of idols, is explored again and concluded (1 Cor 10:15–33). Then, in chapter 11, a new theme is started.

---

9. See Willis, "1 Corinthians 8–10," 103–105. Expanded argumentation is found in Thiselton, *First Epistle to the Corinthians*, 607–612.

Chapter 9 provides concrete examples of what the freedom of the Christian community means in a multireligious society.

4.4 Worshipping Idols that Don't Exist (1 Cor 8–10)
4.4.1 Introduction

1 Corinthians 8–10 is about the eating of food ("meat") that has been offered to idols (1 Cor 8:1).[10] Can a follower of Jesus do that? Some members of the community of Corinth were of the opinion that they could and would even partake of the meals at Hellenistic temples (1 Cor 8:10). Others struggled with that or at least seemed at risk to stumble and fall due to the position of these believers that would continue to participate (1 Cor 8:9–13). It is not exactly clear what Paul alludes to here. It is a well-known fact that Corinth was a prosperous Roman colony that contained a Jewish community.[11] The city had, like many other cities in the Hellenistic empire, a great number of temples for as many gods. Society was controlled by religious ideas and practices. All of life was infused with the presence of the gods and their whims. Everything was focused on keeping the gods happy. That's why it was impossible to separate normal social life from religious. Those who wanted to participate in society had to also keep the religious practices and customs, including the worship of the emperor.[12]

Meals played an important role in social life, especially considering the countless festivals. Celebrations in honor of the gods, but also social happenings such as birth rituals, weddings, and cremations, happened in a temple. The meat that was consumed at these happenings was first offered to the gods and would then be eaten in the temple.[13] The food that was left over would be sold at the market. In that way, regular Corinthians could have it at home as well. That's why the Jewish community would most likely abstain from all meat.

The intertwining of the service to the gods and regular daily life made things pretty difficult for members of the Christian community. Due to their

---

10. This is the most literal rendering of *eidolothuton* (εἰδωλόθυτον), which is a combination of εἴδωλον and θύω. Strictly speaking, it could be about more than just food, but the context clearly points in the direction of food, especially meat (κρέας; 1 Cor 8:13). See Thayer, *Greek-English Lexicon*. See for an overview Thiselton, *Corinthians*, 617–620.

11. Witherington, *Conflict*, loc. 708–709.

12. Wright, "One God," 45–46.

13. Witherington, *Conflict*, loc. 538–614. Excavations of temple complexes have found a number of dining rooms. See Gooch, *Dangerous Food*, viii–xvi, 1–13. Whether these dining halls would also operate as a sort of restaurant during antiquity is not entirely sure.

position in society, those who were well-off were expected at social gatherings that would, nearly without exception, have a religious nature. If they wanted to abstain from the service to idols, it would mean a strong infringement on their social life.[14] The consequences of such isolation would, for those who were less well-off – a significant group of those in the church of Corinth (see 1 Cor 1:28) – be even more impactful. They were almost completely dependent on a patron for their food and livelihood. In exchange for socio-political support, they would be given food and work (patronage). They simply could not withdraw from their (religiously tinted) social duties.[15]

This could be the background to Paul's remarks in 1 Corinthians 8:10 about the joining at the table of believers in a temple. He could potentially be thinking of the offering festivals or another gathering. In 10:27 the meal in question seems to refer to one at someone's home, without a direct link to a temple religious festival. However, that does not mean that there would be no meat that had previously been offered to the gods (see for example 1 Cor 10:28). Either way, Paul is addressing a serious problem that includes more than entering and eating at temples. How are believers to position themselves in a multireligious society?[16] They seem to have no other option than to choose either complete isolation or complete assimilation.[17] The first is impossible; the second theologically undesirable. Interestingly, Paul chooses an entirely different approach to this dilemma.

4.4.2 Idols Don't Exist

Paul ensures there is no misunderstanding about it: believers do indeed have "the right" to eat pagan food that has been sacrificed (1 Cor 8:9), even when it is taking place at a pagan temple (1 Cor 8:10).[18] Even those who are visiting

---

14. Witherington, *Conflict*, loc. 602–605.

15. See deSilva, *Honor, Patronage, Kinship and Purity*, 95–156.

16. This seems to be the primary theme in this letter: the relationship between a value system that is determined by grace, the cross, and resurrection and the value system of the Hellenistic environment. See Thiselton, *Corinthians*, 40. For other introductory questions, see diverse commentaries such as Thiselton, *Corinthians*, 1–52; Fitzmyer, *First Corinthians*, 21–118; Witherington, *Conflict*, loc. 388–705; Fotopoulos, "Arguments Concerning Food," 611–631; Fotopoulos, "Rhetorical Situation," 165–198.

17. Wright uses "dualism" instead of isolation and "paganism" instead of assimilation. Wright, *Climax of the Covenant*, 126.

18. Still, "Paul's Aims," 343–363. Some expositors deny that right, regardless of the location, such as Gooch, *Dangerous Food*, 93: the ambivalences in Paul's argumentation show that Paul strongly rejects judgement of the "strong"; his confirmation is a sham. See also Garland, "Dispute over Food," 173–197. According to Still, this does not hold up. The "rights" that Paul mentions

an unbeliever at home do not have to first ask where the meat came from but can easily eat "whatever is set before" them (1 Cor 10:27). The term *exousia* (ἐξουσία) that in 8:9 is translated as "right," primarily denotes the legal power at the root of it. The translation "liberty" to eat (NRSV, ASV) comes near but has too much focus on the unhindered use of possibilities. The emphasis here is more on the legal aspect, the – God given – authority.[19] The believers have the right to eat everything that is for sale at the market (1 Cor 10:25): "All things are lawful" (1 Cor 10:23).

The argument that Paul uses to defend this position is that there is no God but one in all of the universe and that an idol has no real existence (1 Cor 8:4).[20] The term "idol" here can refer to a statue of a god, like those in the temples of Corinth, but it can also denote the "deity" the statue represents.[21] With this statement, Paul almost literally points back to the core confession of Israel, the *Shema*: "Hear, O Israel: The LORD our God, the LORD is one" (Deut 6:4 ESV; see table 4.1). This is the starting point of faith for every Jew, including Paul.[22] It is also at the center of his argumentation in the following chapters (8–10). However, he does add two points to this confession:[23]

---

in 1 Cor 9, and which he freely gives up, are also real, and thus, that would similarly apply to 1 Cor 8.

19. *LSJ*: "power or authority" to do a thing.

20. Literally put, we know that there is no idol in the cosmos and there is no God but *one* (ὅτι οὐδὲν εἴδωλον ἐν κόσμῳ καὶ ὅτι οὐδεὶς θεὸς εἰ μὴ εἷς). Also possible: "we know that an idol is nothing in this world" (NIV). The latter connects to the characterization of idols in the Old Testament as "nothings" (*hèbèlim*). The structure of verse 4, however, does point in a different direction. The first and second part are formulated in parallel to each other. The second part can only be translated as "there is no God (except *one*)" and not as "God is nothing." That's why it makes sense to translate the first part (there is no idol) in the same way. See Thiselton, *Corinthians*, 630.

21. Prior, *1 Corinthians*, 145–146.

22. Wright, *Paul*, 662.

23. Concerning these additions, the link with the *Shema* has not always been noticed. For example, Fee sees it as a creation of Paul. Fee, *First Epistle*, 374. On the basis of *ta panta*, the underlying background has been found in the Stoa, as seen in the overview given by Thiselton, *Corinthians*, 635. Additionally, the association of 1 Cor 8:3 with Deut 6:5 supports the connection between 1 Cor 8 and Deut 6. Schrage also misses the connection in *Die erste Brief an die Korinther*. Gardner sees it as a possibility that "the strong" are Jewish Gnostics. Gardner, *Gifts of God*, 21.

Table 4.1[24]

Deuteronomy 6:4	1 Corinthians 8:6

κύριος
  ὁ θεὸς ἡμῶν (εἷς ἐστιν)
 	
κύριος εἷς ἐστιν
	εἷς θεός,
	  ὁ πατὴρ
	    ἐξ οὗ τὰ πάντα καὶ ἡμεῖς εἰς αὐτόν
	εἷς κύριος,
	  Ἰησοῦς Χριστὸς
	    δι' οὗ τὰ πάντα καὶ ἡμεῖς δι' αὐτοῦ.

The LORD,
  our God (is the only/one)
 	
The LORD is the only (one)
	there is one God
	  the Father,
	    from whom are all things and for whom
	    we exist
	and one Lord,
	  Jesus Christ,
	    through whom are all things and through
	    whom we exist

He first of all declares that the one God is also the Father from whom everything (*ta panta*) was created and for whom we exist. Paul emphasizes with this that there is nothing and no one that is at the same level as God. He alone is the Creator and all others exist because of him.[25] Creatures are created to honor and acknowledge him. Second, Paul confesses that the one Lord is none other than Jesus Christ "through whom are all things and through whom we exist." Paul places the crucified one, Jesus Christ, right at the center of the most explicit monotheistic confession,[26] not as a second godhead but as the one God himself. God is the Lord and this Lord is none other than Jesus Christ. By christologically reinterpreting the Shema, Paul creates a theological novum that we could call "christological monotheism."[27] In the new dispensation, the confession of Israel has not been set aside but transformed to the reality of God's continued revelation in Christ. In addition, the work of Christ does

---

24. This diagram is based on Wright, "One God," 48.

25. In Gen 1:31, *ta panta* (τὰ πάντα) is used in the Septuagint for everything God has created, just as it is used in Col 1:16–17, 20, and in Rom 8:32 for the glory of the new creation.

26. Wright, *Climax of the Covenant*, 129; Wright, *Paul*, 667; Bauckham, *God Crucified*, 40.

27. Wright, *Climax of the Covenant*, 129; Bauckham, *God Crucified*, 45–79.

not only relate to recreation as is regularly explained.[28] Paul makes no explicit distinction between creation and recreation here. The Father never creates without the Son and the Son does not work apart from the Father. This is how it goes in the Middle East; the son always does what the father would be doing, and the father is always intent upon the work and future of his son. This redefinition of the Shema coincides with what was found in part I: God has created everything for the history of God with human beings and the world. Everything is made by God, for him, and to honor him (1 Cor 8:6). This intention is emphasized again "through Christ," as Christ is God himself, YHWH. Through him everything is there from the beginning and through him all the broken pieces of the world will come back to God's original purpose.

So, if there is only one God and idols do not exist, then eating meat that has been offered to idols has no meaning at all (1 Cor 8:8). All food has been created by God, everything is his (1 Cor 10:26; Ps 24[LXX 23]:1). It simply cannot be of the gods, since the gods do not exist. Of course, Paul cannot deny that there are indeed very many gods. Corinth is full of them. Even the Roman emperor is worshipped as a god. There are many gods and lords in the heavens and on earth (1 Cor 8:5). Even though these gods do not really exist and are "so-called" (λεγόμενοι) gods, for those who worship them they are a reality. They impact their lives and have a certain power over these people. But then again, there is only one God for the believers (v. 6). That is no subjective, postmodern statement for Paul, as if this were to only be true for believers and not for the rest of Corinth. Paul wants to accentuate with this that the body of Christ, in opposition to so many different gods, recognizes only one God, namely the Creator and Savior. The *Shema* is not just the result of argumentation, it's the confession of the covenant.[29] It requires the commitment of all of life to God (see Deut 6:3). According to Deuteronomy 6, the confession of the one God leads to the loving of the Lord with all our heart, with all our soul, and with all our might (Deut 6:5 ESV). It means a life according to the principles of the Torah: life in agreement with how God had intended it to be.

In this way, Paul is resisting every form of dualism that says there are other powers besides God that can claim the world and the believer. Because there is no other God than the one God, believers can continue to participate in daily life without worry or fright. They do not have to withdraw from the world for fear of other powers.

---

28. Wright, *Climax of the Covenant*, 131.
29. Wright, *Paul*, 663.

4.4.3 No Stumbling Blocks

Still, that does not settle all of it. Without taking back any of his recognition of the rights of believers, Paul does make an important sidenote. Everything is permitted but not everything is beneficial and constructive (1 Cor 10:23 NIV). Not everyone possesses the same "knowledge" (1 Cor 8:7). In this chapter (1 Cor 8:1, 7, 10–11), Paul does not mean *gnosis*, "gnostic" or scientific knowledge, but the recognition that there is only one God and one Lord and that idols don't exist.[30] Not everyone entirely shares that knowledge. The authority of the believers *with* knowledge can therefore unintentionally lead to the fall of brothers and sisters with a weak conscience (8:9, 13). Paul is even speaking about "being destroyed" (ESV) or "perishing" (ASV) (ἀπόλλυμι; 8:11), a term that has an eschatological sound to it and is connected to the judgement of God.[31] In his letters to the Corinthians, Paul uses this term primarily in relation to those that do not believe in Christ.[32]

The question is therefore why Paul, all of a sudden, is using such strong terminology. How can he say that a believer with a weak conscience can be destroyed if he or she – tempted or encouraged by the behavior of the believer with "knowledge" – eats food offered to the gods (1 Cor 8:10)? If idols do not exist, it really should not matter if someone is eating anything either with a weak conscience or with knowledge. Either it is sinful to eat the meat offered to idols, and that would go for everyone (both those who have "knowledge" and those who have a weak conscience), or it is not. Of course, intentions are important when evaluating someone's actions. It is possible to commit a sin intentionally or without intention or even awareness. This has implications for the degree of punishment for a specific sin. However, the simple fact that someone does not think something is not a sin does not make it right in God's eyes. Reversely, if someone does think it is wrong that does not imply that God

---

30. According to Fitzmyer, *First Corinthians*, 344. Dawes, "Danger of Idolatry," 88–90. The meaning is close to that of "wisdom" mentioned by Paul in chapters 1–3 (1:17, 21, 30; 2:5; 3:19). Wisdom in wisdom literature is concerned with the recognition of the one God and is closely related to knowledge and insight (see for example Prov 1:7; 9:10; 21:11; Eccl 12:9; Sir 21:13). It is the wise one who lives from the recognition that there is one God. See Job 28:28; Ps 111[LXX 110]:10; Prov 1:7; 2:5 (where the honor/fear for God coincides with "knowledge"/ gnosis of God); 9:10; see also Isa 11:2; 33:6. Additionally, the role and position of Jesus, "through whom all exists" (1 Cor 8:6), in relation to creation, recollects the position of wisdom in Jewish wisdom traditions. Wis 7:21–22, 26; 9:2; Prov 8:22. See Wright, *Climax of the Covenant*, 131.

31. In the Septuagint this is applied to those who have been cut off from the people of the covenant and who are destroyed or who perish. See for example Exod 30:38; Lev 7:20–21, 25, 27; Num 14:12; 16:33; 17:27; Deut 2:12, 21; 4:26; 7:23–24.

32. For example, in 1 Cor 1:18–19; 15:18; 2 Cor 2:15; Rom 2:12; 14:15; see also John 3:16.

agrees. The difference is not in the insights of the person in question but purely in God's norm for life, the Torah.

The crucial difference between believers with and without knowledge lies much deeper. What is at stake here is the fact that believers with a weak conscience are still so accustomed to the worship of idols that they participated in in the past.[33] Therefore, for them, partaking in the meals at the temple is truly experienced as the worship of idols (1 Cor 8:7). The idols are still real to them. When believers with "knowledge" join in the eating at the temples, the believers with a weak conscience do not draw the conclusion that idols do not exist, but that it is apparently no problem to worship idols alongside the one God. That is their sin. They attach meaning to the reality of the idols and because of that fall into real worship of other gods, and that is idolatry.[34] By doing so, they disobey the first commandment of the Decalogue. They break the covenant that is founded upon the Shema.

This is also the reason why their conscience is "defiled" (1 Cor 8:7; μολύνω). The translation of being "bothered" (CEV) by a weak conscience does not reflect the meaning of this term well. Each time it is found in the Septuagint or the New Testament it is used in the cultural context of "desecration" or "being unclean."[35] A "defiled" conscience is for God a "desecrated" or "violated" conscience that requires purification and sanctification. In a legal context, it would be counted as a "guilty" verdict as there is sin involved. In this context, it is not about a believer with scruples feeling bad about doing something out of habit that he or she knows deep down is going against God's commandment. It is not about a believer with a moral dilemma. It is also not about a believer that is being "defiled" or "possessed" by demons and is therefore estranged from God. This is about someone who gave up their exclusive dedication to the one God and the one Lord Jesus Christ by recognizing and serving other gods before God. Hence Paul's sharp words about perishing. The weak believer will not perish because he is going against his own principles, but against those of God. He invalidates the Shema and objectively breaks the covenant with God. Because of that, freedom leads again to bondage (see 1 Cor 6:12).

The "conscience" being spoken of here can be understood as discernment. It seems primarily to be a sort of moral "spiritual compass" that gives believers

---

33. The most obvious reading is συνήθεια, as for example in P46, ℵ, B, 33; the Western chooses συνείδησις, as for example D, G and the Vulgate, but this is easily read as an adjustment to the closing of the verse. See Thiselton, *Corinthians*, 639.

34. According to Dawes, "Danger," 90, and Willis, "1 Corinthians 8–10," 108.

35. See for example Gen 37:31; Isa 59:3; Lam 4:14; 1 Cor 8:7; Rev 3:4; 14:4. See also 1 Macc 1:37; 2 Macc 6:2; 4 Macc 9:20.

an insight into the reality God had intended.[36] It has a kind of prophetic role. When it is "weak" (ἀσθενής), the conscience does not have the power or the ability to fulfill its role.[37] It lacks the right "knowledge" and is not capable of spiritually discerning and debunking the power of the old habit.

This is different from what Paul is addressing in Romans 14 and 15. Those passages are about the weak and the strong who make different decisions about matters that are neither good nor bad. The Romans passage is about food as well, but at the same time, it is about so much more, such as whether or not certain days should have any importance. The difference is that in 1 Corinthians 8 it is about adiaphora. The matter in question is not the food as such, but the temptation to associate with idols. In 1 Corinthians 8 there is no distinction between the weak and the strong, like there is in Romans 14:1 and 15:1, but between believers with knowledge and believers with a weak conscience.[38] It is about the contrast between living a life in the freedom of the covenant and the breaking of it. In Romans it is about two options within the framework of service to God.[39]

This is serious. Because there are believers "without knowledge" and with a "weak conscience," Paul asks believers "with knowledge" to abstain from their "right" to eat meat that has been offered to idols. If "knowledge" is the cause of people for whom Jesus died perishing (1 Cor 8:11), then that knowledge is not functioning as it ought to (1 Cor 8:2; καθὼς δεῖ). It is not in agreement with God's intentions. He does not want for any people to perish (2 Pet 3:9). That is why knowledge can only function through love. Knowledge without love puffs up (1 Cor 8:1). The confession of the one God and Lord is no individualistic confession but a communal one.[40] The church is a body that belongs together (1 Cor 10:16–17; 11:29; 12). If one part of the body suffers or falls away, the whole body suffers (1 Cor 12:26). If, therefore, someone perishes

---

36. Wright, *Paul for Everyone*, 102: "internal compass"; Dawes, "Danger," 96: "internal judge." It is about the making of right moral judgements.

37. See also Rom 5:6 and 8:3. See Reitsma, *God of My Enemy*, 72–74.

38. Cf. Dawes, "Danger," 87. Here, too, it is not about being weak in faith, like in Romans, but about a weak conscience. That is not at issue in Romans. There is no mention of "the strong" in 1 Corinthians at all, even though that is often added in the interpretation. See for example Thiselton, *Corinthians*, 644.

39. Dawes, "Danger," 98; the interpretation that believers with a weak conscience can be tempted to go against their own faith shows that a reading is done in light of Romans 14 and 15.

40. In Deuteronomy, the confession of faith that there is only one God is placed in the context of the fellowship of Israel as a people. God choses Israel as a whole and makes a covenant with the entire community (Deut 7). To have awe for YHWH (Deut 6:2) and to love YHWH (Deut 6:5) means to specifically follow his commandments (Deut 6:2, 6–9). These commandments are related to the relationship with God and neighbor.

because someone in the church thinks he or she can eat anything – that is going against love, the love for God and for neighbor. It is sinning against the body of Christ and thus against Christ (1 Cor 8:12). By the way, being considerate stretches beyond just brothers and sisters. It also applies to Jews and Greeks (1 Cor 10:32). The freedom to eat meat sacrificed to idols should not become a stumbling block to following Christ for anyone (1 Cor 10:33).

When believers are guests in the homes of nonbelievers, there is no problem at all in eating what is served. They don't have to wonder if the food was offered to idols or not (1 Cor 10:25–27). However, if someone points out that it came from gentile temple worship, they are to abstain. Not because it would now create a problem for their own conscience but for the sake of the other (1 Cor 10:29). Moreover, since eating food itself has no additional value before God (1 Cor 8:8) – it does not give the believer a higher status to God nor a lower one[41] – it does not have to be a problem. The highest purpose after all is not someone's own freedom or knowledge but the honor of God (1 Cor 10:31) and the wellbeing of the other (1 Cor 10:33).

Paul supports this appeal to the believers of Corinth in two ways:

1. *The example of Paul.* First, he is pointing to his own attitude. If Paul would cause a brother or sister to fall by eating meat, he would rather be a vegetarian for the rest of his life (1 Cor 8:13). His lifestyle as an apostle has always been focused on not giving any offense to anyone, not to Jews, Greeks, or the body of Christ (10:32–33). That is the example for the Corinthians. In chapter 9, Paul mentions several situations in which he, as an apostle, has forgone his own right (1 Cor 9:15) to eat and drink (1 Cor 9:4), to bring a believing spouse on a journey (1 Cor 9:5), and to receive support for his livelihood (1 Cor 9:6–14). He has consistently made himself a servant to all kinds of people in order to win as many as possible to Christ (1 Cor 9:19; 10:33). He was completely free in doing so (1 Cor 10:23) even though he was bound by Christ and his law (1 Cor 9:19, 21). In the same way that Paul gave up his rights, he is asking the believers of Corinth to do the same.

---

41. What Paul exactly intends this verse to mean is less important in this context. See Thiselton, *Corinthians*, 645–649. The phrase could be used to support the position of both the believers with "knowledge" and those with a "weak conscience." If eating has no specific (spiritual) meaning to God, it should be no problem to participate in the meals at the temple or outside of it; the opposite is just as true.

2.   *Idolatry and demons.* Second, Paul makes it clear in chapter 10 that causing a believing brother or sister to perish is no hypothetical issue. The history of the people of Israel in the desert speaks for itself (1 Cor 10:1–13). All Israelites shared in the spiritual gifts of God, but most of them did not enter the promised land (1 Cor 10:1–5). They worshipped idols (1 Cor 10:7) and were disobedient to God (1 Cor 10:8–10).[42] That is a warning to the church of today (1 Cor 10:6, 11) and touches even believers with "knowledge." Even those who think they are standing can fall (1 Cor 10:12). Even those who participate in Christ can vex the Lord by participating in the sacrificial services of pagans (1 Cor 10:22; cf. Deut 32:12). After all, the pagans sacrifice to demons.[43] That is why those who are participating in the sacrificial services are also in fellowship with demons (1 Cor 10:20).

It seems as if Paul is contradicting himself here. If idols do not exist, how can believers still be one with demons? What does Paul mean?[44] To start with, he repeats his statement that an idol is nothing and that a sacrifice to an idol is therefore also meaningless (1 Cor 10:19). God is the one and only God. Demons are in that sense not gods. All things, including demons, are created by God (1 Cor 8:6).[45] The problem to Paul is the *connection to* demons. He does not want believers to become one (κοινωνός) with demons (1 Cor 10:20). The term *koinōnos* indicates someone who identifies with another, who becomes a "partner" or "companion" to the other. Those who become one with a criminal are themselves criminals (Prov 28:24); a companion in suffering, suffers themselves (2 Cor 1:7). Someone who is one with demons, belongs to

---

42. Paul refers in 1 Cor 10:7–10 to diverse incidents during the journey of Israel through the desert. Several elements can be identified such as the idolatry of the golden calf (Exod 32; cf. 1 Cor 10:7), the punishment of the snakes (Num 21; cf. 1 Cor 10:9), and the history in Num 14:16 – even though it is about 25,000 instead of 23,000 people there that die (cf. 1 Cor 10:8). For the question at hand the details are less important. Israel was disobedient to God and let itself get tempted into worshiping other beings besides the One and that is a warning to the believers in the New Testament. See Fitzmyer, *First Corinthians*, 384–387; Thiselton, *Corinthians*, 722–743.

43. It is not clear what exactly Paul means with the diminutive *daimonion* (δαιμόνιον). To explore that futher, see Riley, "Demon," 445–455.

44. See Gooch, *Dangerous Food*, 87–88.

45. Those who experience a tension here often identify "idols" with "demons." Paul, however, says that there are no idols, which is to say that there are no beings that are equal to God; there is only one God. That does not exclude the fact that demons do exist, but they are created beings. Thiselton is thinking here of powers, *Corinthians*, 775.

them.[46] The problem for Paul here again lies not so much with the eating of the food offered to idols or the entering of pagan temples per se. All things are lawful (1 Cor 10:23). Meat is just meat. By offering it to the gods it has not become contagious, as if consumption alone would be enough to keep believers away from Christ. If that were the case, it would also apply to believers with "knowledge." The problem also does not lie in the location, as if the eating of food offered to the gods is only "safe" outside of the temple complex. If that were the case, eating in a temple would, per definition, also be unacceptable for believers with "knowledge" according to Paul. That is precisely not what he is saying (see 1 Cor 8:10).[47] His focus is on the participation in the *service to* idols.[48] That is still idolatry, even if the idols do not exist. It is a breaking of the covenant because believers would then be worshipping other "gods" besides the one true God. Serving other "gods" besides YHWH is a form of religious adultery.[49] In the end, these "so-called gods" are really just creatures. Honoring them is the primal sin of human beings according to Paul: whoever honors a creature instead of the Creator is exchanging the truth (see 1 Cor 8:2) about God for a lie (Rom 1:25). This breaks the fellowship with God in Christ (1 Cor 1:9). It is impossible to be one with both demons and Christ (1 Cor 10:20–21).

Paul gives two examples to clarify his point. He points to the sacrificial service in the Old Testament and the Lord's Supper. The temple servants in the Old Testament, who ate the offering, were participating in that which the offering stood for (1 Cor 10:18). Whoever participates in the bread and cup, joins (*koinoonia*) in the dying and rising of Christ (1 Cor 10:16; see also 1 Cor 11:24–26). In both cases it is about the condition of the heart of the one who consumes. Pagans who would eat from the sacrifices made at the temple would not automatically participate in the atonement. And whoever would participate in an unworthy fashion in the meal of Christ would not be joining with Christ but would instead call out judgement on themselves (See 1 Cor 11:27–29). The same is thus also true for the eating of food in the pagan temples. It does not automatically lead to fellowship with demons or contamination by demons. It

---

46. To be a companion is comparable to "experiencing *koinonia*," "being one with." *Koinōnia* indicates an intimate connection or to have something in common: 2 Cor 6:4; 9:13; 13:13; Phil 1:5; 2:1; 3:10; 1 John 1:3, 6–7.

47. Both in 1 Cor 8:4, 8, 13, as well as 10:23, 25, 30–31, Paul is speaking about the offering of food to idols in general and in certain locations.

48. According to Willis, "1 Corinthians 8–10," 108.

49. The word for adultery or prostitution (1 Cor 6:18) is also used in the Old Testament to refer to the worship of other gods. See Rev 2:15; 1 Chr 5:25; Ps 73[LXX 72]:27; 106[LXX 105]:39; Hos 3:3; 4:10, 14, 18.

is, however, all about becoming united to the service of idols and, because of that, to demons who are conveniently using idolatry for their own purposes. That is why believers should withdraw from pagan worship services. Paul compares this to the attitude of Israel in the desert. Because the Christian community knows how things ended with the Israelites, it is a firm warning to avoid idolatry (1 Cor 10:14). The temptation exists for everyone (1 Cor 10:12), but it is not beyond the believer's ability nor the outcome that God will provide (1 Cor 10:13).

4.4.4 Excursus: Demons

It is not entirely clear what Paul is picturing when he mentions demons. The term *diamonion* is a diminutive of *daimōn*. *Daimōn* means a lower deity in the Greek world of gods. It is translated as evil spirit, devil, or demon.[50] It is hardly used in the Septuagint (Deut 32:17; Ps 90[LXX 89]:6; 95[LXX 94]:5; 105[LXX 104]:37; Isa 13:21; 34:14; 65:3), and when it appears in the New Testament, it is primarily in the Gospels. The meaning it has there is one of spirits that are bothering people. Paul only uses *diamonion* here and in 1 Timothy 4:1. In Ephesians 6 it is not used, which is surprising because it mentions Satan (*diabolos*) and all kinds of evil spirits in the heavens (Eph 6:11–12; cf. Col 1:16). What he describes in 1 Corinthians 8 is quite down to earth. From that, the following can be concluded:

1. Demons are created beings. If there is only one God, no form or version of dualism is remotely possible. Demons are not at the same level as the Creator. Idols do not exist; they are simply creatures. In our culture, when thinking of demons, images from movies like *Ghostbusters* and *Casper* quickly come to mind. Paul is rather reserved and matter of fact about it.

2. According to Paul, the "weak" believers in Corinth commit the most primal sin of humankind when worshipping the creation next to or instead of the Creator (Rom 1:21, 25). If demons are creations then this is about violating the first commandment and compromising the confession of faith, the Shema. In fact, this would be considered religious adultery.

3. The believers are not being possessed by demons through their service to non-existing idols. In some charismatic circles there is

---

50. See Riley, "Demon," 445.

the idea that people can get "demonically infected" or "possessed." Whoever enters the prayer space of a non-Christian religion or cult, or whoever engages in alternative Eastern healing practices, could become infected with the occult. It is not ruled out that participating in the occult can lead to demonic possession, but what Paul is describing here is not focused on that. According to him, believers are free to turn away from service to idols and turn to fellowship with Christ. There is no mention of power that demons exercise against the will of the believers.[51]

4. With this in mind, it is interesting to study folk-Islam more closely. There are countless rituals and customs that can be dismissed as "superstition" and yet can also be seen as associated with the presence of "powers" and spirits.[52] The question is if these rituals in themselves connect people to the service of idols, or if it is exactly the other way around. Not acknowledging and honoring God alone could be keeping them from the freedom of the gospel. Rituals in that sense then are simply an expression of that. However, this falls outside the scope of this study.

5. The reality of the evil one or the powers of Satan are not denied. However, the New Testament is down to earth about describing these powers, especially in comparison to the speculations found in the literature of the Second Temple period.

4.4.5 Conclusion

The question of how a follower of Jesus should live in a multireligious context cannot be answered with just a few rules of thumb. This is made clear by the example of eating food that has been offered to idols. It is impossible to make one general statement about whether or not it is permissible to eat the meat that comes from pagan temples. The answer is determined by the context and perspective taken. It is never a matter that can be judged in an abstract way.

Paul handles a similar way of reasoning for other delicate themes, such as sexuality. There, too, the same principle is in force: "All things are lawful, but not all things are helpful" (1 Cor 6:12). Sexuality is a gift of creation given to

---

51. The situations that are described in the Gospels (e.g. Matt 9:33–34; 17:18; Mark 7:29; Luke 8:27–38) are of a different kind and are signs of the coming of the new age of salvation.

52. See for example Love, *Muslims*.

a man and a woman who are bound together. In this way, they "become one body" (Eph 5:31; Gen 2:24). Sexuality, therefore, does not exist in a vacuum, but only gets meaning in the context of a relationship. In a relationship of love and commitment, sexuality is good, but in relation with a prostitute it is not (1 Cor 6:16). Factually speaking, it does not have to be very different in practice, yet it is fundamentally different in principle according to Paul. The same goes for the eating of food offered to idols. It does not exist in a vacuum. For those who are exclusively committed to Christ, and who know there is only one God, it is "just" food. For those who serve idols next to the One, the eating of the food opens the door to demons.

4.5 Conclusion: God, Allah, and the Evil One

How can this passage give more insight into the relationship between the God of the Bible and the God of Islamic tradition(s)? Before looking at this, we need to realize that Islam cannot be compared to the polytheistic religion of the Greeks and Romans in Corinth. Muslims do not worship statues; in classical Islam the making of statues in general and of the prophet Muhammad in particular is a very sensitive issue. Islam actually exists because the prophet Muhammad resisted all the gods that the Arab peoples were worshipping in his day. His primary purpose was to get the tribes of the Arabian Peninsula back to the worship of the one God. This is something that needs to be recognized.

4.5.1 There Is Only One God

There is only one God, the Father, from whom are all things and for whom we exist (1 Cor 8:6). No other gods exist. In emulating the people of Israel (Deut 6:4), this is something that cannot be denied by Christians. That means that Muslims *cannot* serve another God, because there *is* no other God. According to classical Islamic tradition, the prophet Muhammad had the intent to bring the Arab peoples back to the service of the one God. Before him, revelations from the same God came to Moses (*Tauwrat*), David (*Zabur*), and Jesus (*Injil*). Due to the fact that these revelations had gotten corrupted by Jews and Christians, Muhammad received them in their purest form.[53] Whatever

---

53. For many Muslims the God of Islam is therefore automatically the same God as in Christianity, even though many Christians, to them, have a wrong view of God. It can be sensitive to them when Christians deny that because it is questioning the core of their faith. However, there are other streams within Islam that recognize far less continuity between the

we may think of this, for Christians to assume that Muslims serve another god and that, therefore, other gods exist, would in fact mean they cease being Christians. Christianity stands or falls on the recognition that there is no other God but the One.

4.5.2 Jesus Christ

That does not settle all of the matter though. Muslims have no issue with the first part of the confession found in 1 Corinthians, namely that there is only one God. Their issue is with the second part, that God is the "one Lord, Jesus Christ" (1 Cor 8:6). The (Jewish) apostle Paul does not reject monotheism with this statement but gives it a reworking. In this, Muslims cannot follow Christians. In Islam, Isa is the most important messenger after Muhammad and very highly revered. He is so perfect as a human being that he cannot be compared with anyone and is almost divine. And yet, he remains a human being.[54] So even though there is only one God, "classical Islam" and "classical Christianity" differ when it comes to their view of the nature of God. How great that difference is depends on the specific Christian or Islamic tradition. Some streams within Islam are closer to Christianity than others and vice versa. Arian Christianity, for example, does not differ much in its view of Christ from classical Islam. Liberal Christianity has often seen Jesus primarily as a rabbi or prophet but not as God. Islamic Sufism has similarities to Christian mysticism in its search for a connection with the divine.

This all means that I propose that Muslims and Christians are talking about the "same" God but that their understanding of God is not the same. It is about the same being, the teacher of our example in 4.3, but Muslims and Christians differ in their view of the nature of that one being (see figure 4.3). Sometimes the views of this one God diverge so much that we can question if we are still talking about the same being.

God of Christians and Muslims because Christians recognize Jesus as God. See Shah-Kazemi, "Do Muslims and Christians," 76–147.

54. Van Gorder, *No God but God*, 66.

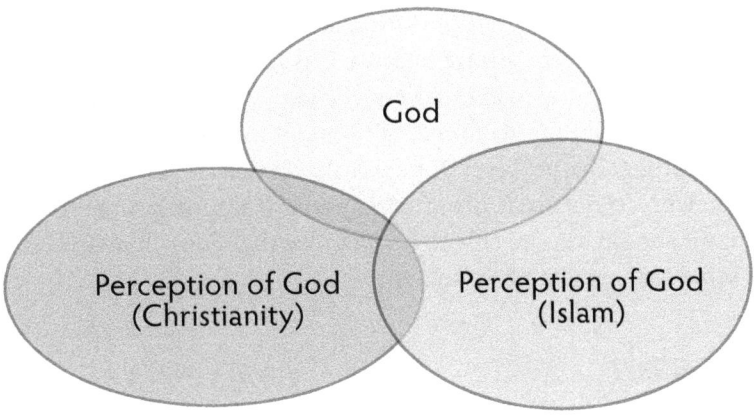

Figure 4.3

4.5.3 Peace as Motive?

Volf, in his book *Allah*,[55] makes the distinction between the "socially relevant" knowledge of God and the "saving" knowledge of God.[56] His focus is thus not on eternal salvation but earthly coexistence between Muslims and Christians.[57] Put differently, Volf designs a sort of political theology with which he would like to motivate Muslims and Christians to live in peace with each other today. According to him, this is only possible when both recognize that in the end, they are both pursuing the one God. Even though their views of God may differ, the objective of their worship is the same.[58] He sees enough commonality with the Christian tradition in certain representatives of Islam to come to this conclusion. He does not deny the differences between Christianity and Islam, however. He continues to hold to the classical faith statements of the Christian faith and the uniqueness of Christ in soteriology.[59] Soteriologically speaking, he would emphasize different aspects than in this political theology.

The surprising thing about Volf's approach is that the prerequisite for peaceful coexistence between people is the recognition that God and Allah are the same. That is also the weakness of his position. The conclusion drawn

---

55. Volf, *Allah*.

56. Volf, 13.

57. Volf, 187.

58. Volf, 14.

59. He explicitly rejects syncretism. Volf, 199.

from Volf's research is its presupposition at the same time. Methodologically speaking, that is not very strong because it is circular reasoning. It prevents the possibility of coming to another conclusion. Moreover, it is also exclusive. Only those that share his starting position will be capable of living in peace with one another. The problem of peaceful coexistence is also and especially with those who do not share his starting point. If we really want to come to a solution, we should also be able to bring those that deny that God and Allah are the same closer together in society.

4.5.4 The Evil One?

There are Christians who connect the God of Islam with the evil one (see ch. 1). The statement made by Paul that serving idols is essentially serving demons seems to allow room for this interpretation. Christians who suggest that Muslims are worshipping a different God than the God of the Bible, and who still hold on to the confession that there is only one God, can therefore only conclude that Muslims worship Satan.[60] Apart from the fact that the evil one, even in this interpretation, is not a god but a created being, it is hard, from a Christian perspective, to defend the idea that Muslims are Satan worshippers. That is far too simplistic and an expression of a very dualistic worldview. It is not something that can be maintained in light of what Paul writes in 1 Corinthians. If something is not from God, it does not mean that it is therefore automatically from the evil one. That does not do justice to the responsibility that human beings have in the complexity of creation. Human beings are not puppets, not of God and not of the evil one. All of creation is the stage that God acts on, but there are also other "actors": the human being with a high level of responsibility, but also the powers, and the spirits in the air, and the evil one. All those actors are playing their role in a complex process of interaction.[61]

The conclusion that Muslims worship another god or the evil one is connected to the rejection of Jesus as the Son of God. If that conclusion is inevitable, then Christians would have to be consistent in admitting that Jews also worship another God. Even though Jesus blames the Jewish leaders in his time of having the devil as their father (John 8:44), that does not mean we can

---

60. It is sometimes said that Muslims worship an idol but that leads to the same conclusion as above. If such an idol is not another god, then it cannot be anything but a creation – which Muslims deny – or a warped image of the One and that is again the first model.

61. See Verkuyl, *Inleiding*, 479, who speaks about a three-dimensional or tripolar view of religion.

simply conclude that Jews are Satan worshippers. That is not a conclusion that many Christians who are critical of Islam would want to draw. And they are, in my view, right. But then that also goes for Islam.

That is not to say that everything Islam stands for, in all respects, is in agreement with the nature of the One. The evil one is capable of misleading people by using religious symbols and systems. Neither Islam, nor Judaism, nor Christianity is immune to that. Christians have to be conscious of the fact that the view of God that exists in Christianity is not identical with God's deepest being. There are forms of Christianity that no longer do justice to the revelation of God in Christ. It could very well be that the evil one has a hand in that.

4.5.5 Trick Question

The question of whether the God of the Bible is the same as the God of Islam cannot be answered with a simple "yes" or "no." If we say that it is about the same God, it needs to be explained that Muslims and Christians nevertheless think very differently about God. Christianity is not Islam, and Islam is not Christianity. If we say that it is not about the same God, then it needs to be explained how this is possible when in fact there is only one God. This is like the trick question: Did you stop hitting your partner? That is an impossible question. Those who answer "yes" will have admitted that they have hit their partner. Answering with "no" is an admission that the hitting is still going on. But those who have never hit the other are not able to answer this question with a simple "yes" or "no." A more extensive explanation is needed.[62] The same goes for the question about the relationship between the God of the Bible and the God of Islamic tradition. Chapman therefore argues for the question to be broken up into smaller questions: (1) Is the Christian *view* of God the same as the Islamic *view* of God? Most Christians would answer that question with "no." (2) Do both views have anything in common? Most Christians would respond with a "yes." The decisive question then is: (3) Do both views have enough in common that Muslims and Christians can use the same word for God?[63] I have answered that question affirmatively here.

62. Chapman, *Cross and Crescent*, 263. The example of domestic abuse is also coming from Chapman.

63. Chapman, 263–264.

5

God, the Holy Spirit, and Experiences of God/god in Islam

"And He made from one man every nation of mankind to live on all the face of the earth . . . that they should seek God, and perhaps feel their way toward him and find him. Yet he is actually not far from each one of us, for 'In him we live and move and have our being'; as even some of your own poets have said, 'For we are indeed his offspring.'" Acts 17:26–28 (ESV)

If a Muslim calls on the name of the Lord, without knowing the Lord, will God hear his or her prayer?

5.1 Introduction

Islam is seen by some Christians as a legalistic, and therefore rather boring, religion. Being Muslim means submitting to the will of God. A Muslim is supposed to direct their lives according to the obligations of divine law, Shari'a. That does not sound appealing to postmodern societies that put a lot of emphasis on freedom, individuality, and authenticity. Discussions in the media about ethical issues such as homosexuality, the position of women, democratic rights and duties, and the ritual slaughter of animals work to strengthen that view. The daily prayer is always the same; there is no singing in the mosque and music is absent. And with all of that, Muslims do not know for sure if all of this insures access into the afterlife by God. You never know if God wants to forgive your sins, not even if you did your utmost to do your best. In short, a Muslim is someone who is denied a certain depth of peace and joy in life.

Let it be clear that is the view that many outsiders, including Christians, have of Islam. Reality, however, is rather different. For example, I have been pleasantly surprised at the exuberant joy Muslims experience during the yearly Feast of the Sacrifice, *Eid al-Adha*. In the Middle East, for hours on end, the minarets fill the air with ecstatic Qur'an recitations. Moreover, the month of Ramadan is a time of joyful repentance and renewal, even though (or maybe because) Muslims abstain from drinking and eating. The daily *iftar* meals with family and friends are some of the most special moments of the year. Muslims can also experience a deep sense of peace when going to Mecca (*hajj*). Evidently, for many Muslims, faith is more than just the compulsory and joyless following of a set of regulations. Many committed Muslims experience peace in their lives through their relationship with God; it gives their lives meaning and fulfillment.[1] Even the lack of assurance of salvation is often appreciated as something positive as it operates as a stimulus to live a devoted Muslim life. Assurance of salvation can easily lead to negligence. Why would you still try your best to live a good life if you already knew where you were going to end up anyway? Of course, there are also many Muslims who are weighed down by the burdens of faith, who recognize the adverse gravity of having no assurance of salvation, and who do not experience a relationship with a good and loving God. In this regard, too, there is great diversity in the Islamic world.

The question is how the faith experience of Muslims – both positive and negative – should be understood. "Experience" is a broad concept,[2] and the focus here is not on what does or does not belong to it. The concern is with how the fact that Muslims say they notice or experience God's nearness in their lives should be understood from a biblical perspective. Can this truly be about the One who has revealed himself through Christ? Or is that option already excluded because Muslims do not recognize Christ as the ultimate revelation of God? What, for example, did Muhammad experience when he got visions and thought the angel Gabriel was bringing him messages directly from God? Where does the peace and joy that Muslims experience in their faith come from; are they from God or not? When Muslims experience their prayers being answered, who is answering them? When Muslims experience healing and other miracles, who is doing these miracles? For Luther, these experiences of Muslims belonged to the *Anfechtungen* (temptations) that could impress Christians and tempt them to convert to Islam.[3]

---

1. See Mallouhi, *Waging Peace on Islam*, 185–239.

2. The concept of "experience" can be about what people go through and encounter, based on feelings as well as knowledge that has been gained through practice.

3. Francisco, *Martin Luther and Islam*, 159–162. Other elements of Islam that made an impression on Luther were the devotion of Islamic clergy, the Islamic devotion to prayer, and the general piety of Muslims.

These questions are part of the search for a biblical-theological view on Islam, the framework of which we have already drawn (part I). The central point is the question of the reality and concreteness of God's presence and work in our world. According to Christian tradition – most specifically found in pentecostal and charismatic circles – this has always been connected to the work of the Holy Spirit. Berkhof typifies the Spirit as "the active presence of God," "God in action."[4] What do the faith experiences of Muslims have to do with the tangible reality of God's work? How does this relate to the work of the Spirit?

5.2 Creation and Religious Experience

In light of the framework of creation set out in part I, we see that experiences of faith are always part of created reality. Being human means to be able to experience reality. Human beings are created to respond to the Creator and creation with their entire being. This is an aspect of being created in the image of God. Human beings are designed in their totality to be connected to God in all facets of their humanity, not just with emotion, will, or mind, but with the deepest layers of their existence. They are also created in order to experience something of God.

This is, therefore, truly about a *human* experience; *humans are* responding to and experiencing something of another reality. It is not as if that other reality is taking over human experience. Theoretically that would be a possibility, of course. In relation to this, diverse indigenous religious traditions in Africa and Asia would think of possession by demons or spiritual powers.[5] The charismatic tradition also reckons with such powers, and in the Roman-Catholic tradition, the office of the exorcist or devil expeller has been recognized for centuries.[6] In such instances of possession, the human being (partially) loses control over themselves. Apart from the question of how to interpret such experiences, it does not evade human responsibility. According to charismatic traditions, people themselves are thought to actively be involved in situations of demonic possession even if just by opening themselves up to certain evil influences. When talking about possession by "powers" or "demons," the boundary between

---

4. Berkhof, *Christian Faith*, 335. The Spirit expresses the personhood of God in its outward actions (Berkhof, 326). Also, in pentecostal and charismatic circles the work of the Spirit is strongly related to experience. See McCarthy, "Spirituality in a Postmodern Era," 196.

5. See also Bowie, *Anthropology of Religion*, ch. 8.

6. See for example Anderson, *Introduction to Pentecostalism*, 211.

one creature and the other is not erased. The same is true for the relationship between God and humankind. When people experience something of God, it does not mean that Creator and creature partially coincide. One of the intentions of the creation story in Genesis is to point out that human beings are not God and God is not a created being.

Religious experiences, therefore, are not really evidence of godly efficacy or presence in themselves. In the same way that religions, simply because they are directed towards the transcendent, cannot automatically be viewed as the work of the one God, religious experiences cannot either. It is not per definition about experiencing the Creator as he has made himself known in Jesus. Religious experiences, too, are not excluded from the brokenness of creation.

It all comes down to the fact that we have to interpret human experiences in the tension between God's good creation on the one hand and the derailment of it on the other hand. Religious experiences are not present in a vacuum. The framework in which these experiences are placed ultimately decides how we are to interpret them. Here, we look at them in light of the revelation of God. With that, it is also said that "experience" is not the final criteria for truth and authenticity as is often thought today in Western culture. What I *experience* as good or bad is not by definition good or bad. People can, whether or not under the influence of drugs, alcohol, or medicine, experience things that are not there. Experience is an instrument like any other instrument of knowledge and wisdom. It is, therefore, not necessarily more, or for that matter less, reliable than rational considerations. Thus, alleged experiences of God and the world have to be connected to the story of God and the world in the same way as more rational truths. Just as the mind is affected by the brokenness of creation – and is therefore fallible – the heart and feelings are as well. Experiences can correspond with how God intended creation to be, but they can also contradict it.

5.3 Islamic Religious Experience and the Spirit of God

We have seen that the Spirit works at the intersection of the times. What God was envisioning at the beginning (the creation) and that which will become reality later on (the glory) is provisionally already present today through the Spirit. The Spirit puts what Christ has done into effect. Through the cross, the day of rest, and the resurrection, the disruption of the old creation is overcome, and the new life has begun. Through the Spirit the new history of God with humanity and the world is taking shape. The religious experience of Muslims should be understood in light of this.

5.3.1 The Spirit and New Life

If we confess that there is only one God (1 Cor 8) and that all of creation is made by God and in one way or another refers to him, then there is no other way but to recognize that the religious experiences of Muslims in one way or another have something to do with this one God. We can understand these experiences as a reaction to the presence of the Creator. Because human beings are created for God, we can understand Islam as an expression of the longing for God. If Muslims say that they have experienced the presence of God, we need to recognize that as a materializing of their "zeal for God." Muslims can experience peace and fulfillment in their faith. They can get joy from complying with the five pillars and devoting their entire lives to the will of God in the form of Shari'a. This cannot be seen apart from the One.

It has, however, also been ascertained that experiences do not simply align in themselves with God's intentions for creation. That only happens when Muslims thank God as the giver of life. That means that they recognize him who in Jesus Christ through the Spirit has fully revealed himself. If Muslims do not do that, even then they may experience peace, but it is incomplete in comparison to God's full intention. Notwithstanding their experiences, they ultimately miss the mark. That is sin, and sin alienates us from God (Rom 1:21). With that, the deep peace will eventually disappear as well.

Before anything else, the Spirit is the one that refers to the new life. He urges people to recognize Christ as the source of that life. If they do that, they will share in that life and move in the direction of Christ more and more: they will be drawn to him (see John 12:32). Wherever Christ works, the Spirit works, and where the Spirit works, Christ works. Joining with the Spirit means joining with Christ and vice versa (see Rom 8:9). That subsequently also means that the Spirit verifies and unmasks any experiences that do not recognize God in Christ. As the *paraclete*, he convicts of sin and righteousness and judgement (John 16:8); the Spirit holds reality up to the light of God's original intent. The cross is the key in all of this. In light of the cross, it becomes apparent how certain experiences can also be experiences of opposition against the Most High. Wherever Christ is kept out of the picture as the full revelation of God and of his purposes for creation, there a disturbance develops in the experience of Muslims. It obscures the view of God. It is there that the experience of the One is imperfect, incomplete, distorted, or even completely out of joint. The consequence of the latter is that the one God can hardly be identified anymore and the presence of the Spirit can no longer be recognized. Even then, the religious experience is still a human response to the one God but in an antithetical sense. Such negative experiences can still reflect something of the Most High, but in contrast to who he really is.

Does this then also count for, for example, Muslim extremists who commit attacks? Although it does not count for all of them, jihadis do sometimes have strong religious experiences. They are touched by the honor of God and are prepared to defend this honor with violence if necessary. For them, it is hard to accept that not everyone is submitted to God and his laws. They try to defend the dominion of God which in their view is realized in a certain form of Islamic rule.

Can we acknowledge this as an experience of the one God? It is a question that needs to be answered very carefully as I would not like to downplay the immense evil caused by extremist groups. In light of the gospel, no form of ideological hate can be explained away. Jesus has given his life on the cross. He did not come to condemn and destroy people but to save them (see Luke 9:56 NASB). He called on his followers to return evil with what is good, to love enemies, to bless those who curse them, and to pray for those who mistreat them (Luke 6:27–28). The experience of the jihadis is therefore not an experience of the one God as he has revealed himself in Jesus Christ. It is the opposite. At the same time, it is biblical to be angry about a world that tramples on the honor of God. God himself is wrathful over people who completely ignore his purposes for this world, who leave his principles behind and trample on his love.

The question is how people should handle their indignation. Do their deeds really represent the heart of God as it has become visible in Christ? When the Spirit directs experiences towards Christ, they are being cleansed, purified, and recreated. That implies a breaking point – a turning point – even if it is experienced as a gradual process. The new life is not an extension of the old. The cross of Christ is in between the two. The revelation of God is not simply linked up to human experiences. The earlier faith experiences of Muslims, however, are not erased but are recreated through death. God does not start all over again as if he recreates human beings from scratch.[7] In Christ, people are transformed with their experiences. Through death there is both a continuity (it is about the same person) and a discontinuity (total renewal). Like a kernel of grain has to die in order to produce fruit, in the same way people's religious experiences need to die with Christ in order for them to carry fruit. *These*

---

7. See Reitsma, *Geest en schepping*, 172.

experiences go into death with the person, but on the other end it is truly *these* experiences that rise out of the grave with Christ.[8]

The example of Muslim extremists clearly illustrates the ambivalence towards religious experiences. Faith experiences are never simply just about God or about the devil as that is an unbiblical form of dualism. Reality is much more complex. Experiences can be designated within the framework of creation where God, human beings, and powers take their positions. Experiences are primarily human reactions that are related to the dislocated factors of creation (psychological and anthropological), with the presence of these powers and with the work of God. Religious experiences are in that sense a reaction to reality in all its many-colored diversity, and they are also marked by that diversity.

It needs to be clear that that which is said here about the religious experiences of Muslims can just as much be said about the experiences of Christians. The Spirit also holds Christian faith experiences up against the light of the revelation of God in Christ. In the same way, these experiences can be interpreted as human reactions to the work of God, but they are not automatically "true" or in line with the purposes of God's creation. If God becomes a tool for a human goal of well-being and happiness, these experiences miss their mark. The Spirit wants to transform these experiences too to ones that are focused on God's reality and the recognition that God has revealed his glory fully in the crucified and humiliated Christ.

5.3.2 The Spirit and the Church

When discussing the Spirit there is still a different aspect that has not been highlighted so far, but which flows forth from what Paul explains in 1 Corinthians 8–10. He does not explicitly talk about the Spirit in this passage, but there is still a very important element here that is of interest to us. Paul takes the Shema, the confession that there is only one God, as a starting point for his view on the eating of meat that has been sacrificed to idols. Because idols do not exist, there is also no problem with the eating of the meat. At the same time, the Shema is no individualistic confession as it constitutes the fellowship of believers. Together they confess that there is only one God. The way in which faith in the one God specifically takes shape in a multireligious society can therefore never jeopardize the community. That's why it can be

---

8. See Reitsma, *Geest en schepping*, 175: there is continuity and discontinuity in the work of the Spirit in relation to creation and thus also to the experiences of that creation.

that the believer would still need to abstain from the eating of sacrificed meat in order to not let brothers or sisters stumble.

In the rest of the letter to the Corinthians, Paul goes deeper into this. Because the one God is none else but the kurios, Jesus Christ (1 Cor 8:6), there is a strong connection between the church of God and the body of Christ (1 Cor 11:22, 27, 29). The church is that body of Christ, and the sincere celebration of the Supper of the Lord is determined by the discerning of that body. The same is true for 1 Corinthians 12–14 concerning the work of the Spirit. The Spirit is not recognized by the gifts of the Spirit (*charismata*), whether spectacular or not, but by the confession that Jesus is Kurios (1 Cor 12:3). In this way, the Spirit creates a new fellowship of people who belong to Christ; through one Spirit they were all baptized into one body (1 Cor 12:13, 27). With that, the framework is set for the employment of the gifts of the Spirit. These are meant for serving each other and building up the church (1 Cor 12–14). All parts of the body, no matter how different, are inseparably linked; if one member of the body suffers, all suffer together; if one member is honored, all rejoice together (1 Cor 12:26). That is why love is essentially the deepest secret of the body of Christ and the work of the Spirit (1 Cor 13).

Recognizing the work of the Spirit, the norm is eventually not the experience but the connection to the body of Christ. The love of Christ has become visible through the cross and it takes shape in the church of God. This determines how we interpret experiences. In the midst of all the experiences of Muslims, the Spirit eventually always creates a new community of people who follow Jesus. That is very telling in the context of collectivistic cultures. In the end, the church of Christ is not determined by family or tribal affiliations but by the focus on Christ. How exactly that materializes is dependent on the context.

5.3.3 Answers to Prayer and Miracles

Can it be said in relation to this that Muslims' experiences of answered prayers have anything to do with God? If Jesus emphasizes multiple times in John that the prayers of the disciples are heard if they are prayed in his name (John 14:14, 26; 15:16; 16:23–24, 26), how can the prayers of Muslims be answered? Praying in Jesus's name is impossible for Muslims. They could, however, easily pray many of the Christian prayers, such as the Psalms and other parts of the Bible. Yet, praying in the name of Jesus is a form of faith in and devotion to Jesus Christ and his work. That would cross a boundary for Muslims. Still, Muslims testify to answered prayers: a child who is healed, a job that has been provided, food that has been received. If we do not want to ascribe these answered prayers to the devil – which would be in line with what was described earlier as too simplistic an approach – then, one way or another, it would have to be connected to the works of God and his Spirit. Or is that unthinkable?

In this context, it is good to realize that in general God does not answer prayer because of the faith of the one who prays or on account of the words and formulas used (see Matt 6: 7–8). The only basis for God to answer prayers is the work of Jesus Christ. However, that does not mean that God cannot or does not want to hear the prayers of those who do not know Christ. If that were the case, Paul – with his appeal to the Old Testament – could not say that "everyone who calls on the name of the Lord will be saved" (Rom 10:13 NIV). Whoever needs salvation is after all not a faithful part of the covenant yet, and whoever is already saved does not need to call on the name of the Lord for this. Thus, Muslims who call on the name of the Lord will be heard by him.

When it comes to prayer, I see two differences between the followers of Jesus and Muslims. Those who are connected to Christ and his work and who pray in his name would know the heart of the Father better and therefore also be more equipped to pray according to his will. They would acknowledge the Father through Jesus Christ and thank him for answering their prayers. Those who do not know Christ in this way will ascribe their experiences to other powers or influences. The same is true for other miracles and healing. God does not only heal Christians. The difference is that Christians would recognize, when they are healed, that it is a gift from God and an act of the Holy Spirit. Which is no different from when a healing takes place through the use of doctors and medicine. Ultimately, it is still God who heals people through the use of doctors. It does not matter if those doctors recognize that. In all cases of healing it is the one God who heals people. What the fruit of that healing will be depends on whether people acknowledge that God, in Christ and through his Spirit, has done this or whether they ascribe the healing to other "gods" or powers.

5.4 Conclusion

The faith experiences of Muslims can be seen as experiences of God, through his Holy Spirit. However, these experiences are not the criteria for understanding who God is in the deepest sense. Having "experiences" does not say anything about the "truth." They are not, in themselves, connecting us to the One. Some experiences are more of an expression of resistance against God and a concession to the evil one. The question is therefore what Muslims do with their experiences. Emotions are normal human responses, but in the brokenness of each day, we are called by God to handle these emotions in a way that fits the new life. That is why there is the commission to interpret these experiences and to focus them on the one God. We will have to interpret and verify the experiences of the presence of God. To what extent do they do justice to who God is in the deepest sense? In what way are they reflecting life as God had ultimately intended? The Spirit, as the power of the new life, holds these experiences up against the light of the cross of Christ. That is true for Christians no less than for Muslims.

Part III

The Church

A Vulnerable Community

6

The Church and the Kingdom of Christ

"The cross is all about the redefinition of power, God's power made known in weakness."[1]

"Giving up power is the prerequisite to love."[2]

"The Bible expounds a theology of weakness."[3]

"God is the first victim of war in his name."[4]

6.1 Introduction

The nature of the church can only be understood within the tension between God's original purposes for creation and the disruption of it. Just like in Islam, the worldwide church of Jesus Christ has so many different manifestations that it is impossible to discuss all the variations. Nevertheless, several principles should be recognizable in every context: typical character traits of the church. In this chapter, we are focused on the question of what kind of community the church is (6.2) and what the nature of this community characterizes (6.3).

6.2 A Provisional Community

The Christian church can be typified as the community where the contours of God's original purposes for his creation are becoming visible. The new life that

---

1. Wright, "Jesus, Israel, and the Cross."
2. Campolo, *Choose Love Not Power*, 14.
3. Dawn, *Royal Waste of Time*, 237.
4. Mallouhi, *Waging Peace on Islam*, 26.

Christ has made possible through the cross, the day of rest, and the resurrection is taking shape in the church. God created the world for the covenant between himself, human beings, and all of creation. The purpose was a community of people that would honor God and rule the earth on his behalf. All that is finally being realized in the church of Christ. It is the new creation. The old has gone, and the new has come (2 Cor 5:17).

The church does not emerge as a new community out of the blue. God first chose the people of Israel. However, Israel was not the final goal of God's plan but the instrument with which God showed all of creation why he had made the world. It was about a community of people that would live according to his purposes. In Abraham, *all* the nations are blessed. That is becoming a reality in Christ. In him, God returns to his people in order to restore the whole creation. The church of Christ is the redeemed people of Israel together with the Gentiles who are incorporated into Israel.[5] John continuously makes the connection between the followers of Jesus and the people of the old covenant. They show by their faith in Jesus that they also truly believe in the Torah (John 5:46–47). They are the sheep that are led by God, the Good Shepherd himself, and not by the untrustworthy leaders of Israel, the hired hands (John 10). God had already announced this in Ezekiel 34. The disciples of Jesus are compared with branches of the true vine (John 15), as Israel was compared to a vineyard in the Old Testament. Israel did not bear fruit (Isaiah 5:1–7); the new people of God, however, bear much fruit by remaining in Jesus. As the faithful Israel, they worship in Spirit and truth (John 4:23). Something of God's original intentions with the world becomes visible in this eschatological community.

All of this, however, is happening in the middle of a still broken reality. The fullness of the new creation has not yet come; the Spirit lives in the church as the *first* gift of the coming glory. In the church of Christ, God is recognized as the Creator of life and honored for his saving act of sending his Son, Jesus Christ. The church has a representative role: by worshipping God, the Christian church does what the rest of creation is still neglecting. In doing so, it points back to the beginning but also to the future, to what is still to come. Soon, every knee shall bow in the name of Jesus, and every tongue will confess that Jesus is Lord, to the glory of God the Father (Phil 2:10–11).[6] The church functions as God's ambassador. It presents in its nature what God envisioned with creation. The church testifies to that purpose with its existence. It shares what has been entrusted to it. The church itself is still part of a broken reality. It is not entirely

---

5. See Reitsma, *God of My Enemy*, 104–107.

6. Paas, *Vreemdelingen en priesters*, 185–187.

the way that God would like it to be. The church is exposed to the temptation to be like other nations in their ethics, in society, and even in politics.

This will be explored more fully here. What does it mean that the church has its own provisional nature? How does it relate to the rest of creation? And to Islam? What characterizes the church?

6.3 The Nature of the Church[7]
6.3.1 From Threatened Minority to a Privileged Power

The conversion of Emperor Constantine in the year AD 314 was a symbol for the change of the position of Christianity in the world. Before Constantine, the church was a threatened minority. It did not have access to the power structures of society and could only influence through character and presence. After Constantine, the church became a tolerated and later privileged community. Eventually, Christendom even became the state religion. Only those who were part of Christianity could fully participate in society.[8]

Because of this, the church, in a way, became a community like all others in this world. Due to this development, the conversion of Constantine is sometimes called "the fall of Christianity."[9] The church got a position at the center of power politically, socially, and economically. From that moment forward, it was able to actively and, if needed, violently influence world events. Christianity not only became attractive due to its message – because people were so touched by the gospel that they would eagerly accept to follow Jesus as Lord – but also because of the societal advantages it offered. The church could even enforce faith, baptism, churchgoing, and membership to the church.

This actually led to a connection between the cross and sword that would never really get disconnected in the future history of Christendom. The impact of this can hardly be underestimated. The importance of this turning point in history might even be greater than the influence of the Enlightenment on European Christendom.

It is good to realize that this change in the position of the church was never comprehensive; the church did not always, or everywhere, have a position of power. In various parts of the world, the church has never had full access to power. For example, it is currently vulnerable in different parts of the Islamic

---

7. This paragraph comes from a part of Reitsma, *De kerk*. It has been edited and elaborated upon here.

8. Hill, *History of Christianity*, ch. 3.

9. G. J. Heering, *De zondeval*.

world where it is completely dependent for its wellbeing on those in power. Still, this turning point has in various traditions consciously and subconsciously led to the idea that the church is called to regain paradise and, if necessary, to do so with force. When the church expands its influence in the world, God's dominion is increased. World history in this way practically coincides with salvation history and the church (or a Christian government) with the kingdom of God.[10]

We can compare the Constantinian transformation that took place within Christianity with the change that the migration (*hijra*) of Muhammad brought within Islam. In AD 622, the beginning of the Islamic calendar, Muhammad left Mecca for Medina and went from being the prophet of a threatened minority to becoming the statesman of an Islamic majority. He became the leader of both the spiritual and the political community of Muslims. The divergent visions regarding the connection between these two aspects, which manifested themselves emphatically at the succession of Muhammad, is the primary reason for the great contrast between Sunni and Shi'a Islam.[11] This contrast has most likely had more influence on the development of Islam than the confrontation between Islam and Christianity. For radical Hanbali Sunnis, Shi'a heresy is more dangerous for "true" Islam than Christianity or Judaism.[12]

If Christianity and Islam are comparable players in so many respects, they can easily become rivals. At various times in history that has led to armed conflicts. It is in the places where Christendom wants to manifest itself socially and politically that it comes into conflict with the type of Islam that aims for the same, and vice versa. The explicit connection between faith and sword has given Islam a negative image in the Christian (and Western) world and Christianity in the Islamic world. Christian theology, from the beginning of the Constantinian era, has continuously had to ask itself how the cross and power relate to each other and if these two can go together at all.

I want to look at that question by investigating how John positions the new creation in a world that is not yet redeemed. This tension between old and new is experienced in the entire Gospel according to John. There is a contrast between light and darkness (John 1:4–5; 3:19–21; 8:12; 12:35–36, 46), between above and below (John 8:23), and between being of this world and not of this world (John 9:39; 12:25, 31; 18:36). Occasionally, John uses the term "kingdom

---

10. See Reitsma, *De kerk*, 3–5. For the example of *Pseudo-Methodius* see below 10.6.

11. See Rippin, *Muslims*, 122–123.

12. Nasr, *Shia Revival*, 54. Sunni Islam emphasizes more strongly than Shiism that God's sovereignty manifests itself in the societal superiority of Islam. Nasr, 57–58.

of God" or "kingdom of Jesus" to denote the new life (John 3:3, 5; 18:36). By doing so, he is bringing this new life up to the level of the rulers of this world. "Kingdom" or "kingship" (βασιλεία) can relate to rule as well as the area over which this dominion is exercised.[13] In either case, it is the relationship between faith and power which occupies us here. The very fact that John rarely uses the term kingship/kingdom is significant. It is used only five times in three verses (John 3:3, 5; 18:36), while the Synoptic Gospels use it more than 120 times.

In John 3, Jesus speaks with a Jewish leader about the kingdom of God. In 18:23–27, during his trial, he discusses the question of who the king of the Jews is with a representative of the Roman emperor. This is not a coincidence. John most likely wrote his gospel, as is commonly held,[14] during the last quarter of the first century (after AD 70). That period was marked by increased tensions. The Christian church found itself between a rock and a hard place: on the one hand, Judaism; on the other, the Roman Empire. The confession "Jesus is Kurios" brought the church into conflict with Judaism, because only YHWH was recognized as Kurios, and also with the Roman emperor who claimed this title for himself.[15] It is clear that speaking about the kingdom of God and the kingdom of Jesus would have to be understood in that context, especially because, in John 18, both groups are actively present. It is possible that John was seeking to encourage the Christians who were banned from the synagogue and persecuted to keep believing.[16] It could also be that he wrote for a wider Christian audience in Asia Minor (or even outside of that), which clashed with the Roman authorities. Either way, in both passages – John 3 and John 18 – the focus is on the relationship between the new creation and the existing social realities and "kingdoms." From that, we can deduce something concerning the nature of the Christian church in relation to the power structures of the world, especially those of Islam. The church does not coincide with the kingdom, but it does make up a part of that kingdom. It is the believers in Christ who can enter the kingdom because they are born again (John 3:3, 5). They are the fellowship of the new life (see 6.3) and therefore the people who belong to that kingdom.

---

13. See *LSJ*.

14. According to Keener, *Gospel of John*, 140–142; Kümmel, *Einleitung in das Neue Testament*, 211. The author most likely comes from a Jewish environment or is influenced by the language and thinking of the Old Testament. See Davies, "Reflections," 44.

15. It is known, for example, that Domitian explicitly let himself be called Lord and God. Cassidy, *John's Gospel in New Perspective*, 14; see John 20:28. When Christians wanted to escape persecution, they had to worship the image of the emperor, renounce Christ, and bring an offering to the Roman gods. Cf. Kierspel, *Jews and the World*, 216–217.

16. According to Boer, *Johannine Perspectives*, 69; Davies, "Reflections," 52.

Our attention is here predominantly on the second part: the trial against Jesus and Jesus's pronouncement that his kingdom is not of this world (John 18:36).

6.3.2 The Kingdom of Jesus and the World (John 18:36)

The eschatological king

In their conversation with Pilate, the Jews accuse Jesus of pretending to be the king of the Jews. The real complaint they have against Jesus is one of blasphemy (see for example John 5:18; 8:59; 10:33), but that accusation is not relevant to Pilate. It is initially not even mentioned and is only brought up in John 19:7. When Pilate asks Jesus directly if he is the king of the Jews, Jesus responds that his kingdom is "not of this world" (18:36).

We will need to understand this expression of Jesus against the backdrop of the expectations of Judaism during the Second Temple period. Earlier we saw that the Jewish people lived in expectation that God would return to his people in the final days in order to reign as king again. Even though he was already king *de jure*, he would then also unmistakably be king *de facto*.[17] In this way, the long-awaited time of salvation for Israel and the nations would start (see 3.2). When Jesus, in John 18, speaks about his kingdom, it needs to be understood against that background: Jesus is the eschatological king in whom YHWH is returning as king to Zion. That is exactly the accusation against Jesus, that he claims to be the king of the Jews (John 18:33). For the Jews that is exactly what is blasphemous because, in so claiming, he is making himself equal to God (John 5:18; 10:31–33).

This identification of Jesus with God as the eschatological king is especially confirmed with the entry of Jesus into Jerusalem. Jesus is riding into Jerusalem on a donkey as the prophet Zechariah had prophesied: "Rejoice greatly, O daughter of Zion! . . . Behold, your king is coming to you . . . humble and mounted on a donkey" (Zech 9:9). The spectators are pointing this out as well. They call Jesus the "king of Israel" (John 12:13) and welcome him as the Blessed One, "who comes in the name of the LORD" (Psalm 118[LXX 117]:26).[18] In other words, Jesus is the king of Israel, or as Pilate puts it, the king of the Jews. With the triumphant entry of Jesus into Jerusalem, YHWH returns to Zion.[19]

---

17. Wright, "New Testament and the 'State,'" 12.

18. In the Gospel according to John, the Jews mainly use the title "king of Israel" in a respectful way. See for example 1:50; 12:13. When there is talk about Jesus in a contemptuous way, the term "king of the Jews" is used. See 18:33, 39; 19:19, 21.

19. Brunson, *Psalm 118*, p. 179, 283. For a lengthy discussion, see especially ch. 7, p. 265–284. See also Wright, *Victory*, 651.

Of a different nature

During his defense, Jesus clarifies that his kingdom is different from what Pilate and the Jews are imagining. His kingdom distinguishes itself in two ways.

1. *Not of this world.* This kingship is, like Jesus literally says, not "of" or "from" this world (ἐκ τοῦ κόσμου τούτου; John 18:36). The word "of/from" is used by John throughout his gospel to specifically indicate "origin." This origin implies a character that is in line with that origin. For example, those who have accepted the Word and believe in him are born "of" God and not "of" the will of a human being or "of" the flesh (John 1:12–13). That is not to say that they do not have biological parents but that their nature is not just coming from natural origins. Even though they remain "earthly" people, their origin, and, with that, also their character, has changed. The same is true the other way around for the Pharisees who actually are "of" this world (John 8:23). This means more than the Pharisees simply being "inhabitants of the earth" in comparison to, for example, angels. It is a qualification of their origin as being "of" this world and of their character as being in line with this origin.[20] It shows what the Pharisees ultimately belong to. This is primarily seen through their resistance to Jesus, who is not "of" this world (8:13, 47).[21]

In this context, the picture "of this world"/"not of this world" is further defined with the picture of "above/below." Jesus is from "above," which is to say from the world of God. His origin and therefore his nature and essence are characterized by God himself, and thus also by the grace and truth of the new covenant, the eschatological life. Contrarily, the Pharisees are from "below," which is the territory where the adversary of God – the ruler of this world – exercises his power (John 12:31; 14:30; 16:11).

Therefore, the term "world" has an ambivalent character for John, as it depends on the perspective from which reality is seen. It is about two ways of being.[22] From God's perspective the world is the reality that he created. It is the world that reminds us of the fact that God has had a purpose with creation from the beginning. This world is the place the Word has come into (John 1:9–10), the world that is so loved by God that he gave his only begotten son to save it (John 3:16). From the other perspective, which is emphasized by John, the world is primarily a reality characterized by sin (1:29; 16:8). It is

---

20. See Keck, "Derivation as Destiny," 283. Origin also determines someone's destination: the one who is not born of water and Spirit – and who has therefore not received the eschatological life of the new covenant – shall also not be able to enter the kingdom. See John 3:5.

21. See Keck, "Derivation as Destiny," 280–281.

22. Bruce, *Gospel of John*, 192: "realms"; cf. Lindars, *Gospel of John*, 558: "spheres of relationships" and "orders of being."

the degenerated creation. As such, the world rebels against God and refuses to acknowledge Christ as the one sent by the Father (John 5). It also does not know the Father (John 17:25) and hates Jesus and his followers (John 7:7; 15:18–19). This world is cloaked in darkness (John 8:12; 9:5).[23]

It is evident that John means more with "the world" than simply "humanity." It is a total concept that covers all of created reality, in which humanity has a central role.[24]

2. *Not forced.* Another striking characteristic of Jesus's kingdom is that it is not one that is realized by force. His servants did not fight to keep him out of the hands of the Jews. That would, after all, be the minimum that you would expect of your subjects: that they would protect their king.[25] Like a rabbi has disciples, in the same way kings and rulers have "servants."[26] Jesus, however, does not have servants who will, if necessary, use violence in order to stand up for him – even though Peter saw that differently (John 18:10). Jesus is consciously choosing to drink the cup that God has given him (John 18:10–11). The kingdom of Jesus is not to be defended, nor expanded, through violence.

When saying that the kingdom of Jesus "is not of this world," it says something about the origin and nature of this kingdom. It does not have its roots in the world marked by rebellion against God, by sin and darkness, but in God himself. This kingdom is of another nature than the empire that Pilate represents, and that the leaders of the people of Israel are showing complete loyalty to (John 19:15). The rule of Christ as the eschatological king of the world brings the world back to its original purpose. It is becoming God's good creation once more. This is not something that can be accomplished through the worldly conquering of people and territory. The problems run much deeper.

That is not to say that the kingdom of Jesus is disconnected from the reality we live in. John does not account for a gnostic or platonic dualism between an

---

23. "World" here is about more than a principle of sin or evil. Kierspel, *Jews and the World*, 213. Otherwise, the positive remarks about the "world" in John would be without meaning. The principle of evil in John is inseparably linked to the concrete reality of creation. This concrete world is "locked in persistent rebellion against its creator" (Carson, *Gospel According to John*, 468).

24. See Kierspel, *Jews and the World*, 213–214. Sometimes interpreters think of "humanity" because John presents the "world" as an active person. For the meaning of John 18, it does not matter as much. For an overview of the different meanings see Kierspel, 13–36.

25. Striving or fighting (γωνίζομαι) means to put effort into creating something, into winning a price, or as in this instance, into protecting the king. For the latter, it is unthinkable that it does not go hand in hand with "fighting."

26. See also John 7:32, 45–46; 18:3, 12, 22; 1 Cor 4:1.

"earthly," material kingdom and a "spiritual," immaterial kingdom.[27] Otherwise, John would not put so much emphasis on the Word "becoming flesh" (John 1:14). John paints a picture of Christ as the eschatological king and his kingdom as the realization of the promises of the Old Testament concerning the new covenant. That is extremely "materially" and even "politically" tinted. The rule of God is breaking into the world.[28] The new period of salvation is breaking out and making progress in the reality of creation, and it is a threat to all the powers that are not submitted to God.

There is a dynamic tension here. For the kingdom of Christ is taking shape within our reality, but it cannot be realized through earthly means. It is of a completely different nature than all the earthly kingdoms, and it can hardly be described with earthy terms and concepts. Perhaps that is why John is very restrained in the use of the term "kingdom."[29] He describes the content of the kingdom mostly with other words, like eternal life (John 3:16) or salvation (John 3:17; 5:34).

To bear witness to the truth

After Jesus has first explained what the kingdom is not, he explains what it does mean – namely, "to bear witness to the truth" (John 18:37). To that end, Jesus was born and has come into the world.[30] Here, it does not really matter how we interpret the answer that Jesus gives to Pilate's question of whether he is a king after all. The "you say that I am a king" can be read as a denial: "you say so, so those are your words, not mine." Generally speaking, however, it is seen as an affirmation: "indeed, you say so."[31] In the latter case, verse 37 is a further explanation of the kingship of Jesus. In the first case, it is more about a description of Jesus's mission in general, which is inseparably connected to the kingdom of Jesus. One way or the other, the ambivalence of the term kingdom is clearly present in the way Jesus answers. "You say so," then, should be more

---

27. See Smith, *Theology of the Gospel of John*, 10–16.

28. See Wright, "New Testament and the 'State,'" 13.

29. "Kingdom of God" in John 3:3, 5; "My kingdom" in John 18:36 (three times). The Synoptic Gospels use "kingdom" (of heaven/of God) far more: fifty times in Matthew, fourteen times in Mark, and fifty times in Luke. Green, McKnight, and Marshall, *Dictionary of Jesus*, ch. 5.

30. John 18:37 is the only place that the birth of Jesus is mentioned in all of the Gospel according to John.

31. See for example, Blaß, Debrunner, and Rehkopf, *Grammatik des neutestamentlichen Griechisch*, §441.4, 451.1. See also Diebold-Scheuermann, *Jesus vor Pilatus*, 37.

or less read as, "if you want to say it that way, that's fine, but what I mean by kingdom is rather different from you."[32]

Jesus makes this statement about bearing "witness to the truth" during his trial when he is asked about his identity. For Pilate, this question is not much deeper than whether or not Jesus is the king of the Jews and thus a threat to the Roman Empire. For the evangelist John, it is about something entirely different – namely, if Jesus, as the king of the Jews, is indeed God returning to his people in order to rule as king. Witnessing to the truth is connected to that. As we have seen, for John, truth, together with grace, forms the essence of the new covenant (John 1:17; see ch. 3). Jesus testifies that in him the *true* eschatological life has come. Jesus himself *is*, after all, *the* truth and *the* life (John 14:6). What Jesus does bears witness to the fact that the Father has sent him (John 5:36; cf. 5:17). That is especially true of his suffering. At the cross, Jesus calls out "it is finished" (John 19:28, 30). He uses almost the exact term here that Genesis uses for the finishing of the creation (Gen 2:1–2 LXX).[33] The *true* eschatological life, the new creation, does not come through power or might but is realized on the cross.[34] In this way, we meet with the fundamental characteristic of the kingdom: it is inseparably linked to suffering.

Suffering

The structure of John's description of the trial against Jesus is concentrated on the accusation that he is the king of the Jews. The account of the evangelist includes seven "acts." In the center, as a hinge point in the trial, is the passage of John 19:1–3.

(1) John 18:28–32	Conversation between the Jews and Pilate about Jesus and his crime.
(2) John 18:33–37	Conversation between Jesus and Pilate about Jesus and his crime.
(3) John 18:38–40	Jesus is not released, but a criminal is.
(0) John 19:1–3	Jesus, the king of the Jews.
(1') John 19:4–7	Conversation between the Jews and Pilate about Jesus and his crime.

---

32. See for example, Lindars, *John*, 559; Wright, "New Testament and the 'State,'" 12: "Jesus accommodated himself to the language of his day, what he *meant* by it was something quite different." Cf. Brown, *Gospel According to John*, 853–854: this is not "affirmative" but a "qualified answer."

33. Τελέω instead of συντελέω.

34. Cf. Koester, *Symbolism in the Fourth Gospel*, 202.

| (2') John 19:8–12 | Conversation between Jesus and Pilate about Jesus and his crime. |
| (3') John 19:13–16 | Jesus is not released but convicted.[35] |

The emphasis lies on the ridicule of Jesus as the king of the Jews (John 19:1–3). This is how the king-who-is-not-of-this-world is treated. His "honor" lies in mockery; his crown consists of thorns. The eschatological king is a king who suffers. He is flogged and lets himself be mistreated. John is preparing his readers for what is to come. After John 19:1–3 it is no surprise anymore that this king is executed on a cross. Neither is this a tragic end of the trial against Jesus. A careful observer would recognize the climax here that is slowly developing throughout the gospel, from the prologue onward. He came to his own and his own people did not receive him (John 1:11). When Pilate wrote an inscription on the cross in three contemporary world languages that Jesus was the "King of the Jews," he unintentionally and unknowingly spoke the truth (John 19:19–20). At the cross, the true nature of Jesus's kingship was revealed – namely, that it is not of this world. That is how the king of Israel is coming to Zion. The suffering of Jesus as the king of the Jews is the inauguration of the new time of salvation.

6.4 Conclusion: The Church as "Minority"

The church of Christ takes its identity from the new life that has become a reality in Jesus Christ. It is the fellowship of the kingdom of Christ and therefore also not "from" or "of" this world (John 15:19). The church takes an entirely unique place in the midst of all the kingdoms of this world. As the nation of the king, the church is not a political power, and it therefore does not fight with the rulers of this world for world domination. The church is in a category by itself. Its nature and origin do not lie in the world that is estranged from God but in God himself. Its character runs completely counter to the broken creation. That is why the followers of Jesus are not fighting for dominion in *this* world.

In relation to Islam, I would characterize the fellowship of the church theologically as a "minority." That is not a quantitative qualification but a qualitative one. It is not primarily about "size" or "numbers" but about "nature" and "character." Even when the church is numerically a majority in society,

---

35. Keener, *Gospel of John*.

it remains according to its nature a "minority."[36] The new life is a life without power. A minority without force is not able to impose its will on the majority. That is the nature of the church. When it lets go of this fundamental principle, we can wonder if the church has not compromised its identity as the church of Christ.[37]

In the context of Islam, the characterization of the Christian church as a "minority" raises the question of whether we voluntarily submit to a system that, by Bat Ye'or among others, has been called *dhimmitude*. *Dhimmitude* is the whole system in which Jews, Christians, and Zoroastrians are subordinate to Muslims, both legally and socially. Christians, in classical Islamic jurisprudence, are recognized as a protected community, the people of the covenant (*ahl al-dhimmi*). In exchange for their loyalty to the Islamic regime and the paying of a reasonable tax (the *jizya*), they receive religious, economic, and political freedom.[38]

> At the core, non-Muslims, especially Jews and Christians, are people in Islam who are to be protected due to a treaty with God and his messenger, and they should enjoy full freedom everywhere under Islamic rule.[39] It is primarily an obligation for Muslims and not a form of religious discrimination against non-Muslims in favor of Muslims.[40] In line with this, there are statements in the Qur'an and Sunna that call Muslims to treat non-Muslims in a friendly and just manner, as long as they do not form a threat to the faith of Muslims.[41] Muhammad is supposed to have said that whoever harms a *dhimmi* would offend the prophet and whoever offends the prophet offends

---

36. The concept of "minority" has multiple meanings. See Reitsma, "Strangers in the Light," 211–212. It can mean (1) numerical minority (half minus one) or (2) a specific group of people that is ethnically, culturally, or religiously distinct from the majority. In many countries, being a numerical minority is accompanied with subordination. In the West, that is officially not the case. Every minority has the same rights and duties as the majority and the discrimination of minorities is forbidden by law. That does not mean that discrimination does not happen.

37. We could therefore describe this character of the church as being strangers in this world rather than being at home here, as the church does not really belong in this world. The term "minority," however, more strongly denotes the fact that believers do not possess means of (manipulative) power in society.

38. Doi, *Shari'ah*, 427, 429.

39. Ellethy, *Islam, Context, Pluralism and Democracy*, 123.

40. Ellethy, 127.

41. Surah 60:8–9 (Sūrat al-Mumtahanah). The only time the Qur'an speaks about the *dhimmi*, it concerns a covenant to protect what has been entrusted to them: Surah 9:8–9 (Sūrat al-Tawba); Ellethy, *Islam*, 123.

God.[42] This means that there have been times that Jews and Christians could fully participate in Islamic societies. There have, however, also been times when the dhimmi-status was interpreted far more negatively. Christians and Jews have often been subjected to strict discriminatory rules. For example, under certain forms of dhimmi-legislation, Christians were not allowed to build new churches or restore old ones, and Christians could not hire Muslims or buy land from Muslims. They could not marry a Muslim without converting to Islam, and the witness of one Muslim had the same power in court as that of two *dhimmis*. Also, their clothing and posture had to express that they were (literally and figuratively) inferior to Muslims.[43] This often led to the persecution of *dhimmis*. Overall, we can say that the situation for dhimmis improved as Islam got stronger and worsened when Islam weakened.[44]

Does the characterization of the Christian church as a "minority" not mean that, by definition, we have submitted to the Islamic ideal? According to Bat Ye'or that is not what Christians should ever do. She cites Bashir Gemayel, who, after being elected president in 1982, during Lebanon's the civil war, said, "Henceforth, we refuse to live in any 'dhimmitude.'"[45]

When I characterize the Christian church as a "minority," it is different from a voluntary acceptance of subordination. It also has nothing to do with the fear of Islam or a premature capitulation in order not to offend Muslims. The self-identification of the church as a "minority" is a conscious decision that comes from and is qualified by the nature of the kingdom of Jesus Christ. That is entirely different from the way in which classical Islam gives meaning to the word "minority." When Jesus explained that his kingdom was not of this

---

42. Doi, *Sharī'ah*, 430. Cf. Ellethy, *Islam*, 125, and Ayoub, "*Dhimmah* in the Qur'an," 103. They refer to a tradition that declares that the prophet had said, "Whoever kills a man who has received the *dhimma* from God and the *dhimma* of his prophet, shall not smell the scent of paradise" (according to Abu Hurayrah).

43. Berger, *Klassieke sharia*, 83, 84. Ye'or describes such discriminatory measurements against *dhimmis* in chapter 2, *Dhimmi*, 51–77. The negative elements are related to the so-called "Pact of Omar" that is supposed to have been written by the second caliph, Omar. Most likely, however, this document dates from a later time period. Moreover, there are also multiple versions in circulation. See Chapman, *Cross and Crescent*, 328–330.

44. Berger, *Klassieke sharia*, 84. For a thorough overview of the legal position of *dhimmis*, see Chehata, "Dhimma." For an overview of the position of *dhimmis* throughout history, see Cahen, "Dhimma." See also McAuliffe, *Qur'ānic Christians*.

45. Ye'or, *Dhimmi*, 404.

world, he also gave a different meaning to kingdom than the Jewish community and the Roman authorities did. He did not withdraw from the reality of the powers that be, but he was present among them in an entirely different way of being. With his kingdom, Jesus is not one of the parties that are fighting for power. His authority is also not of a higher or stronger form of the same kind; it is about a power of an entirely different character. Earthly rulers like Pilate (and the emperor) do not, therefore, have any authority over him, unless it is given to them from above (John 19:11). The power of Jesus does not express itself socially in the same way that the kingdoms of this world do. The cross is a complete redefinition of power.[46] The witness of Christ, who was prepared to suffer and die at a cross, "demonstrates most graphically that God does not work through the power structures and ideologies of this world. Furthermore, on the cross he exposed and triumphed over all the principalities and powers of politics, economics and religious institutions."[47]

When I characterize the church as a "minority," I do so specifically in light of this redefinition of power. As said, I use this theological qualification in order to show that the church does not principally participate with the ongoing power plays of society. But does that mean that the church does not exercise any influence in the world? Christians who take their calling seriously are present in society. That means that they have influence and influence is a form of power. Even a hermit who completely withdraws from society and lets himself be walled up in a cave in Lebanon has a deep effect on the community in his area. However, the Christian community needs to be conscious about the way in which it exercises that influence. Every form of manipulation or political, societal, or economic power that is used to strengthen or grow the church is contrary to the gospel. The only power that the church of Christ has is the power of the cross, meaning unconditional and self-sacrificial love. That is power without a sword.

---

46. Wright, "Jesus, Israel and the Cross."
47. Dawn, *Royal Waste of Time*, 47; cf. Col 2:15.

7

The Church and the People of Israel

"The challenge for the church at this point is to explain to Muslims that the alliance with the Jewish people does not detract from both the uniqueness of Jesus Christ as Lord and Savior and from the universal meaning of his salvation work. As far as the confessed alliance with Israel might give the impression that God's Kingdom is of this world after all and that the church similar to certain movements in Islam is focusing on conquest and possession of territories as a sign of true faith, this will have to be contradicted pertinently"[1]

"Combined with prejudice against Arabs and Muslims, this [pro-Israeli] bias has meant that Christians have been unable to make a positive contribution to implementing justice and peace in the Middle East. It also explains, to some degree, why many Arabs and Muslims are suspicious of the West and Western Christianity."[2]

7.1 Introduction

In the relationship between the Christian church and the Islamic community, "Israel" is a sensitive topic. The church is inextricably linked with Israel through Jesus Christ, a faithful Jew from the line of David. The New Testament is a continuation of the "Jewish" Bible. Even though there are black pages of anti-Semitism in the history of the church, protestant and evangelical churches in

---

1. Reitsma, *Integrity and Respect*, 22.
2. Moucarry, *Faith to Faith*, 281–282.

the Western world believe that the church is inseparably connected with the people of Israel.[3] The church and synagogue share, each in their own way, the Tenach as the revelation of God and serve, again in their own unique ways, the same God of Abraham, Isaac, and Jacob.

This is different for the Islamic community. Classical Islam has a connection to Judaism. Jews, after all, as "the people of the book," have received revelation from God and serve the same God. There is an Islamic tradition, however, that is convinced that the Jews did not preserve this revelation in a pure way, and therefore Judaism is inferior to Islam.[4] This hierarchy has often led to tensions throughout history. The establishment of the state of Israel, in the heart of the land of Islam, has put a strain on the relationship between Islam and Judaism. Different Muslims worldwide believe the establishment of the state of Israel to have been unjust.[5] Before 1947, Jews only inhabited 5.8 percent of the land and made up one-third of the population. In the UN Partition Plan, however, they received more than half of the land.[6] Besides that, the land of "Palestine" has a special status for Muslims. After Mecca and Medina, Jerusalem is the third holiest city in Islam.[7] Most Muslims would desire nothing more than to see the land come under Islamic rule again.[8] However, it is good to realize here that within Islam an enormous variety of views on the land of Israel exists. There is a lot of internal debate about this. Many Muslims are committed to peace with Israel and are working on a viable solution to the problems of the Middle East. In 2005, the Arab League even offered to completely normalize all relations with Israel on the basis of the UN Partition Plan of 1948.[9]

---

3. See also *Israeli-Palestinian Conflict*, 40–41, 46, 51. The Protestant Church in the Netherlands even mentions this in its church statutes (art. I-7).

4. See Vajda, "Ahl al-Kitāb."

5. See Al-Faruqi, "Islam and Zionism," 261.

6. Pappe, *Ethnic Cleansing of Palestine*, 29–33. After the war for independence, Israel even owned 77 percent of the land. Burge, *Whose Land? Whose Promise?*, 39.

7. The direction of the prayers was originally towards Jerusalem. According to tradition, Muhammad – literally or in a vision – made his heavenly journey there on a horse (Surah 17:1, Sūrat al-Isrā). See Badawi, "Jerusalem and Islam," 138–139. The value that the city and the land of Israel/Palestine has in Islamic tradition is, however, larger than the text itself seems to suggest and largely became important when the possession of the land was contested – for example, during the Crusades. See Reitsma, *God of My Enemy*, 131.

8. According to Al-Faruqi, "Islam and Zionism," Islam and a Zionist state will never go together. The only option is for Jews to live as the protected people of the book in an Islamic state. Al-Faruqi, 262.

9. In 2007 the Arab League confirmed the so-called Beirut Declaration of 2002 in which the League, upon the initiative of Saudi Arabia, offered to Israel the complete normalization of relations on the basis of the UN Partition Plan of 1948. BBC, "Arab Leaders Relaunch Peace Plan."

The seemingly unconditional support given to the state of Israel by Christians on the basis of certain interpretations of the Bible is hard for many Muslims to understand. This great loyalty to Israel has a negative impact on the relationship between Christians and Muslims, not just in the Middle East. For many Muslims, it makes the gospel sound unjust and therefore not credible. Christian Zionism, especially, is a sensitive topic for Muslims as well as for the majority of Christians in the Middle East.[10] The thought that the establishment of the state of Israel is a fulfillment of God's promises in the Old Testament, and that Israel has a God-given right to the land, puts the relationship under a lot of pressure. This has, therefore, occasionally been called one of the greatest stumbling blocks for the proclamation of the gospel.[11]

That is why, in this chapter, we will have to carefully define what we mean with the "inseparable connection" between the church and Israel. What is it saying about the nature of the church? What influence does this loyalty have on the relationship between the Christian church and Islam? In my book *The God of My Enemy: The Middle East and the Nature of God*, I give a thorough biblical-theological analysis of Romans 9–11 in light of the questions raised by Arab Christians about the establishment of the state of Israel. These same questions play a role in connecting to Muslims. I will now connect the key points of that book with the framework set out in part I of this book and apply it to the relationship between the church and Islam.

7.2 Inextricably Linked

For Western Christians, it is not hard to understand that Jesus Christ is the connecting link between Israel and the church. The church is the fellowship of Jews and Gentiles who confess that Jesus is the Messiah. The church can only understand itself in connection with the people of Israel in the Tenach. However, when we attempt to further specify what this means, things get more difficult. Does it mean that Christian fellowship is inseparably connected to the *state* of Israel that explicitly claims to be a *Jewish* State? Or does it mean that the church enters into a dialogue with Israel concerning the interpretation of Scripture and the coming of the kingdom of God?[12] Does it mean that the church should *refrain* from witnessing about Jesus Christ as the Messiah? Does

---

10. Middle East Council of Churches, *What Is Western Fundamentalist Christian Zionism?*

11. Chapman, "Evangelicals," 150.

12. Kerkorde Protestantse Kerk in the Nederlands, art. I-7.

it come down to the fact that the church unconditionally supports the Jewish community in and outside of Israel economically and/or politically?

With *whom* is the Christian church actually connected? When we reference "Israel," do we mean the Judaism of the first century? Or of today? Both fundamentally differ from the Judaism found in the Old Testament. Are we connected with those in the Middle East who have a deep longing to strive for a "greater Israel" in preparation for the coming of the Messiah? Or do we choose the side of the orthodox Jews who see the establishment of the state of Israel as an act of disobedience to God because only the Messiah can bring the people of Israel out of exile?

As long as we do not explain exactly what we mean, we cannot solemnly declare that we are "inseparably linked with Israel." But that is exactly how the problem remains hanging in the air, abstract and virtual. As long as the "theory" is not actualized anywhere, we are not really saying anything at all. That is where the question arises: What are the contours of this inseparable connection between the church and Israel? And what does it mean for the church in relation to Islam?

7.3 Basic Principles

The foundation for the inseparable link of the Christian church with the people of Israel is Jesus Christ. He is first of all the Messiah of Israel. As we have already observed before, in him the long-awaited time of salvation for Israel was realized. We concluded from different texts in the Gospel of John that the content of the new covenant, life as God had intended from the beginning, becomes reality in Jesus (see ch. 3). Similarly, Paul writes about this by calling Jesus the "end" (*telos*) of the law, the Torah (Rom 10:4). We saw that the term *telos* is practically identical to the concept that is used in Genesis 2 (LXX) for the finishing of creation. Jesus completes the righteousness that the law demands. With righteousness, Paul means God's faithfulness to the covenant, as this is seen in the covenant partner who stands in a right relationship to God.[13] It describes life as God envisioned it from the beginning. That becomes a reality in Christ: "Just as the law enshrines the righteousness of God for Israel, so Jesus is an expression of that same righteousness, in personal, living form."[14] In him, Israel, together with all of creation, reaches its destiny. The Torah is therefore not abolished by Christ. The requirements of the law still

---

13. See Reitsma, *God of My Enemy*, 69.
14. Motyer, *Israel in the Plan of God*, 92.

stand, even though the law itself is not capable of realizing what it demands (Rom 7) because it is weak due to sin (Rom 8:3). Jesus has conquered sin and that is how the requirement of the law, righteousness, is being fulfilled by the Spirit in those who believe (Rom 8:4; 9:31).[15]

From this basic foundation, we can gain more insight into the relationship between the church of Christ and Israel as a people (7.3.1) and as a land (7.3.2).

7.3.1 Israel as the People of God[16]

What is the position of the people of Israel today? Are they still the people of God? Each answer raises new questions. When answering *negatively*, the question is if we can still trust God. If he can go back on his unconditional love for Israel, he could go back on his grace for the church of Christ as well. What then would distinguish him from an arbitrary God? When we answer the question *affirmatively*, on the other hand, it raises other questions: would non-Jews then fully belong to the people of God? Or is he some sort of tribal God, who, in the Middle East, has chosen Israel – over and against Muslims but also over and against Arab Christians and Jews who confess Christ as Messiah.

The election of Israel goes back to the calling of Abraham. In the chaos of the disrupted and broken creation, God worked from the very first Sabbath to restore his creation. God calls Abraham and creates a name for him (Gen 12:1–2). Abraham is given a promise: in him all other nations and all the families of the earth shall be blessed (Gen 12:3; 18:18; 22:18). The promise of a large offspring and its own country is given to one single *creature* for the blessing of *the whole creation*. The particular exists for the universal. Because God wanted to save the world, he chose Israel. God wanted a fellowship of people that would reign with him over creation. By the election of a community, salvation comes to the nations in an exemplary way. Salvation is relational. God saves the world through people who are chosen and sent; we are saved in and through a community. This community and this "dependence of one another, is not merely part of journey toward the goal of salvation, but it is intrinsic to the goal itself." That is the "logic of election."[17] It is by grace that Israel is the people

---

15. See Reitsma, *God of My Enemy*, 73; the relationship between "law" and "reality of the law" is like the relationship between the blue prints and the realization of the building or like that between a photo and the person of whom the photo is taken. For the relationship between the new life and the law, see Reitsma, *God of My Enemy*, ch. 4, 65–83.

16. For a more thorough discussion, see Reitsma, *God of My Enemy*, ch. 5, 87–127.

17. Newbigin, *Gospel in a Pluralist Society*, 82–83; for a thorough explanation of this logic of election, see 80–88; cf. Reitsma, *God of My Enemy*, 153.

of God, not because it was greater than other nations (Deut 7:7). Without the gracious intervention of God, Sarah would have never had children, Ishmael would have had the rights of the firstborn, and Isaac would not have existed. The same is true for Isaac and Rebekah. Without God's gracious intervention, the covenant with Abraham would have been continued with Esau and not with Jacob. Israel would not have existed (Rom 9:6–8). All of this resounds when Paul compares Israel to an olive tree. God planted Israel like a tree without Israel providing any particular reason for such favor. The root is God's grace, as is seen in the election of Abraham, Isaac, and Jacob. The tree is not chopped down; God did not go back on his election. But there are natural branches that have been cut off and wild olive branches that have been grafted in (Rom 11:17).[18] Insofar as the Israelites do not believe in Jesus as the Messiah, they are to be compared to the natural olive branches that are broken off. Insofar as the Gentiles do believe in Jesus as the Messiah, they will be like wild olive branches that have been grafted in among the people of God.

All this means that, *from God's perspective*, the people of Israel today are still the chosen people (Rom 11:29). In the coming of Christ, and his work, God does not act differently from the past. In Christ God is also working out his salvation by grace. Insofar as Israel believes in the Messiah, Israel will also experience the blessings of that faith. That does not happen automatically. Not all who are descended from Israel are also Israel in the truest sense of the word (Rom 9:6). The election remains the same, even if Israel does not believe in Christ, but disbelief puts its relationship with God under pressure. There is a judgement coming for the branches that were broken off (Rom 11:22).

The image of the olive tree also illustrates that the Gentiles are a full-fledged part of the people of God thanks to Christ. If Israel, after all, was chosen to be God's people out of grace, then there is no single reason why the Gentiles cannot also belong to the people of God. They are grafted into the one tree with the same root. The nations of the earth also share in the blessing of Abraham (see Gal 3–4). In that sense, the church, consisting of Jews and Gentiles in the

---

18. It literally says that the wild branches are grafted (ἐγκεντρίζω) "in them" (ἐν αὐτοῖς). This has been explained and translated as "taken the place of" (CEV) or "among the others" (NIV). Both are possibilities. Even when we follow the first interpretation, still the text does not support the classical replacement theory because, according to Paul, it is not the church that has taken the place of Israel. The Gentiles share in one salvation in Christ together with the Jews who believe in Christ.

New Testament, is not a new entity in God's history, but the eschatological continuation of the people of God in the Old Testament.[19]

The nature of the Christian church is therefore determined by the history of God with Israel. That history reveals God's elective love as it ultimately becomes reality in Christ. In history, it is also revealed that God's actions toward the Gentiles are part of the identity of Israel. Israel is chosen for the restoration of the whole creation and therefore fulfills its purpose when all the nations shall acknowledge Christ. That is the fullness, the completion, of Israel. That is when the nation is finalized, like creation was finished on the seventh day.

This is why there is ultimately only one people of God, and they consist of Jews and Gentiles. There is one olive tree, with natural and wild branches. The distinction between those who belong to the church of Christ and those who do not is a greater distinction than within the church between Jews and Gentiles. The people of God have undergone a transformation with the coming of Jesus: it has changed from a national ethnic group to a universal community that contains all languages and nations.

7.3.2 Israel and the Land[20]

Does the connection of the church with the *people* of Israel imply the same connection with the *state* of Israel? The latter plays an even larger role than the first in the relationship between Muslims and Christians. The establishment of the state of Israel has put the relationship between Muslims and Jews on edge. The question is what the coming of Christ means for our relationship to the land of Israel. Although the theme of the land is not explicitly discussed anywhere in the New Testament – it is not even mentioned in the list of privileges for Israel in Romans 9:4–5 – there are three thought patterns in Paul that help us in this respect and point in a particular direction.

1. *Law and land.* According to the Judaism of the Second Temple period, the Torah can only be completely fulfilled in the land. A large part of the regulations of the Torah are related to the land. The ultimate goal of the law is that Israel will serve God in the land completely and, in that way, truly be the people of God. The reverse side to this is that the gift of the land is conditional. Only when Israel stays true to the commandments will it be allowed to live in the land (see Lev 18:2; cf. Lev 18:24, 28; 20:22). The law can therefore only

---

19. Or "the salvation, historical consequence of the election of Israel." Reitsma, *God of My Enemy*, 120.

20. For a more thorough discussion, see Reitsma, *God of My Enemy*, 129–162.

really be fulfilled *in* the land, but at the same time, Israel can only *remain* in the land if the law is followed completely.

As long as the power of sin reigns in this world, that obviously leads to a paradox. It is only in the land that the law can be fulfilled, but only when the law is completely fulfilled is Israel allowed to stay in the land. If no one is righteous (Rom 3:10), Israel will never be able to live in the land and really serve God. This paradox is solved in Christ. He is the righteousness, the fulfillment of the law. That means that everyone that is in Christ, and thus righteous, may live in the land. Only "in Christ" does the land come to its full meaning for Jews and Gentiles.

2. *The promise to Abraham.* Paul comes to the same conclusion when he speaks about the covenant with Abraham (Gal 3). Those who have been grafted into Christ form the offspring of Abraham. They are therefore also Abraham's heirs and share not only in the promise of a great nation that would be a blessing to all the nations but also in that of living in the land (Gal 3:29; 4:28; cf. 3:22). The promise, thus, applies to Jews and Gentiles alike who believe in Christ and therefore gains a universal character. That is why, in Romans 4:13 – a departure from the original formulation in Genesis 12:7–8 – Paul calls Abraham heir of the "world," the cosmos, instead of heir of the land.

3. *The creation.* Paul speaks in an indirect way about the land when he talks about the creation. When the people of God are transformed from a national *Jewish* community into a community from all languages and nations, that also has implications for the land. Because, if all who are "in Christ" take possession of the land, it would be impossible for the promised land to contain that great a multitude. The transformation of the people of God also leads to a transformation of the meaning of the land. The scope of Paul's vision of the land is therefore *the whole creation* (Rom 8). We have now come full circle. From the beginning, God has had the purpose of bringing the entire world under his rule. God's election of Israel is motivated by his longing to save a *community* of people. Salvation comes to us in an exemplary way through the community of the people of Israel. Similarly, the election of the land is motivated by God's longing to save people as actual tangible creatures. Salvation therefore comes to us, in an exemplary way, through the election of the *land* of Israel. In the same way that the community of Israel highlights what God ultimately had in mind for all of humanity, the land of Israel reveals what God ultimately had in mind for the whole of creation.

God does not break his promises to Israel. He actually fulfills them, though in a way that is infinitely greater than Israel could have imagined.[21] God had promised Israel the land of Canaan; he fulfills that promise by giving Israel, together with the Gentiles, not only the land of Israel but the entire world. That is no "spiritualizing" of the promise of the land, in which the earthly reality evaporates. In Christ, too, it is about the concreteness and material reality of salvation. The new covenant is realized *in* the land. That land now actually comprises all of creation.[22] Whoever still longs to go back to Canaan is, in a way, taking a step backwards in the history of salvation; why would you want to light a candle when the sun is shining?

Since the coming of Christ, we can no longer discuss the land apart from him. That observation relativizes the meaning of a specific place on the Mediterranean Sea. Because, if the full righteousness, the new life, has been realized in Christ, then obedience in the land can never provide more than we have already received in Christ. The land cannot bring us closer to God than we already are in Christ.

It is understandable that Israel longs to live securely in the land of their forefathers. That is entirely legitimate. However, it does not have any historical salvific meaning. God's visions for Israel and the world are so much bigger than solving the problems of the Middle East. It goes much further than the return of the Jews to a piece of land. God is out for total victory over sin and the renewal of the entire creation. The purpose is that the *whole* earth will be filled with the knowledge of the glory of the Lord as the waters cover the sea (Hab 2:14). The land has been transformed from a strip on the east side of the Mediterranean to a creation-enveloping empire where God is king over Jews and Gentiles. That kingdom is not of this world. It comes through the way of the cross, not through the conquest of territory.

---

21. See Reitsma, 129: "If God promised Israel the land, is he then unfaithful to himself if he gives his people, together with the Gentiles, the whole creation?"

22. According to Paul, the "land" does experience a transformation in this context. Because the land in the old *aeon* is intrinsically connected with sin and brokenness, the restoration of the kingdom in the land can only entail a complete renewal of the land. Thus the promise of the land is fulfilled literally: the new creation is "material" in nature but in a way that far exceeds our human understanding of what land and "the material" mean. See Reitsma, *God of My Enemy*, 145–149, 152.

7.4 Conclusion: The Church, Israel, and Islam

What does the preceding mean for the nature of the church and its relationship with Islam?

7.4.1 Connected with the God of Israel

That the church is inseparably linked with Israel, first and foremost, means that the church is inseparably connected with the *God of Israel*. Ultimately, it is not about Israel but about God as the creator of heaven and earth. In order to realize his original plan, God chose Israel. That was unconditional love. There was no single reason in Israel itself why God started out with this group of people. It was the smallest of all nations (Deut 7:7), and according to Paul, it was stubbornly disobedient (Rom 10:21). That says everything about God: his deepest nature is unconditional love. He chooses that which has no prestige, that which is lost. He cares about those who do not want to know him (see Rom 5:8). This becomes explicitly clear in the coming of Jesus as the climax of God's journey with Israel. His kingdom is characterized by the cross on which he gave his life for all – Jews and Gentiles alike.

This is the history of God with Israel that determines the identity of the church of Christ. The church can only speak about God as the God of Israel. That is not because of the *people* of Israel but because of the *God* of Israel. If he went back on his choice for Israel, then there would be no hope for anyone, neither Jew, nor Christian, nor Muslim. A God that does not fulfill his promises is unreliable and unpredictable.

That God is the God of Israel is sensitive in the Middle East because "Israel" is automatically associated, or even identified, with the *state* of Israel, an economic, political, and military power. The God of Israel is the God of the enemy. What this means for the state of Israel is a separate matter (see 7.4.2). But that God is a graceful God who does not go back on his promises for the *people* of Israel is also the only source of hope for Christians and Muslims. After all, his unconditional love means that no one is excluded from the kingdom of God. If God elects the people of Israel, then anyone can belong to God. If there is hope for Israel, there is hope for all the nations. This is because Israel exists for the whole of creation. The renewed creation offers a place to a community that consists of all languages and nations of the world.

If God in his grace had not focused on the whole of creation, then Israel would have never existed. Encountering Islam could remind Israel again of the fact that it is itself chosen in order to be a blessing for all people. Could reaching Muslims with the gospel help awaken Israel anew? Paul was focused on the Gentiles in order to make Israel jealous and thus to save some part of it (Rom 11:11–15). Wouldn't it be possible that Muslims, especially, who begin following Jesus and appropriating the gifts and promises offered to Israel for themselves could make Israel jealous?[23] Could the conversion of the nations that have threatened Israel the most have more impact than all the words of the Torah and the prophets combined?

We can conclude that being inseparably linked with the people of Israel should, in any case, not have to be at the expense of a connection with the Christian church in the Middle East. Arab Christians are, after all, part of the same body that exists of many members from all nations and languages. In that sense, they are closer to the Western church than the branches of the people of Israel that have not accepted Jesus as Messiah. Neither can the connection with the people of Israel be at the expense of the connection with the rest of creation, no matter how little that creation is living up to God's purposes. The Christian church shares God's passion in Jesus Christ for the whole world. It is, in that respect, also connected to Muslims, albeit in a very different way. This connection is founded upon God's mission to restore the entire original community of creation.

7.4.2 Connection with People and State?

In passing, I wrote that the inseparable connection with the *people* of Israel does not mean that the Christian church is similarly connected with the *state* of Israel.[24] In light of God's purpose with creation, we would need to be extremely careful about drawing a direct line between the promises of the Old Testament concerning the land and the establishment of the state of Israel in 1948.[25] It is questionable whether the modern state can be compared to the theocratic ideal from the Tenach because, as a nation and political entity, the state is a modern and secular phenomenon. It has its roots in the Enlightenment and only developed after the two World Wars. But even besides that, the Tenach does not give a unified picture of the way in which Israel needs to be governed.

---

23. See my reasoning concerning the salvation of Israel and the Gentiles in Romans 11 in Reitsma, *God of My Enemy*, 111–116.

24. Several synod reports make the distinction between Israel the people group, the land, and state. See for example *Israël, volk, land en staat: Handreiking van de Generale Synode van de Nederlandse Hervormde Kerk*, 1970. Still, the state is mentioned here as a sign. In *Israeli-Palestinian Conflict*, the connection between people, land, and state is made more strongly than in earlier reports.

25. See Reitsma, *God of My Enemy*, 153–155.

The people asking for a king was an expression of unbelief and disobedience; it revealed a rejection of God as king (1 Sam 8:7). In other places, the kingdom is spoken off as the ideal for a society that lacks direction, where everyone does what they think is right in their own eyes (Judg 17:6; 21:25). Even if a direct line could be drawn from the form of governance found in the Old Testament to the modern state of Israel, this form of governance would still be only a shadow of what God had in mind in the deepest sense. Just as the life that is described in the Torah – righteousness – has been realized in Christ, in the same way, the ideal of the kingdom of Israel in the Tenach is realized in the kingdom of God in Christ. That kingdom includes all the earth and all the nations. Because it is not of this world, it also cannot be realized through the means of earthly kingdoms. It comes through the death and resurrection of Jesus Christ and not through weapons and earthly governments. Christianity therefore has a different "territorial nature" than the main streams within Judaism and Islam. The ultimate ideal is not a piece of land near the Mediterranean Sea but new heavens and a new earth in which righteousness will dwell (2 Pet 3:13) and where there will be no more sin or death.

It will not come as a surprise that this vision is a significant stumbling block for dialogue with the Jewish community. For many Jews, the state of Israel is an inseparable part of their *Jewish* identity. For them, connection with the Jewish people cannot be separated from solidarity with the state of Israel.[26] However, that is certainly not the case for the entire Jewish community. There are, as mentioned, Orthodox Jews who see Israel as the fruit of unbelief because the establishment of the state is reserved for the Messiah.[27] Therefore, it is not a form of anti-Semitism when I cannot see myself as inseparably, religiously connected to the *state* of Israel. I do not deny Israel its right to have a place in this world, nor do I dispute Jewish self-determination. But, on the basis of God's revelation in Jesus Christ, I cannot endorse the justification of that self-determination. I am not connected to Israel's own ideals, despite their origin in the Tenach. They ultimately fall short of what God has in mind for Israel. His vision goes far beyond the ideal of a safe state in the Middle East: God is aiming at the complete salvation of Israel and the whole of creation. It is with *that* vision that I am inseparably connected through Jesus Christ.

---

26. Response of the NIK (Dutch Israelite Church community) to the Islam Memorandum, Integrity and Respect of the Protestant Church, https://www.nik.nl/2012/10/wederkerigheid-ontbreekt-in-protestantse-islam-nota/, accessed 1 March 2020.

27. For example, Neturei Karta and the Satmar Hasidim oppose Zionism, see Ravitzky, "Zionism and Orthodox Judaism"; cf. see also Rabkin, *In naam van de Thora*.

All of this implies that God does not inevitably side with the state of Israel or with the Palestinians. He is in Christ focused on a kingdom that embraces all the nations of the world. Muslims are not by definition God's opponents when they are critical of the state of Israel. Nor can Christian supporters of Israel be counted automatically as siding on the side of God. The core of the matter lies much deeper. In his history with Israel and the nations, God has revealed his heart and shown his true nature. That is a challenging message for Muslims, Jews, and Christians. God shows his majesty by first connecting himself to an insignificant people like Israel and then humbling himself in Jesus Christ to the point of death on a cross. That is how great his love is for his creation.

If the Christian church wants to reflect the nature of God, it cannot take sides in the conflict in the Middle East. The church represents in its nature the "righteousness" that God had in mind since the beginning of creation: a community of all creatures who would live in *shalom/salaam* with God and with each other. The church itself is the symbol of reconciliation; the wall that kept Jews and Gentiles separated has been broken down by Christ on the cross (Eph 2:14). That is why the church should primarily be focused on the reconciliation of those who are known to pass for "irreconcilable." Like the good Samaritan, the church is called to attend to the victims of injustice, no matter if they are Jews, Muslims, or Christians.[28]

7.4.3. Anti-Semitism

Being connected to the *people* of Israel means that the church has to continuously be aware of the problem of anti-Semitism and fight against it. Christians tend to think that Islam is in itself anti-Semitic, since they perceive a persistent Muslim resistance to the state of Israel, which is seen as anti-Semitism.[29] It is true that we can witness different kinds of anti-Semitism in the Middle East, but it is doubtful that this can be ascribed purely to Islam as a religion. Jews have not suffered more in the Islamic world than they did in Christian Europe. As we've seen, in classical Islam, Jews, together with Christians, are seen as a protected minority (*ahl al-dhimmi*). Yet even though Jews have known relative religious, social and economic freedom in exchange

---

28. See Reitsma, *God of My Enemy*, 192–198.

29. In some responses to the Protestant Church's Islam memorandum *Integrity and Respect*, the objection was that there was too little attention given to the danger of Islam and that it needed a stronger emphasis on supporting Israel against the threat of Islam. See Koffeman and Reitsma, *Vervolgnota*, 17.

for a special tax, they have also been considered lower in rank than Muslims. Therefore, the Jewish community has often had to deal with discrimination, even with persecution. Still, their position has generally been better than in the Christian world. At least the Islamic world has never known a Holocaust. It is therefore too simplistic to state that Islam is anti-Semitic. We do see a rise of anti-Semitism in the Arab world due to the rise of the Zionist movement in the nineteenth century. The establishment of the state of Israel has been a strong incentive in this development.[30] Many young Muslims make a clear distinction between Judaism and Zionism.[31] Anti-Zionism can only be labeled as anti-Semitic if Zionism coincides with Judaism. The latter is not the case, since an important part of Orthodox and Liberal Judaism opposes Zionism.[32] However, we must realize that the line between anti-Zionism and anti-Semitism is more blurred in real life than it might be in theory. Those who resist Zionism will often not make a clear distinction between the system and the people who are supporting that system.

In meeting with Muslims, the connection with the people of Israel means that the church should not avoid the problem of anti-Semitism. But in the light of the history of Christianity, that requires a certain level of modesty.[33] Resisting anti-Semitism does not just come from the connection between the church and Israel, even though it remains an important factor. Even replacement theology – the doctrine that the church has replaced Israel – does not legitimize anti-Semitism. God has made every human being in his image, no matter their race or ethnicity. Anti-Semitism, therefore, is diametrically opposed to God's purposes for creation, just like any other form of racism or discrimination.[34] Every form of contempt for people on the basis of race, ethnicity, sexual orientation, or gender is foreign to the gospel. In the same way that anti-Semitism contradicts the nature of the church because it is connected to Israel, every form of racism contradicts the nature of the church because it is connected to the whole of creation. If the church distinguishes between

---

30. Jansen, *Van jodenhaat naar zelfmoordterrorisme*. From the overview it is clear that – without looking at the exceptions – anti-Jewish sentiment has been increasing in the Middle East mainly from the nineteenth century onwards. Two things happening simultaneously does not necessarily imply causality, but a relationship between the rise in anti-Semitism and the Zionistic developments of the nineteenth century is certainly plausible.

31. See Van Wonderen and Wagenaar, *Nader onderzoek beelden*, 6. See also Van Wonderen and Wagenaar, *Antisemitisme onder jongeren in Nederland*.

32. See for example Torah Jews, "Anti-Semitism and Anti-Zionism Are Unrelated."

33. See Jansen, *Christelijke theologie na Auschwitz*.

34. Reitsma, *God of My Enemy*, 127.

one or another form of racism, and resists one form of racism more than another, it is no longer a witness to God's grace. In this way, the sensitivity in the Christian community to rising anti-Semitism should evoke a similar sensitivity to other forms of racism, including increasing islamophobia inside, and outside, the church.[35]

---

35. See Green, "New Study."

8

The Church and the Context of Islam

"To the Muslim I became a Muslim?"[1]

8.1 Introduction

In the Islamic world, Christianity is still seen as a Western religion. Many Muslims think that the West is Christian and that Christianity represents Western values. At first that may seem startling because Christianity has unmistakably Eastern roots, and it is inseparably linked to the people of Israel. The church of Christ is the eschatological continuation of the Old Testament people of God to whom, in Christ, other nations belong as well.

However, Christianity separated itself early on from Judaism and even dissociated itself from it. Over the course of history, Christianity's center of gravity shifted more and more to the West. Especially after the decrease of Eastern Christianity due to the rise of the Mongols, the centre of Christianity was virtually limited to Europe. During the colonial period, this Western Christianity spread all over the world through missions. Moreover, with the gospel, Western culture was also exported. Sometimes that was happening unwittingly, at other times very deliberately. Because Western culture was so strongly linked with the Christian faith, it was seen as higher and more civilized than other cultures.[2] When discussing the multicultural and multireligious society of today, that sentiment sometimes surfaces again in relation to Islam.

---

1. Woodberry, "To the Muslim," 23.
2. Gort, "De vis en het water," 15.

113

Critics believe that Islam does not fit the Judeo-Christian culture of the West.[3] Islam supposedly does not share the fundamental values of democratic civilized Western society, such as the equality of men and women, the freedom of expression, and the freedom of religion. To this day, Muslims in the twenty-first century are, at times, shamelessly labeled as people with a lesser and non-civilized (desert) culture,[4] an attitude that is almost similar to that at the height of the colonial period.

This raises the question of what the relationship is between the gospel and the cultural context in which it is proclaimed. Christianity has often dealt differently with this question than Islam has. In Islam there is a strong connection between the Arab context of the prophet Muhammad and the content of the faith. The Qur'an should be recited in Arabic; a translation is no longer the true Qur'an. The example of the prophet is normative to the life of a Muslim and that, therefore, also affects his cultural context.[5] In Christianity, the gospel is often proclaimed through interaction with the culture. The essence of the gospel has taken on a specific form and shape in a diverse range of cultures without compromising its central message. Is this also possible for the cultural context marked by Islam? Whoever says "yes" to that question will have to explain how the fundamental differences between Islam and Christianity should be dealt with. Whoever says "no" will have to explain the nature of the relationship between the gospel and culture. What does it mean for Muslims who want to follow Jesus? Can they remain in their own culture or must they adopt another culture?

The question about the relationship between the gospel and culture in the evangelical protestant tradition is primarily asked in the context of missiology.[6] That is understandable. Whenever the gospel is shared in a new cultural context, the question is how the message can be translated meaningfully into that context. However, this question is not just reserved for missiology. The gospel that is shared in another cultural context is itself already contextually defined. It is the gospel that has taken shape in the

---

3. *Volkskrant*, "Wilders." See also "Afschaffen artikel 1 valt slecht. Wilders komt met programma," in *Nederlands Dagblad*, 22 March 2006, 3.

4. For instance, the late Dutch politician Pim Fortuyn. See H. Wansink, "Fortuyns Kruistocht'inKruistocht," in *De Volkskrant* 22-12-2001, https://www.volkskrant.nl/nieuws-achtergrond/fortuyns-kruistocht~bbea6496/, accessed 1 March 2020.

5. For both aspects, see Rippin, *Muslims*, chs. 2 and 3.

6. See, for example, Hesselgrave and Rommen, *Contextualization*, 200. "Contextualization . . . has to do with . . . all of those activities involved in carrying out the Great Commission."

culture of the Christian church that is sharing it. A "culture-less" gospel does not exist.[7] The Christian community has to continuously ask itself how it relates to the context in which it exists. This is about the nature of the Christian community as it takes shape in both an Islamic and non-Islamic context. That clearly has a missional aspect, but it is more than that. That is why the issue of the relationship between the gospel and the cultural and religious context of Islam is raised here, in the section dealing with the nature of the church. How does the church, as a new fellowship of the kingdom, relate to the cultural and religious context of Islam?

8.2 Exploration: The Church and the Context of Islam
8.2.1 C1–C6 Spectrum

In 1998, John Travis created an overview of the kinds of churches found in the Islamic world. He described six forms of "Christ-centered communities," C1–C6 (see table 8.1 on pages 118–119).[8] The C1 churches are the least contextualized. They don't use insider language – the language of the local Muslim population – in their gatherings, and they use the same traditional church forms and rituals that are seen in other parts of the world. The C5 communities are on the other end of the spectrum and distinguish themselves far less from their environment. C6 has a rather specific character. They are communities of Muslims that have Christ at the center but keep this hidden from their community. They are not, therefore, directly recognizable as Christian. The people in these communities are seen by the Islamic community as Muslims and identify as such. They do fall within the spectrum because the emphasis is on "Christ-centered," but, due to their secret nature, research on these communities, or description of them, is complicated. To what extent are these believers still "Christ-centered," and if they are "Christ-centered," are we still talking about contextualization?[9]

There are four (of the five) kinds of Christian communities that are more (C5) or less (C3, C2, C1) adapted to their environments. The C5 communities stay more strongly within their social and religious Islamic context. They see themselves as Muslims who follow "Isa Al Masih" – Jesus the Messiah.

---

7. According to Newbigin, *Pluralist Society*, 189.

8. Travis, "The C1 to C6 Spectrum," 407–408. The C in C1–C6 does not stand for "contextual" or "contextualized" but for "Christ-Centered Communities."

9. See Strengholt, "Contextualisatie," 38.

Everything that contradicts the gospel they reinterpret or reject. The most crucial transition is from a C4 to a C5 community.

The model that Travis created is a typical example of how the conversation about contextualization is constantly placed in the context of missiology. Travis, with his classification, gives a *description* of how churches in Islamic contexts are expressing the Christian faith. It was not meant as a prescriptive model for missionaries,[10] but it did start functioning that way. To really reach Muslims with the gospel, churches should become far more contextualized and thus move from C1 to C5. That development is, to a certain extent, brought about by the model itself. Travis suggests that C1 believers are less contextual than C5 followers of Jesus. With that, an indirect prescriptive element is present. In the missional approach to Islam, this prescriptive element has received more and more emphasis.[11]

Critical questions can be asked of Travis's model. Strengholt summarizes this critique in three points.[12] (1) To start with, Travis's thesis that there is a great cultural divide between the C1/C2 churches and the Islamic community is too general. In any case, that divide, according to Strengholt, does not exist between Islam and the oldest churches in the Middle East. The Oriental church already existed before Islam came into being. The tension between these traditional churches and their context is not different in the Islamic world than elsewhere. Strengholt suspects that contextualization has rather taken place in the opposite direction. Islam, when spreading, has adjusted itself to the already existing Oriental-Christian culture. (2) Next, contextualization, to Travis, primarily has to do with the external design of the church – such as language, liturgy, music, and rituals. He gives little to no attention to the theological aspects. That is, however, precisely where the important differences between Islam and Christianity lie. His spectrum would likely look very different if theological factors were determining the categories. (3) Lastly, Strengholt points out that the reference for contextualization according to Travis is the mosque. The context, however, concerns all aspects of life, not just the mosque.[13]

---

10. Travis, "C1–C6 Spectrum."

11. Strengholt, "Contextualisatie," 39.

12. Strengholt, 36–39.

13. For the latter, see Howell and Paris, *Introducing Cultural Anthropology*, 27.

We can wonder if this criticism does justice to the intention Travis had. His original article about the C1–C6 communities is not more than an inventory, a sketch-like description of his observations. It does not give the impression of a thorough sociological or cultural-anthropological exposé. Still, the critical questions are important when considering Travis's observations, especially the issues that are crucial for the relationship between the church and the context of Islam.

Travis's classification has led to a lot of discussion on whether or not there is enough basis for legitimizing C5 fellowships within the Christian tradition.[14] Is it possible that Muslims follow Jesus while staying in their own Islamic context? Does that mean the Qur'an still has authority among these believers and that Muhammad is still seen as a prophet? Does this mean that they still go to the mosque, participate in the five daily prayers, practice the five pillars, and celebrate Islamic festivals? There are many witnesses among Muslims who do just that, but who, in doing so, are fully focused on Jesus Christ instead of on the Islamic traditions. Is this, then, primarily a kind of contextualization or is it – like critics are claiming – a form of syncretism, a sort of Chrislam? Vice versa, the question is what the alternative would be. Does the following of Jesus mean that new Christians have to adopt an entirely different social and societal culture? Which culture should that be? There is no culture that is religiously or ideologically neutral; each context is imbedded with worldviews, norms, and values. To answer these questions, we will first have to clarify the terminology that is used.

---

14. For a thorough overview of the C1–C6 debate, see Sleeman, "Origins," 498–566.

Table 8.1

Christ-Centered Communities (according to John Travis)				
C1	C2	C3	C4	C5
Traditional church using outsider language	Traditional church using insider language	Contextualized Christ-centered communities using insider language and religiously neutral insider cultural forms	Contextualized Christ-centered communities using insider language and biblically permissible cultural and Islamic forms	Christ-centered communities of "Messianic Muslims" who have accepted Jesus as Lord and Savior
Being church in the traditional sense	Being church in the traditional sense	Being church in an adjusted traditional way, with variations	Church form is closely related to the cultural Islamic context	Church remains legally and socially in the Islamic community
Coming together in a building that is recognizable as a church	Coming together in a building that is recognizable as a church	Coming together in a building that is recognizable as a church or is neutral	Coming together on neutral territory, no association with church	Coming together on neutral territory within the Islamic context
No insider language in the services	Specific Christian form of insider language in the services	Neutral form of insider language in the services	Insider language in the service that is common for Muslims	Use of insider language that is typically Islamic

Christ-Centered Communities (according to John Travis)				
C1	**C2**	**C3**	**C4**	**C5**
Western cultural forms of being church, cultural divide between C1 churches and Muslims	Western cultural form of being church, cultural divide between C2 churches and Muslims	Religiously neutral form of being church, Islamic elements are filtered out, less cultural foreignness	Culturally "Islamic" forms and customs, praying while holding hands up, no alcohol or pork	Rejection or re-interpretation of Islamic thinking that is not consistent with Christian faith
Some Christians with a Muslim background, calling themselves Christian	More Christians with a Muslim background than C1, calling themselves Christian	The majority are Christians with a Muslim background, calling themselves Christian	Mainly Christians with a Muslim background, seen by Islamic communities as Muslims, calling themselves followers of Isa al-Masih	Christians with a Muslim background, seen by Islamic communities as Muslims, calling themselves followers of Isa al-Masih, participation in Islamic services varies.

8.2.2 "Culture," "Context," and "Contextualization"

So far, we've talked about culture and context as if they are monolithic concepts. That is not the case. Culture has been defined in many different ways.[15] The nuances of the term are, for our present purpose, not very important. The common factor in all definitions is that "culture" is primarily a "total way of

---

15. Kirk mentions four definitions. Kirk, *What Is Mission?*, 85.

life."[16] It is about the particular identity of a certain community – in worldview and behavior – which differentiates it from other communities.[17] "Context" includes more than culture; it is about the whole of reality in which the gospel takes shape. Still, I would not want to separate these two terms from each other too much. In light of the framework set out in part I, I would define context and culture together as the concrete reality of creation as it is taking shape through human beings.

"Contextualization" means that the gospel in all of its diversity is becoming a concrete reality in the totality of the context of creation. This is more than simply translating the gospel into a previously unknown context.[18] It is about the way in which the gospel is being expressed in all areas of life.[19] "Contextualization" is more comprehensive than other concepts like "accommodation," "indigenization," and "inculturation." In Roman Catholic circles (primarily among the Jesuits), "accommodation" has signified the adapting of the gospel, in language and cultural practice, to a non-Western context. "Indigenization" has been used more in the protestant tradition to denote the process that would ensure that missional churches would become *self-supporting* and led by local Christians. Lastly, "inculturation" has focused the attention on how the gospel enters a certain culture and how it transforms that culture.[20] The term "contextualization," on the other hand, offers more space for the mutual interaction between the gospel and the context.[21]

When thinking about the contextualization of the gospel in relation to Islam, here too, we need to watch for essentialism.[22] Culture is a complex

---

16. Howell and Paris, *Cultural Anthropology*, 36.

17. Hofstede, Pedersen, and Hofstede, *Exploring Culture*, loc. 236. See also Hofstede, *Cultures and Organizations*, 585, as cited in Lewis, *When Cultures Collide*, loc. 607. "Culture" helps "to describe a reality that people experience, the behaviors and assumptions common to a group that distinguish one group from others." Howell and Paris, *Cultural Anthropology*, 25.

18. Bevans classifies the translation model as one of the forms of contextual theology. Bevans, *Models of Contextual Theology*, 37–53. For Hesselgrave and Rommen, contextualization is the same as "translation." Hesselgrave and Rommen, *Contextualization*, 200.

19. See Conn, "Contextualization," 44–45, as cited in Hesselgrave and Rommen, *Contextualization*, 34. Conn's critique is that evangelicals are primarily focused on the translation of the gospel to other cultures but forget they themselves are also defined by culture.

20. For more on this terminology, see Tennent, *Trinitarian Missiology*, 345–346; Costa, *One Faith, Many Cultures*, xii; Kirk, *Mission*, 89–90.

21. In this way, I hold together the distinction that Bosch, in following Waldenfeld (1987), makes between the inculturation/translation model and the socio-economic model. See Bosch, *Transforming Mission*, 421. See also Gort, "De vis en het water," 18–20. For an overview of the development and usage of the term contextualization, see Hesselgrave and Rommen, *Contextualization*, 28–32.

22. Coe, "Contextualizing Theology," 20–21, cited in Gort, "De vis en het water," 19.

phenomenon that is continuously in motion. Not only do cultures differ from place to place, but even within one context, there are varieties. Not to mention that people can combine very different cultures and cultural expressions within themselves.[23] There is, therefore, not one single Islamic culture or context. There is always a complexity of factors, like religion, ethnicity, history, economy, and environment. These factors interact and work together. Even though it may seem at times that all Muslims worldwide experience and express their faith in the same way, when looking closer, it is clear that that is not the case.

8.3 Contextualization and Islam

Contextualizing the gospel in the world of Islam is founded on two principles: the reality of God's creation and the incarnation of Jesus.[24]

8.3.1 Contextualization and Creation

If "culture" and "context" refer to the concrete reality of creation as it takes shape in and through human beings, then "contextualization" is an ambivalent term.

Cultural diversity

The great cultural diversity in the world is desired by God. It is the consequence of the great diversity of creation. This diversity of creation leads to cultural diversity. God created every human being in his image with a great variety of characteristics. He created human beings as male and female. Every human being and every community of people is expressing life in a unique way. In this way, the variety in creation leads to many different contexts and cultures. A diverse spectrum of climates with a diverse variety of flora and fauna has created a range of different societies. Life in the tropics is shaped differently from areas with a sea or land climate. In Genesis, that diversity is not yet seen in detail, but the potential is there. Human beings are created in the image of God with the freedom to develop that creative potential. The richness of cultures is part of the vision that God had from the beginning.

The question, therefore, is if that is also true for religious diversity. In cultural anthropology, religion is often seen as a part of culture.[25] Although

---

23. See Howell and Paris, *Cultural Anthropology*, 27. This is why, according to Howell and Paris, culture is something learned, adaptive, shared, and integrated. Howell and Paris, 36–38.

24. Bevans, *Models*, 12.

25. See Howell and Paris, *Cultural Anthropology*, ch. 9.

that is not incorrect, we need to go deeper than that. We have defined Islam as an expression of the fact that human beings are created by God (see ch. 4). It is a human attempt to do justice to the presence of God in creation. With that in mind, religion is also more than an aspect of culture. It actually gives meaning to all the other cultural elements. It is the foundation for everything that human beings do. Religious diversity is connected to the diverse ways in which human beings express their longing for God.

Contextualization, therefore, is closely related to the cultural diversity of creation. In this world, God establishes a relationship with human beings and that relationship takes shape in a great diversity of contexts. Therefore, even the religious diversity in the world is, in a sense, an expression of the fact that creation can only be understood in relation to God. Contextualization implies that the diversity of creation is meant for and devoted to the one God and his plan for creation.

Cultural diversity disrupted

The downside to this is that cultural diversity is also part of the disruption of creation. This is already clear in Genesis 11 in relation to language, a fundamental aspect of the way in which people live together. The great diversity of languages works as a curse and is a painful sign of the distortion of the creation community.[26] It creates confusion; people no longer understand each other and part ways. According to Genesis, this is a display of God's judgement. When people seek to make a name for themselves and want to be like God, diversity derails. That is not only true for language but for all aspects of culture.

The derailment of diversity can lead to extremism. The absolutization of one's own culture, for example, does not leave room for people who are different. When ethnicity is glorified, it results in racism, xenophobia, discrimination, and exclusion. If that is combined with violence, it deteriorates into forced prostitution, slavery, or ethnic cleansing. The absolutization of culture is often a sign that someone is unable to deal with the diversity that God has installed in his creation. Whoever (or whatever) that is different becomes a threat to one's own identity. Those who call the culture (and religion) of Muslims backward are treading on thin ice in my view.

Another way in which diversity can derail is found in the relativizing of cultural diversity. This means not just that every culture is equal in value and

---

26. Even before Genesis 11, different languages existed (Gen 10:5), and in that sense, this is a clear illustration of the ambivalence of culture. The diversity of languages is not only a sign of the disruption of creation, it also represents the vastness of God's presence – it is essentially impossible to represent God's nature with one single language.

worth, but it also indicates that all elements of any particular culture are equally valid. Cultural relativism in an academic sense emphasizes that every culture can only be understood from within itself. It is nearly impossible to evaluate a culture from another reference point. Ideological cultural relativism takes it a step further in stating that no judgement of any elements of other cultures is possible at all. Due to the fact that all cultural expressions are equal in value, no evaluation of what in a specific culture is good or bad can be made. Such cultural relativism ignores the distortion of creation. In such a perspective, even what is purely evil becomes relative – it can no longer be seen as evil for everyone, always and everywhere – which is a sign of distortion in and of itself.

All of this also applies to the phenomenon of religion as an essential part of culture. As was seen, religion cannot, in itself, automatically be defined as an expression of a relationship with God. It can also develop as a form of *resistance* against the Almighty, a way in which human beings want to manifest themselves over and against God. It is also possible that human beings are seeking to find their eternal happiness on their own by means of religious rules or enlightenment. In that case, God has become redundant. The distortion of religion does not just appear as violent extremism but has to do with religion in all its facets, including peaceful mediation or diaconal benevolence. This derailment is not limited to Islam; it is just as much found in Christianity and other religions. Zeal for God does not in itself lead to "knowledge" or a connection with the Almighty. Contextualization also means that the gospel, as a counterculture, holds up the distorted cultural reality against the light of God's original purposes.

In summary, on the basis of God's purpose in creation, we can say that contextualization means that the gospel gets a concrete shape in each culture. This is inherent to the diversity of God's creation. But it is equally the case that the gospel is always counter to the distortion of that diversity of cultures. It reminds the world of God's original purposes.

8.3.2 Contextualization and the Incarnation[27]

Fortunately, the ambivalence of reality does not have the final word: in Christ, God's intentions with creation are realized again. As we have seen earlier, creation becomes visible in this broken world as a spot of light around the cross. John connects creation explicitly to the incarnation. The Word who

---

27. A few of the principles about the incarnation, and the Jewishness of Jesus, are a summary and application of what I have discussed more thoroughly in *The God of My Enemy*, 39–64.

was with God in the beginning, and through whom everything has come into existence, has become "human" (John 1:14). This confirms in a different way what we saw in the previous paragraph.

God became a Jew

The fact that the Word became flesh means that God has entered our world and became a part of it. The Word has not become "human" in the general sense but "human" in the specific context of Judaism in the first century. In Jesus, God became a Jew.[28] Jesus lived, thought, and acted as a Jew of the first century. For one thing, this shows God's loyalty to his election of Israel and his original intentions for creation. God had promised Abraham to bless all the nations through him, and this is the way that God has gone through history in order to fulfill that promise. That Jesus is a Jew shows that God does not go back on his promise. Moreover, it shows that the gospel is not an abstract dogmatism that is passed on to the world in a generic way. The message is coming to us in human likeness; it becomes flesh and blood in the culture and context of Israel. In order to realize his purpose with creation, God becomes part of it. The gospel is therefore contextual to the core and does not exist separately from the Jewish context. That, too, is a sensitive topic for Muslims (and Christians) in the Middle East. The Jewish Jesus reminds them of the situation in the Middle East. *Jews* have driven Palestinians from their homes and have founded a Jewish state on the land that was in the hands of Muslims (and Christians). Muslims worldwide feel connected to this issue. Still, the Jewishness of Jesus is an integral part of the gospel. If we abandon that, the gospel ceases to be the gospel. However, that does not mean that the *state* of Israel is an integral part of the gospel, as we have seen in the previous chapter.

God is not a Jew

God becoming a Jewish human being means, at the same time, that the "Jewishness" of Jesus is not absolute. The idea of God becoming human could indeed suggest that. If God has made himself known in the Jew Jesus, that could mean that the new life in Christ could only become a reality in the form of Judaism. The new creation would then only know a Jewish culture. Followers of Jesus would have to become Jewish in order to really share in it. That would lead to the absolutizing of culture that we have earlier explicitly rejected.

---

28. Though it has not been defined which version of Judaism is characteristic of Jesus's Jewishness. Perhaps the tables should be turned, and we would need to conclude that Jesus defines true Judaism. For a more thorough discussion, see Reitsma, *God of My Enemy*, 50–51.

The matter has to be understood differently. The incarnation does not just emphasize that Jesus is Jewish but also relativizes that Jewishness at the same time. For it is *God* who became a human being. Jesus as the Messiah of Israel is also the Lord of creation. That means that Jesus also transcends his Jewishness, for if the Jewishness of Jesus is essential to the nature of revelation it would imply that God himself is "Jewish." That is a step too far. We would then also need to conclude that God is a man because Jesus as a human being was male. God, however, is not a human being, even though we can only speak about him in human concepts and images. Therefore, God is neither a Jew nor a man.[29] The essential nature of the Creator of all the nations cannot be contained in any one category of creation (including the Jewish one).

In this we sense the same dualism we have found in the context of contextualization and creation – namely, that the gospel completely enters creation yet without becoming domesticated by it. True life is present in Jesus as the incarnated Word, but it does not coincide with the distorted reality. On the contrary, real life critiques the broken reality. That is why Jesus was critical of Israel insofar as it was not living up to God's purposes. Jesus realizes the life that the Torah requires; the justification of the law is fulfilled in him. That is why Jesus, in a way, is showing what true Judaism entails. The meaning of true Jewishness lights up in Jesus.

The question is whether relativizing Jesus's Jewishness also relativizes his true humanity. Does this not lead to a form of Docetism? Do we also call into question the contextuality of the gospel? Instead of absolutizing the Jewish culture, do we end up with an absolute relativization? The answer depends on how "being truly human" is defined. Is that defined by ethnicity or – with regard to the maleness of Jesus – gender? Chapter 2 showed that human beings are created in the image of God: they stand as ambassadors in a special relationship to God and to the rest of creation. This determines the essence of the human being regardless of gender. Both the man and the woman are created in the image of God (Gen 1:27). If gender does not determine truly being human, then neither does ethnicity or other aspects of being human.[30] The decisive

---

29. The expression Paul uses in 2 Cor 5, that we have known Jesus "according to the flesh" but not anymore now, seems to mean the same thing. See Reitsma, 44–45.

30. Essentially, that is also why the church ultimately resisted slavery, the unjust treatment of men and women, racism, and apartheid.

factor is our relationship with God. The same is true for the incarnation. It is not Jesus's being Jewish which is decisive but his being human.[31]

Jesus's transcending of his Jewishness does not mean that being Jewish is now irrelevant. Transcending is not the same as leaving behind or abolishing. It means that Jesus enters into the context of Judaism but does not completely coincide with that context. He is not just the savior of Israel but of the whole world. That is why the Gentiles, through Jesus, can also be part of the people of God as Gentiles. They do not need to take on Jewish culture and context (Acts 15:19, 28).[32]

Both aspects – that Jesus is Jewish and that he transcends his Jewishness – are coming together at the cross. The one who was cursed by the Jewish law is being recognized by the law of God as the righteous one. The crucified one is raised. With that, not only is judgement passed on contemporary Judaism, but the Torah is also being fulfilled in an unexpected way. Jesus is the reality of true humanity; he has reconciled God and human beings and has settled the distortion of creation: "What human beings truly are, how God has meant life in the deepest sense, cannot be understood by looking at a broken creation. In the same way that God has created a reality that can only be recognized as a spot of light around the cross, this also applies for what it means to be human."[33]

With the incarnation, God is showing that he wants to be present in the culture and context of human beings. He is coming to where we are. However, he does not let the context remain as it is. He is coming in order to restore the original purposes of that context. He is saving us from the distortion. "The Jewish man Jesus has become equal to us in all possible ways, whether we are male or female, Jew or Gentile, Western or Asian,"[34] but his work is not according to the broken nature of that context. In all diversity he is restoring what it means to be truly human. That is why the cross and resurrection are the secret of contextualization.

In 1 Corinthians 9, Paul connects the incarnation with his own ministry. He does not want, in any way, to be a hinderance to the gospel of Jesus Christ

---

31. It is for this reason that the writers of the New Testament, at theologically crucial points, do not emphasize the Jewishness of Jesus but the fact that he was human. See Phil 2:5–11; John 1:14. It is striking how even in the letter to the Hebrews the "Jewishness" of Jesus hardly plays a role where it could have been theologically decisive.

32. Becoming conformed to the Jewish Jesus, therefore, also does not mean that everyone should adopt the Jewish culture and religion but that we will reflect his character. 2 Cor 3:18; Rom 8:29; Col 3:10.

33. Reitsma, *God of My Enemy*, 60.

34. Reitsma, 60.

– not for the members of the Christian community nor for Jews and Gentiles. That is why he has given up all his rights and privileges as an apostle (1 Cor 9:15, 23). Paul has become a Jew to the Jews (1 Cor 9:20–21), a slave to the slaves, and weak to the weak (1 Cor 9:19, 22). Paul became something to everyone in order to save them – even if just one (1 Cor 9:22). He is able to do so because the gospel eventually transcends and breaks through the context. "Being Jewish" or "being non-Jewish" is not decisive in following Jesus, neither is being a man or a woman. Paul is fully free because of Christ. He is not even under the law but can in all freedom place himself under the law and make himself subservient to others (1 Cor 9:20). In this way the gospel is fully contextual. People hear the gospel within their own frame of reference. At the same time, the gospel also transcends culture and confronts it with the cross. The cross is folly to those who are perishing, a stumbling block to Jews and Gentiles (1 Cor 1:18, 23): "For the foolishness of God is wiser than men, and the weakness of God is stronger than men (1 Cor 1:25).

8.4 Conclusion: A Contextual Gospel

On the basis of both creation and incarnation, we can conclude that concerning contextualization in relation to Islam we always have to keep the two perspectives together. On the one hand the gospel is present in the form of the concrete culture and context of Islam, on the other hand it also calls that context into question. True contextualization according to Newbigin implies that the gospel "comes to life" in a certain culture without ceasing to be the same authentic gospel. It means that the gospel is "at home" in a culture without being domesticated.[35]

8.4.1 Gospel and Culture

The gospel and culture cannot simply be separated from each other, as if they relate like different layers of an onion.[36] The message can only come to us in a form from our own world. We can only understand what comes to us in our own images and experiences, otherwise it is irrelevant; it does not touch *our* lives. If this was not the case, the gospel would be gnostic or docetic and it is not. It is very concrete. Similarly, we can only respond to the gospel message with the help of forms, rituals, and expressions that have meaning within our

---

35. Newbigin, *Pluralist Society*, 142, 144.
36. Stackhouse, "Contextualization," 6. See Newbigin, *Pluralist Society*, 189, 191.

own culture. Even the Bible is contextual. The message is partly characterized by ancient Eastern culture and partly by the Jewish-Hellenistic culture of the first-century Middle East. Jesus himself is a Jew. Who he is, what he does, and what he says are influenced by that context. That is how God reveals himself in the midst of the contingency of existence. Contextualization is therefore a continuous interaction between gospel and culture.[37]

8.4.2 The Gospel in the Context of Islam

If reality, in all of its diversity, is an expression of God's creative actions, then there is no context in which the gospel cannot somehow take shape. If there is only one God, "the Father from whom are all things," "and one Lord, Jesus Christ, through whom are all things" (1 Cor 8:6), then all of reality is through him. Everything is his. There is no form of expression that cannot be employed by the gospel. That is true for all of the C1–C6 Christ-centered communities that Travis describes. Every form or thought is available to the church. Paul writes that even the eating of food offered to idols in the temple is no problem for the believer who knows that there is only one God. Should Christians in the context of Islam be worried, then, about the use of forms and ideas that are also used by Muslims? Would Paul's exhortation not also mean something to Muslims who follow Jesus and give expression to their faith in their own social context? Would that not offer room to pray in the Mosque, participate in Ramadan, eat halal, continue to refer to God as Allah – and participate in various other cultural practices? If God fully entered into the context of first-century Judaism, would not the church, then, be permitted to fully enter into the context of Islam? If Paul can become a Jew to the Jews, and become as one without the law for those without the law, could not the church of Christ be able to be "Muslim to the Muslims"? According to Paul, that all depends on whether or not one recognizes that the one God has fully revealed himself as the Lord Jesus Christ.

The other side to this is that culture and context also share in the distortion of creation. The context of Islam is, in all its diversity, also an expression of rebellion against the one God. There is never a direct connection between the gospel and a derailed and broken context. The gospel is not fully determined by the context but also critiques the culture. The church is the fellowship of the

---

37. Strengholt, *Gospel in the Air*, 8–9. Strengholt mentions six contextualization warnings that underline this interaction. See also Niebuhr, *Christ and Culture*, who defines this relationship as Christ above culture, against culture, in paradox to culture, and transforming culture.

kingdom that is not of this world. That is why being church does not simply correspond in all ways to the world of Islam. In the midst of any cultural context, there is a need to constantly search for concepts and images, language and forms, that present God's new reality in the midst of any particular context without taking away the cultural resistance against the gospel. It also clashes. The gospel unmasks the degeneration of creation and critiques the world. If the gospel of the cross no longer collides with the context of Islam, does that not imply that it has been robbed of its power? A message that is in harmony with Islamic culture does not liberate it.

This does not mean that the church should, by default, disapprovingly dispose of everything Arab or Islamic. The new creation is not the liberation of people out of their own context in order to take on a different, Western culture instead. Western culture, too, is ambivalent and deeply touched by the distortion of creation. The gospel means that the context *itself* is being renewed. It is about a liberation of the *degeneration* of a culture so that it can reflect God's original purposes again. That means that Muslims who start to follow Jesus do not have to adopt Western norms, values, and habits, nor take on Western social-political choices and forms. Neither is it necessary for the church to take on Western forms, habits, and customs when it comes to the arrangement of church services, the use of language, rituals, music, and songs, its leadership, its membership, or how the gospel is worded. Insofar as "Christianity" is seen as a particular system, no one needs to join "Christianity" in order to follow Christ. Muslims who start to follow Jesus are at the beginning of an exploration; they are testing how they can do so in their own social context. How do they keep the balance between their context as a part of God's good creation, on the one hand, and its distortion on the other? Different followers of Jesus will answer that question differently, as it partly depends on their context. This matter does not just play out in the context of Islam. It is the calling of every Christian community.

8.4.3 Contextualization in Context

We need to be cautious as Christians from one particular culture in determining what correct contextualization looks like for Christians in another culture. The risk is that we base our judgement on the cultural form the gospel has been given in our own culture instead of on the gospel itself. That is true for Christians in the West who have trouble with C5 or C6 Christians in the Islamic world. It is also true for Christians in the Middle East (especially Muslims who are following Jesus) who have trouble with how the Western church is trying to contextualize in a postmodern world. The way in which the church relates to Islam is especially hard to judge from a different context. However, I do not advocate for a form of cultural relativism, as if the contextualization of the gospel should not be subject to critical evaluation. The point is that every Christian community should be consciously aware of its own contextualization. It suits the church to be humble. Only then can we discuss the right relationship between gospel and culture across the boundaries of different cultures. In the end, it requires the meeting of Christians from very different cultures in order to discover the wealth of the gospel. In that process, however, the encounter with Muslims and Islam also plays an important role. Their very different religious context is precisely what forces the Christian church to think about its own faith and its own connection to a particular social-cultural context. This meeting can help the Christian community discover its blind spots and see how its forms, customs, habits, and even its way of explaining the Bible, or theological emphases, are marked by culture.

It will be seen that we should not label Western culture as "Judeo-Christian" all that fast. Of course, there have been centuries in which Christianity was the dominant religion in the West, and that has had influence on the norms, values, and arrangement of society. At the same time, we should be cautious with this label. What is so Judeo-Christian about Western culture today? The justice system does not come straight from the Christian tradition but is based on a Roman form of justice. If we objectively look at Western norms and values, we discover that there are not that many Judeo-Christian principles present today. There is just as much in Western culture, if not more, that is contrary to the basic values of the Christian faith than it has in common with them. Not to mention that most Jews consider it a form of patronization and annexation to connect Judaism to Christianity in this way. In light of all this, Western Christians should wonder how they can say that Islam is not compatible with Western culture but Christianity is. What does that imply? Has the gospel been adjusted so much that it seamlessly fits within a Western lifestyle and alongside Western norms and values? Is there still a critical interaction possible between the gospel and culture or have we actually created a compromise?[38] That question is important in every context where gospel and culture interact and the Christian community is engaged.

---

38. With respect to intercultural theological conversation, Van den Toren speaks about triangulation. This discussion is about a trialogue: apart from the interaction between two (or more) conversation partners, each from their own cultural contexts in which the gospel is taking shape, there is the third (or really *primary*) reality of God in Christ. See Van den Toren, "Interculturele theologie als driegesprek," 29.

8.4.4 No Stumbling Blocks

When speaking about the relationship between the church and the context of culture, it is good to remember Paul's warning not to make those who are not yet free from their previous lives nor those who are outside of the church stumble. Especially for new followers of Jesus from a Muslim background, certain cultural and religious forms can create confusion. They can also create misunderstandings within the Islamic community and create the impression that there is no difference between Islam and Christianity. It is best to avoid such stumbling blocks. Which is equally true for any church in any context.

Paul places his remark in 1 Corinthians in the framework of "spiritual adultery." The relationship with God is broken when someone, due to the form and content of what he or she does, gives his or her heart to someone or something other than the one God. Even the *virtual* allowance of another lover in an exclusive relationship of trust puts love under pressure. In the context of Islam that is also decisive: does the way we engage with forms and customs in the Christian community do justice to the one God, "from whom are all things and for whom we exist," and the Lord Jesus Christ, "through whom are all things and through whom we exist" (1 Cor 8:6)?

8.4.5 Contextualization and Muslims Who Follow Jesus

Muslims who start to follow Jesus and seek to remain in their own context, often get the accusation that they are doing this in order to escape suffering and persecution. Setting exceptions aside, in general this is not true. Reality shows that C5 communities are most definitely experiencing opposition and persecution. Muslims in these communities, in contrast to the "outside category," the C6 believers, are not following Jesus in secret. They are standing up for their faith in Jesus as Messiah and receiving questions about their faith. In some situations, there are even legal consequences. In many cultures, it's practically impossible to change religions. In such circumstances, followers of Jesus with a Muslim background remain under the personal and family law for Muslims, which is different than that for Christians. Even when that is not the case, C5 believers who remain in their context are not doing so in order to make the gospel easier. It primarily offers them the opportunity to share their faith in Jesus with others. When they exit their community and join another community with another cultural context, their message becomes farfetched and hard to understand. Rather than the gospel itself, the stumbling block becomes its strange form and content.[39]

Apart from this, people always experience their faith from within the context of their own history and culture. The transition to the belief in Jesus does not mean that all the experiences of the past are wiped away. Who is in Christ has become a new creation (2 Cor 5:17) but is not recreated from scratch. That is to say, God does not start all over again with people once they get to know Christ. People are not saved *from* but *within* and *with* their context. Their past is in a way born again and renewed through baptism. That means that there should be room for these new believers to experience their faith in such a way that it connects to their personality, their past, and their culture. The Spirit, as a "critical authority," will transform these experiences from the inside out.

In this context, it is important for the Christian church to think about how it can create space for other ways of expressing faith and being church. If Muslims are starting to follow Jesus from within their own culture and context, they will do so in their own way. That way is just as legitimate as every other expression of Christian faith that is focused on and led by the Spirit of Christ. It is even possible that the influx of new believers can inspire traditional churches towards renewal. That can happen through Muslims who start to follow Jesus locally, but also through the migration of Christians either as refugees or otherwise. They can challenge the church worldwide to be open to the new ways in which the Spirit might be leading.

---

39. Van der Poll has discovered a comparable motive among Messianic Jews who, for purely missional reasons, stay within their Jewish social and religious contexts. Van der Poll, *Sacred Times.*

9

The Church and Persecution in the Context of Islam[1]

"Most of the Bible is written by persecuted believers to strengthen other persecuted believers."[2]

"Suffering is not the negation of worship – it is part of it. True worship can only be expressed from a position of suffering, because worship connects the believer with the reality of God and of his love. Worship connects us with God's pain over a broken creation."[3]

9.1 Introduction

A study on the relationship between the church and Islam cannot ignore the fact that, in many countries where there is an Islamic majority, Christians suffer for their faith. At least, the majority of incidents against Christians are reported in these countries. As was mentioned earlier (ch. 1), this is true for seven of the top ten countries on Open Door's *World Watch List* (2020).[4] Although there are some academic concerns with the use of this list both within and

---

1. This chapter is a deepening and elaboration of thoughts I have set forth in "Health, Wealth and Prosperity," 164–181.

2. Boyd-MacMillan, *Faith That Endures*, 17.

3. Reitsma, "Strangers in the Light," 222–223.

4. See the website Open Doors Analytical (http://opendoorsanalytical.org/) – specifically the sections "World Watch List Documentation" and "Country Dossiers." Use the password "freedom" to access the site. North Korea, India, and Eritrea are the three non-Islamic countries of the ten countries that top the list. In Eritrea, however, half of the population is said to be Muslim.

outside of Open Doors,[5] the results signal that there is an issue. Christians are experiencing hard times in Islamic countries. That is especially true for Muslims who start to follow Jesus as the Messiah. They experience opposition, expulsion, or violence.[6]

This chapter does not discuss the question of whether this kind of enmity is or is not inherent to Islam. There are many different opinions on this, including among Muslims themselves. There are Muslims who use Islamic texts to justify the persecution of Christians because they are unbelievers or apostates.[7] Other Muslims use other passages within the same sources to show that Christians are actually equal; they seek to protect them.[8] The classical schools of jurisprudence – both Sunni and Shi'a – all consider apostasy as punishable by death. Different Muslims will interpret this justification of the death penalty differently – for instance, due to the fact that apostasy was originally considered a type of treason. Leaving Islam in a time of war would imply leaving the Islamic community and defecting. In this chapter, the focus is on the question of how the suffering of the Christian church in the context of Islam should be understood within a biblical-theological framework. What do suffering and

---

5. Open Doors has devoted a lot of academic attention to the methodology behind the World Watch List. See Open Doors, *Complete World Watch List Methodology*. The list therefore can be said to provide a reliable indication of what is happening around the world. For that purpose it should be used. As a statistical tool it does not and cannot give an interpretation of the facts. It does not put persecution in a theological context, neither does it give a complete picture of all the motives and issues that are involved in situations of persecution. It needs similar reports on other groups to put the persecution of Christians into perspective. Unfortunately, those limitations are easily forgotten when the list is presented in the public domain. It is sometimes used as the last word on – in our case – the relationship between Islam and Christianity or as an instrument for political pressure. Sometimes the context of failing states and situations of war are forgotten (even though they are referred to in the "World Watch List Documentation" and "Country Dossiers" sections of the Open Doors Analytical website). Numbers are also prone to abuse by groups of people for their own interest. Finally, there is an embedded tension in the World Watch List, namely that it connects statistical facts to a theological or ideological concept. Persecution is an interpretation of facts, which is dependent on the perspective used. All of that, however, is beyond the scope of the list itself.

6. See Meral, *No Place to Call Home*.

7. Christians are, after all, guilty of the only sin that cannot be forgiven according to Islamic traditions, namely that of *shirk*, which is to ascribe companions or partners to God, which is also called polytheism. In the eyes of the Islamic tradition, true Christians are the ones who distance themselves from this fallacy and who "follow Isa in the Islamic way." This is, however, not about the historic or living community of Christians but about a "conceptual idealization." McAuliffe, *Qur'anic Christians*, 287.

8. According to the *Marrakesh Declaration*. The Qur'an speaks both positively as well as negatively about Christians and, in the end, how Christians are seen and treated depends on the hermeneutical choices that Muslims make. See Chapman, *Cross and Crescent*, 281, 287. See also Ayoub, "Nearest in Amity," 187–211, and Ayoub, "Muslim Views of Christianity," 212–245.

persecution have to say about the nature of the Christian community? How do they relate to the calling of the church in the context of Islam?

9.2 "Religious Persecution": Definition
9.2.1 Restrictions to a Theological View of Persecution

At first it seems that religious persecution is a matter that needs little explanation. The common perception is that Christians in the Islamic world experience discrimination and violence simply because they believe in Jesus Christ. In mainstream classical Islam, Christians may be seen as a protected minority, but the step towards being a *discriminated* minority is a small one. Christians have often experienced, and still experience, subordination in the Islamic world. Those who are considered less than others can also count on having less rights. The transition from discrimination to persecution is made even more easily. Christians who suffer in the Islamic world nearly always do so due to their faith.

When we look at the suffering of Christians in the context of Islam more thoroughly, however, it is seen that it is more complicated than the picture I just drew. The concept of "religious persecution," for example, does not give an objective description of what Christians experience; it is a certain theological interpretation. It is also used by organizations such as Amnesty International and Human Rights Watch for everyone who suffers because of his or her beliefs. Christian organizations like Open Doors, Voice of the Martyrs, or Barnabas Fund, however, would not use it so easily for what non-Christians experience because the concept is used in the Bible primarily for what Jesus and his followers are experiencing (see John 5:20; Acts 9:5; 26:11; 1 Cor 4:12; 15:9; *diōkō*). It seems to be an important "identity marker" for the Christian community in the New Testament (Matt 5:10–12; Rom 8:17).[9] According to Paul, "all who desire to live a godly life in Christ Jesus will be persecuted" (2 Tim 3:12).

I will mention two aspects that we need to take into account when speaking about suffering in relation to religious conviction today:

1.   "Religious persecution" does not just affect Christians. There is an endless number of non-Christians who suffer in the same way

---

9. In the Roman Catholic tradition martyrs are highly revered. That is not only evident from the martyr calendar but also from the fact that martyrdom is a highly regarded factor in beatification and canonization. According to Pope Urban II, those who died during the Crusades in the battle for the promised land would go straight to heaven.

because of their faith, beliefs, or life convictions. Some are persecuted for political-ideological reasons, others because they stand up for justice and resist (dictatorial) regimes. Muslims, too, suffer due to their faith. Sunni ISIS-Muslims in Syria and Iraq did and do not just fight Christians and Yazidis but also Sunni and Shi'a Muslims who they deem "apostates." The primary victims of Boko Haram in Nigeria are Muslims. In Pakistan, the lives of Ahmadiya Muslims are often in danger and it is nearly impossible for Shi'a Muslims to live out their faith publicly in Saudi-Arabia. "Religious persecution" is therefore not just a problem for Christians. Statistics show that Christians are not persecuted more often or more severely than non-Christians. In 2011 Pew Forum reported that Christians are persecuted in 130 countries and Muslims in 117.[10] This does not say anything about the actual number of Christians, but it does seem to indicate that they are persecuted slightly more than Muslims are. De Wever, however, points to the fact that there are more Christians in the world than Muslims, and thus it would seem logical that under identical circumstances more Christians would be persecuted than Muslims. When we take this into account, it seems that Christianity does not stand out. According to Wever, Christians in the Islamic world are not even the "favorite" enemy.[11]

2. Contrary to the persistent image, Christians are not always suffering in the context of Islam *due to their faith*. There are often multiple factors at work, such as ethnicity, economic standards, or political preferences. Christians in the Middle East who are victims due to civil wars or international conflicts cannot simply be counted as persecuted due to their faith. However, it also cannot be ruled out because Christians could be more vulnerable due to their faith than other groups in society, and if they practice nonviolence on principle, they can become an easy target because of their faith. However, the question is if faith is then the primary reason. There are

---

10. Pew Forum, "New Pew Forum Report."

11. Wever, "Christenvervolging." In practice, it seems that it is not easy to accurately establish the number of people who are persecuted for their faith. In 2014 there was even a decrease in the number of countries with religious restrictions, even though religiously related terrorism was on the rise. See Pew Forum, "Trends in Global Restrictions."

various situations that demonstrate a more complicated picture.[12] If for years Christians have chosen the side of a dictatorial leader, can we still call it persecution when people take revenge on them during a change of regime? Is it persecution when Christians are facing the consequences of Western (often interpreted as "Christian") colonial and military interventions in the Islamic world? When Christians suffer in the context of Islam, we need to be careful to not be too quick in labeling it "Christian persecution." Organizations like Amnesty International, Human Rights Watch, and Open Doors are continuously pointing out that reality is very complex and that there are always multiple factors at work when Christians are suffering.

If "religious persecution" is not exclusively or primarily experienced by Christians, and if not every form of suffering that Christians experience can be called "persecution," than what is the meaning of "suffering for Christ's sake"? Does it even exist? Can it be demonstrated in the context of Islam?

9.2.2 Definition

For the sake of argument, it is necessary to first carefully define the term "persecution." In general, we could say that persecution is always about the violation of human rights. But not all violations of human rights can also be labeled as persecution. The boundary between the two is not very clear. Does the concept of persecution primarily apply to "extreme" forms of suffering, such as torture, prison sentences, or even death? Or do other forms such as bullying, harassment, and discrimination belong to it too?[13]

Tieszen has made an attempt to create an all-inclusive definition of persecution in which the above-mentioned factors are considered. He differentiates between three levels: (1) general persecution, (2) religious persecution, and (3) religious persecution of Christians, theologically speaking. The first is every form of hostile or unjust action with one or more motives, directed at a specific individual or group of individuals, resulting in varying levels of harm (considered from the victim's perspective).[14] The second level

---

12. The policy statement on religious persecution from the Conservative Christian Political party in the Netherlands (SGP) looks at a diversity of factors that can lead to religious restrictions and persecution, one of which is "failed states." See Krooneman, *Een ongemakkelijke waarheid*, 9.

13. Open Doors distinguishes between "squeeze" and "smash" – between slowly being squeezed and being hit hard – but sees both as forms of persecution. Lowry, "Understanding." See also Boyd-MacMillan, *Faith That Endures*, 85–100.

14. Tieszen, "Towards Redefining Persecution," 163.

is comparable but with the difference that these actions are directed at one or more believers of a particular religion or belief system and have religion as their primary motivator.[15] The third level concerns persecution that is specifically focused on Christians *purely and only* on the basis of their Christian identity.[16]

Even though this definition does much to clarify the term and gives the suffering of Christians a unique position, it still does not completely satisfy. Tieszen creates the impression that the three levels can be easily distinguished from each other and perhaps even separated. In order to determine whether or not something is truly religious persecution or not, Tieszen – in following Marshall – asks, for example, the question of whether that persecution would have also happened if the individual or the group in question had no religion or a different religion.[17] This assumes that religion and other factors can easily be separated from each other. In the West that may (partly) be possible, but that is unthinkable in non-Western cultures. An ethnic conflict in the Middle East is often also a religious conflict and vice versa. Religion is an essential part of the identity of a group or an extended family. An attack on an ethnic community is therefore also always an attack on their faith. That is one of the reasons why Christians are sometimes targeted by Muslims while their actual focus is Western economic, political, or military intervention in the Islamic world. As we have seen in chapter 8, Christianity is viewed by many Muslims as Western and the West is viewed as Christian.

More substantial is the objection that this definition aligns a theological approach (level 3) with a sociological one (level 1 and 2). In truth, it is about two different perspectives on the same reality. Sociologically speaking, level 3 could also be a subcategory of level 2. Multiple subcategories of this level would be possible, such as the persecution of Muslims, Buddhists, Yazidis, etc. Due to the theological component – it is about a Christian view on the persecution of Christians – Tieszen makes it a separate category. That theological perspective is, however, also possible for levels 1 and 2. It would imply an interpretation of persecution in general (level 1) and of religious persecution (level 2) in light of the gospel.[18]

Organizations like Amnesty International and Human Rights Watch do not consider the third level as a separate category. They do not judge discrimination

---

15. Tieszen, 165.

16. Tieszen, 168.

17. Marshall, "Persecution of Christians," 5.

18. There are also comparable theological perspectives possible from other religions, like an Islamic perspective on the persecution of Muslims, Christians, and others.

and violence against Christians any differently than discrimination and violence targeted at non-Christians. Freedom of religion is one of the rights that has been established by the Universal Declaration of Human Rights, and it applies equally to Muslims as it does to Christians. When minorities in a society are facing difficulties, it does not matter if they are Christian or Muslim. The danger here is that the religious motivations of those who persecute Christians (or Muslims) can easily be overlooked.

Christian organizations who stand up for the rights of persecuted Christians concentrate far more on the theological perspective. It is not unthinkable that this perspective may get confused with the sociological one. A biblical interpretation is then seen as a sociological one and vice versa. If Christian organizations see the persecution of Christians as the consequence of their dedication to Jesus, their suffering could gain a higher status than the suffering of non-Christians.

In order to also support that status sociologically, some Christians have the tendency to exaggerate the suffering of Christians. That is possible by using statistics that supposedly show that more Christians are being persecuted than non-Christians. In truth, the numbers of persecuted Christians usually do not represent hard facts but estimations. It is practically impossible to verify what the numbers are based on. Besides that, statistics fluctuate depending on what definition is used. For example, if all the Christians who lost their lives in World War II were viewed as martyrs, it would give a very skewed picture of Christian persecution.

Marshall, for example, mentions that two hundred million Christians have experienced extreme forms of persecution (mass murder, torture, rape, etc.). Four hundred million Christians, according to him, experience discrimination or legal limitations. Marshall does not explain what these numbers are based on. "Discrimination" and "legal limitations" are very general terms.[19] And are these yearly figures or the total number of Christians during a certain time period? Others are still – unjustifiably so – holding on to the idea that there are one hundred thousand Christian martyrs a year. That number was originally introduced by the Center for the Study of Global Christianity. It's generally known that this number is incorrect and based on the wrong extrapolation of statistics.[20] Open Doors continues to try to give a global indication of the number of Christian martyrs per year, placing it at 4,344 in 2014 and 7,106 in 2015. In 2016 the number of martyrs radically dropped to 1,207. Even the

---

19. See Marshall, *Their Blood Cries Out*, 4. See also Marshall, "Persecution of Christians," 163.
20. See Alexander, "Are There Really 100,000?"

destruction of Christian buildings, such as churches or community centers, was halved in 2016 compared to 2015. In 2017 the number of Christians killed for their faith rose again to 3,066 and in 2018 to 4,305, which is still lower than 2014, while 250 million Christians supposedly experienced some form of persecution.[21] In 2019 a reported 2,983 Christians were killed for their faith. It is not completely clear where these huge differences come from. It can be due to a different way of counting, better research methods, or a true fluctuation in persecution. It might also show the difficulty of providing reliable statistics. Open Doors tries to give an interpretation of these variations in their World Watch List documentation.[22]

Statistics are prone to be manipulated. By adjusting the definition of "persecution," it can seem as if there are suddenly more or less people who are persecuted. The most extreme example is the statement that all Christians who died during World War II died as martyrs for their faith: claiming the Holocaust as the ultimate example of Christian persecution.[23] At the same time, there were people who, due to their faith convictions, helped others to go into hiding and were then arrested. In short, statistics say very little.

The suffering of the persecuted church can also be exaggerated in order to emphasize that Christians suffer far more than non-Christians. For the sake of that image, the truth is sometimes skewed. Even persecution can, in that way, become an instrument in the hands of the Western church to exercise a certain form of power in the Muslim world and enforce Western norms and values. Schirrmacher points out that Christians are not immune to this, especially when it could increase financial support. Websites, such as Facebook, and other social media outlets also ensure that incorrect information can easily be shared and last for a long time.[24] Ultimately, Christian organizations do not help the persecuted church by encouraging inaccurate information.

The most important question that Tieszen's definition raises, therefore, is how the theological perspective relates to the sociological one. Is the suffering of Christians, because of their faith, different in nature from the suffering of non-Christians? Should the Christian community respond differently to the suffering of non-Christians than to the suffering of Christians? In order to

---

21. For the statistics for 2019, see Open Doors, *World Watch List 2019*.

22. http://opendoorsanalytical.org/wp-content/uploads/2020/01/WWL-2020-Compilation-of-main-documents.pdf.

23. Castelli, "Praying," 329.

24. See Thomas Schirrmacher, "Falschmeldungen zur Christenverfolgung," blog 13-12-2014.

answer that we need to first clarify what suffering and persecution have to do with the nature of the Christian church.

It is clear that when we reflect on suffering and persecution, we tread on holy ground. It is that ground that, as Stanley Jones mentions, has been sanctified by blood and tears.[25] The experience of sorrow and loss is so drastic that academic reflection can only be done with the utmost caution. The challenge is to take the traumatic experiences of Christians (and others) seriously and, at the same time, interpret them with integrity in the light of the new life in Christ.[26]

9.3 Suffering with Christ

In light of the framework we have sketched earlier, we focus here on what the evangelist John and the apostle Paul have to say about the church in relation to suffering. Both bring up suffering and persecution as the consequence of the tension between the new life of the Spirit and the old life of brokenness.

9.3.1 In the World You Will Have Tribulation (John 16:33)

The reign of Jesus, as we have seen, does not come with might or violence but through the way of the cross. The king of Israel and the world takes the road of suffering and demise. That is how the new life comes, through the death and resurrection of Jesus Christ. From the very beginning of his gospel, John writes that the new life clashes with the powers of the old era: "He came to his own, and his own people did not receive him" (John 1:11). The Jewish leaders resisted Jesus, the Romans join in. As long as the new life has not come in full glory, it also means that the community of Christ will suffer. The followers of Jesus are – just like Jesus – not of this world (John 15:19; 17:14, 16). Their nature is determined from "above" and therefore the world hates them too (John 15:18–19). The "servant is not greater than his master," and the world will persecute the believers just like they first persecuted Jesus (John 15:20). The church suffers because of the name of Christ (John 15:21).[27] They will be put out of the synagogues, and people will think they are serving God by killing them (John 16:2).

---

25. See Jones, *Christ and Human Suffering*.
26. See Castelli, "Praying," 330.
27. Causal διὰ τὸ ὄνομά μου (dia + acc).

It is thus part of the essence of the fellowship of the kingdom of Jesus that his followers will have tribulation (θλῖψις) in the world; they will experience "oppression" or "persecution." Jesus prepares his disciples for this and encourages them for when it will happen. He has overcome the world (John 16:33). In this way, John encourages the church of his time to continue to believe despite the resistance from both Jewish and Greco-Roman circles.

9.3.2 Suffering between the Ages

Similarly, Paul emphasizes that the believer suffers "with Christ" (Rom 8:17),[28] but he takes it even a step further than John. The church suffers with Christ in order that it may also be glorified with him (Rom 8:17). Suffering is not only the inevitable consequence of the connection with Christ but also a necessary condition for sharing in his glory. Paul speaks in Romans 8 – as we have seen in chapter 3 – about the suffering of the church in the context of the contrast between old and new (Rom 6:21–22; 8:1). In Christ, the new era of salvation for Israel and the nations has come, even though, at the same time, the old creation is not yet over. The powers of sin and death have, in Christ, been replaced by the power of the Spirit and life (8:2), but they have not yet disappeared (8:11). The inheritance – the fullness of glory (8:17–18, 21, 23) – has not yet come. That is also the reason why all of creation, including believers, are still suffering and experiencing labor pains (8:21–23). They look forward to the moment that the glory, of which the Spirit is the first gift, will fully break through (8:18–23).

It is at this specific point in time, *ho nun kairos* (Rom 8:18), that the church of Christ is suffering. *Kairos* often refers to a critical moment (Rom 5:6), and it is more a theological than a chronological qualification in Romans 8:18. This time is a significant moment in the history of God.[29] It is the time between the beginning of the new era of salvation – the final breakthrough of the fullness of the new *aeon* – and the disappearance of the old *aeon*. The characteristics of that time determine also the characteristics of the suffering of the church of Christ. It is a time characterized by (1) the continued presence of the powers of the old creation, and (2) the reality of the new life in Christ, the fullness of which is about to break through.

---

28. Paul literally writes: you suffer together (συμπάσχω) and you will be glorified (συνδοξάζω). In light of the aforementioned "being heirs with Christ" (συγκληρονόμοι δὲ Χριστοῦ) that can only be interpreted as "suffering and being glorified with Christ."

29. See Christoffersson, *Earnest Expectation*, 128; "the decisive moment." The metaphor of labor pains that Paul introduces (8:22) points in the same direction. It is a crucial moment.

The powers of the old creation

Life in a disrupted creation brings suffering to the believers. They are not yet delivered from the power of death (Rom 8:10), which expresses itself in different kinds of suffering. This suffering is suffering in solidarity with Christ. His suffering was – albeit in a different way – also the result of the powers of sin and death (Rom 6:10; 8:3). The believers are, through baptism, united with Christ and his cross (Rom 6:4–5) and therefore share in his suffering.[30]

The "suffering with Christ" in Romans 8 is regularly interpreted as "religious persecution."[31] The primary argument for this interpretation is that persecution is always suffering that is related to faith in Christ (see Matt 5:10–11; 10:18; Acts 5:41). Still, this interpretation of Romans 8 is not tenable for two reasons.

First, the New Testament never calls persecution "suffering *with* Christ." The term *sumpascho* (συμπάσχω) is only used by Paul once, in 1 Corinthians 12:26, and it is absent in the rest of the New Testament.[32] In 1 Corinthians 12:26, it indicates the communal (*sun*) suffering of all members of the body of Christ. The emphasis lies on the common aspect of suffering. When one person shares in the suffering of another, both are equally touched by it. *Sumpascho* never means suffering *for the sake of* or *because of* someone else.[33] In every passage where Paul uses the word *sun* in relation to Christ, it is either about connection with the cross and the suffering of Christ or with his resurrection and coming glory.[34] When speaking of persecution, Paul prefers to use the term *diōkō*.[35]

Second, the context of Romans 8 points in another direction. The suffering of the believers needs to be understood in the context of the greater perspective of the suffering of all creation (8:18–22). Suffering with Christ is to experience the suffering that also affects the rest of creation – namely, futility (8:20) and corruption (8:21). The suffering of creation differs from persecution. It can only be explained as the power of death that manifests itself in creation. It goes without saying that the believers' suffering, then, is more than just

---

30. See Fitzmyer, *Romans*, 502. In Phil 3:10, Paul explains the same relationship between "knowing" Christ, sharing in the sufferings of Christ, and becoming like him in his death (συμμορφιζόμενος τῷ θανάτῳ αὐτοῦ).

31. Penner simply assumes that Romans 8 is about persecution. Penner, *In the Shadow*, 197–201. See also Ignatius, *Epistle to the Smyrnaeans*, ch. IV.

32. It is rare in classical Greek. See *LSJ*.

33. For that the New Testament uses other expressions such as suffering "on account of" or "for the sake of" (ἕνεκα of ὑπέρ) the name of Christ. For ἕνεκα, see for example Matt 5:10–11; 10:18; Mark 13:9; Luke 21:12; and Matt 10:39; Mark 8:35; Luke 9:24. For ὑπέρ, see Acts 5:41; 9:16; 15:26; 21:13; cf. Eph 3:1.

34. See Reitsma, "Health, Wealth and Prosperity," 176.

35. For διώκω, see Rom 8:35; 1 Cor 4:12; 2 Cor 4:9; Gal 1:13, 23; Phil 3:6.

persecution. Paul explicitly mentions various forms of suffering in Romans 8:35: tribulation (θλῖψις), distress (στενοχωρία), persecution (διωγμός), famine (λιμός), nakedness (γυμνότης), danger (κίνδυνος), and the sword (μάχαιρα); each of these are manifestations of the power of death.[36] One of them is persecution,[37] but it is not the only one. In a similar way, Paul sums up all sorts of suffering in 2 Corinthians 12 as different aspects of the same thing. The weakness of the believer consists of insults (ὕβρις), hardships (ἀνάγκη), persecutions (διωγμός), and calamities (στενοχωρία) (2 Cor 12:10). The power of Christ is completed, or fulfilled, in all that suffering (2 Cor 12:9; τελειόω).[38] In the same way, the term *pascho*, without *sun*, is used in the New Testament to both denote suffering in general[39] and persecution.[40]

Paul, therefore, does not explicitly distinguish between persecution on the one hand and other forms of suffering on the other when speaking of "suffering with Christ." He uses the overall concept of suffering with Christ, which is the result of the continuing presence of the powers of the old creation.

The new life

Suffering with Christ is subsequently also determined by the reality of the new life. Because Christ paid for our sins (Rom 8:3) and the power of death is forever defeated (Rom 6:10–11), the character of the suffering of the church has been transformed. The powers at this moment in time are no longer present in the same way as they were before the coming of Christ. They are no longer able to separate the believers from the love of God in Christ (Rom 8:39; cf. 8:31–39). Death no longer has the final word. That is why the believers are suffering in expectation. They wait eagerly for their adoption as children (*huiothèsia*), which is the redemption of the body (8:23). The bodies of the believers will in the future be permanently and ultimately redeemed from mortality. In the Spirit, as the firstfruits, that glory is already present (8:23), and in this way, the Spirit is also the guarantee that the full glory will break through. The Spirit of him who raised Jesus from the dead dwells in the believers and will soon also

---

36. Wright, *Justification*, 207.

37. Romans 8:36 is a quote from Ps 44[LXX 43]:23.

38. "May rest upon me" (ESV) is a rather poor translation. It indicates here the realization or completion of something – the power that reaches what it exists for – namely, the strengthening of the believer in weakness.

39. See Phil 3:10; Matt 17:15; 27:19; Acts 28:5; see also Matt 16:21, where it is about more than just persecution.

40. See 2 Cor 1:5; 2 Thess 1:5. Acts 9:16 is about persecution but uses the expression "for the sake of the name of Christ" (ὑπὲρ τοῦ ὀνόματός), not "suffering with Christ."

give life to their now mortal bodies (Rom 8:11). Paul is most likely thinking here of the resurrection of the body, of which he also writes in 1 Corinthians 15. Once the glory has come, the power of death will be permanently gone. That expectation marks the suffering of the believer. The suffering with Christ is not the agony of death but labor pain (8:22–23). It is not the kind of suffering that announces the end of God's work but the full breakthrough of the new life. Just like labor pains are the prerequisite for the birth of new life, suffering with Christ is the prerequisite for sharing in the glory of God (8:17).[41] Just as there is no other way for Christ to enter glory than through suffering, in the same way there is no way for those who are in Christ to share with him the blessings of the new time than through suffering with Christ, by dying and rising again (see Rom 6). In this way, the coming glory is already paradoxically present in suffering with Christ. It is about to break through and is therefore passionately longed for. In the different forms of suffering, believers may recognize the signs of the fast-approaching glory. Suffering is suffering in hope (Rom 8:24). That is why suffering can in no way take away from the glory that is to come and is not worth comparing with that glory (8:18). It affects all of creation because all of creation will be redeemed with the believers and will share in the freedom of this glory (8:21).

In conclusion, the unique character of the suffering of the church is determined by the life "between the ages." At the crossroads of the old and the new, the suffering of the church has a very specific character. The believers, in their suffering with Christ, are connected to all of creation because they are suffering as a consequence of what has gone wrong in God's history with heaven and earth. Their suffering is entirely different from what the world experiences outside of Christ because it is marked by the glory of Christ that is already present through the Spirit of Christ. Their groaning in suffering as a consequence of death is a groaning in the pains of childbirth which announces the new life. That is why the suffering in a broken world is part of the essential nature of the church. If it wants to share in the fullness of the new life, it will also need to suffer with Christ. That is not a glorification of suffering, for it is contrary to God's intentions. The brokenness of creation and God's good intentions are not related as two sides of the same coin. One day the distortion of creation will be fully dealt with. Once the glory breaks through in fullness, sin and death will cease to exist and God will wipe away every tear from the eyes of the believers (Rev 7:17; 21:4).

---

41. Εἴπερ as fulfilled condition; see Blaß, Debrunner, and Rehkopf, *Grammatik des neutestamentlichen Griechisch*, §454.2; also see Fitzmyer, *Romans*, 502; "if indeed."

9.4 Conclusion: the persecuted church and Islam

We can now draw several theological conclusions about the suffering of the Christian church in the context of Islam. The paradox of the old and new creation sheds light on suffering in relation to the nature of the Christian church, as well as the relationship between the theological and the sociological perspectives.

9.4.1 Suffering and the DNA of the Church

Suffering is an essential characteristic of the church of Christ in a distorted creation. Because the church is a new creation, its nature is at odds with the powers and structures of the broken reality. That unavoidably brings suffering. The Christian church clashes, as the community of the kingdom of Christ, with the kingdoms of the world. If that was not the case, then, in its nature, the Christian church would be no different from distorted creation. Even more so, it would cease to be the church of Christ. In that sense, suffering belongs to the DNA of the church in *this* context. It is therefore not surprising that the church in the context of Islam is a suffering church. It is far more surprising that the church in the West is not experiencing affliction. We could even question if the situation of the church as a minority in the Islamic world is not more consistent with the true nature of the church. If the church is an entity that reveals the kind of life that is so contrary to the old *aeon*, then the church can only be present in this world as a suffering community.

9.4.2 Suffering in Different Forms

When suffering belongs to the essence of the church in *this* world, then we cannot make a theological distinction between "suffering in general" and "persecution." For Paul, that distinction does not exist. According to him, the powers of the old age, sin and death, assert themselves in many ways: in the form of suffering as a consequence of the brokenness of creation but also in the form of hatred and opposition that lead to discrimination and persecution. In practice, it is hard to determine exactly where we should draw the line between religious and non-religious factors, between religious persecution and suffering in general. When Christians receive less help from the government after a natural disaster than Muslims do, is that suffering a form of persecution or is it simply the consequence of the distortion of creation? If Christians die during a civil war, are they the victims of religious persecution if one of the groups in that war was Islamic? In short, suffering in this world is always a very complex phenomenon. Suffering is never simple.

In meeting persecuted Christians, I've noticed that some of them have a hard time accepting this. "Simply" suffering seems so trivial and senseless, while "suffering for the sake of Christ" is honorable. It is seen as the expression of dedication to Jesus Christ, and it is appreciated as a sign of loyalty and perseverance – which is why it is not meaningless and not a waste of opportunities and talents. The first Christians rejoiced "that they were counted worthy to suffer dishonor for the name" of Jesus (Acts 5:41); they considered it a joy to suffer while doing good and thus walk in the footsteps of Jesus Christ (see 1 Pet 2:20–21; 4:13). When persecution is aligned with "suffering in general," it seems as if "persecution" also becomes trivial, as it no longer has any unique value.

Still, that is not necessarily the case. Both forms of suffering are shocking and expose the contrast between the old and the new life. Both show that the new life has not come in its fullness yet, and both are equally painful. It is precisely because the believers share in the new life that the reality of the old life is so bitter. That is true in relation both to opposition from outside the church and to the brokeness of creation. If the powers have been overcome, it stings that they still assert themselves. It is as shocking as when people during a war are still being shot at after a cease-fire has taken effect. Similarly, it is shocking that disease and death still defeat tens of thousands of people every day even though Jesus has conquered disease and death. It is just as bitter as when those who were liberated from the German concentration camps after World War II still died from exhaustion on their way home, even though the enemy had been defeated. It is *because* believers have received the Spirit as the first gift of the future glory that they still suffer due to the brokenness of creation and the opposition of its authorities. Theologically speaking, there is no difference.

Ultimately, it is also true that both forms of suffering pose the same challenge for the church of Christ – namely, to stay faithful to Christ. When Christians are persecuted, they are called to persevere through the pain and sadness and to keep believing that God will cause all things to work for good for those who love him (Rom 8:28). If they suffer as a result of the brokeness of creation, the challenge is the same. In every situation it is all about trusting that God's grace is enough (2 Cor 12:9).

9.4.3 Suffering and Persecution Is Not Exclusive to Christians

When suffering is a result of the presence of the powers of the old *aeon*, it also affects nonbelievers. The brokenness of creation concerns everyone. That is not just true for suffering in general but also for suffering in the form of injustice and suffering because of religion, ethnicity, political preference, or gender. What Paul says about suffering and persecution in no way excludes the fact that non-Christians can also be "persecuted" and "hated," even though it is not for their faith in Christ.[42]

We may conclude that when believers suffer, this suffering has changed in character due to their connection with Christ. For their suffering is no longer a sign of despair but of hope. It is not the agony of death but of labor pains. It points to the glory that is coming and in the Spirit is already present here and now. It is no longer a sign of failure – of the history of God, human beings, and creation – but evidence that the new life has arrived. All this is not just true for hardship, hunger, or poverty but just as much for persecution and the sword. All suffering for believers has come to announce God's glory. Believers *sometimes* suffer "for the name of Christ." They always suffer "together with Christ," both when they are persecuted and when they suffer in other ways.

That means that, from a sociological perspective, believers can experience exactly the same suffering as nonbelievers. They do not suffer more or less than others. That is true both qualitatively and quantitatively. For example, Christians are not persecuted more often than Muslims, and their suffering is not by definition harder than the suffering of non-Christians. Sociologically speaking, they may be identical, but theologically there is a great difference. The suffering of a follower of Jesus has to do with his or her relationship with Christ; it has become a sign of the coming fullness of the new life.[43]

9.4.4 Suffering and the "Prosperity Gospel"

If suffering belongs to the DNA of the Christian church, it implies that we need to be utterly critical of the so-called "prosperity gospel."[44] The theological vision behind "the health, wealth, and prosperity gospel" poses that God will always bless his people both materially and spiritually. Put differently, whoever believes does not have to be sick or suffer but will always be doing well and prosper. Because Christ has overcome sin, the consequences of sin for a Christian are

---

42. That is level 2 from the definition of Tieszen.

43. In 2 Cor 2:15–16, in a different context, Paul says something similar. The believers are the aroma of Christ. For those who are saved it is delightful, "a fragrance from life to life," for others it is "a fragrance from death to death." In this way, suffering is for those who are saved as labor pains and for those who are lost as the agony of death.

44. In truth there is a great diversity of movements. That is why Fee speaks of prosperity *gospels*. Fee, *Disease*. For references, see Reitsma, "Health, Wealth and Prosperity," 164–181.

also overcome. And if that is not the case, it means the believer lacks faith, has not fully surrendered to God, or was disobedient to him.

Such a vision clashes, first of all, with the reality of the persecuted church in the Islamic world. It is even an insult to that persecuted church. Christians suffer in this context namely *for the very reason* of their dedication to Christ. They experience difficulty precisely because they do not want to give up their faith in him. Second, the "prosperity gospel" is also opposite to what we have learned from John and Paul. Suffering for them does not indicate a lack of faith and commitment. The very fact that the church represents the new life makes it suffer in a unique way. If the church of Christ does not experience opposition in this world, we have to question whether it is still faithful to the gospel.[45]

Still, the health, wealth, and prosperity gospel has a point. There certainly is a link between Christ's victory over death and sin and the blessing that is associated with it. Sin is the cause of the distortion of creation and the suffering that accompanies it. Conversely, does that not also mean that if that sin is taken away, the distortion of creation would also be reversed? The work of Christ, after all, contains the renewal of the whole of creation, which becomes as God had intended it in the beginning, and that is without sickness and death (cf. John 5:1–9). The resurrection body no longer knows disease or death.

The "prosperity gospel," however, derails in two ways – with respect to (1) time and (2) quality. Concerning the first, the "prosperity gospel" does not give enough attention to the fact that the fullness of salvation is still at large. We are living in the *kairos*-moment. What the prosperity gospel is claiming for *right now* does not become reality yet until the full revelation of glory. That does not, of course, exclude signs of that glory in the present. Second, the "prosperity gospel" is satisfied with a very limited quality. The blessing that the prosperity gospel promises largely stays within the parameters of the current status of creation. God's salvation and deliverance do not rise above the restoration of life under the conditions of the old creation. The glory that God has prepared for his church, however, is a total transformation of reality (see 1 Cor 2:9).

---

45. It needs to be noted that proponents of the prosperity gospel do not deny that there are Christians who suffer and who do not prosper. Different reasons are given for that such as the lack of faith, the presence of sin, evil powers, and the devil, the lack of perseverance, the not claiming of victory, and as a last resort, the fact that God in his sovereignty may have different plans or that it remains a mystery. See, for example, Ouweneel, *Geneest de zieken!*, 378–379.

Part IV

The Church and Islam

A Vulnerable Relationship

10

Vulnerable Love

"When Muslims hear the Christian proclamation of love wrapped in the cloak of angry polemics, it becomes an alien threat instead of divine revelation."[1]

"If your brother does not understand you, perhaps it is because you do not love him."[2]

10.1 Introduction

The Christian church is the restoration of the community of creation in Genesis. In the church it becomes visible how God has intended life to be, namely as a covenant of love between God, human beings, and the rest of creation. That new covenant is present in a world that has not yet been fully redeemed. The fullness of the new life is still to come. The church, too, is still awaiting the ultimate redemption from the powers of sin and death. As the first gift of the glorious future, the Spirit of God connects the church with what is still to come.

If we let the reality of these words sink in, we must highly value the position and calling of the church. After all, in it the contours of the life that the Almighty had in mind from the beginning have become visible. The church is the visible expression of God's creational love and represents the Creator in his creation. That unmistakably gives the church its identity. In a certain way it is very *exclusive*. If God in Christ through his Spirit has overhauled the distorted creation, the church is not just a random group of people, but the result of God's work. That is not insignificant. The church holds up a mirror to the world and criticizes the distortion of creation. It unmasks evil by what it is.

---

1. Van Gorder, *No God*, 23.
2. Van Gorder, 6.

Despite this high calling, humility is appropriate because, in this broken world, the church and Christianity do not fully overlap with the kingdom of God. The church has betrayed its identity repeatedly throughout history. It shares in both the brokenness and imperfection of the world of Islam, as well as in its longing for wholeness and fullness of life. The church is not the ultimate goal of God's work; the covenant of God with all of creation is. When looking at it this way, the church is also very *inclusive*.

For "exclusivity" and "inclusivity," Volf uses the terms "exclusion" and "embrace," albeit in a different context.[3] The gospel calls on the followers of Jesus to love and *embrace* their enemies. That, however, does not mean that the victims of violence and injustice must naively conform to evil. On the contrary, evil needs to be opposed and *excluded*, otherwise society will become impossible to live in.[4]

When it comes to the relationship between the church and Islam, both the synthetic and the antithetic approaches, as described in chapter 1, are inadequate. The synthetic approach is not able to do justice to the exclusivity of the creative work of the triune God. The identity of the church is essentially exchanged for the greater mystery that both Christianity and Islam point to in their own way. The antithetical model, meanwhile, leaves far too little room for the inclusivity of the gospel. The suggestion is created that Christianity completely overlaps with the kingdom of God, with Christians representing all that is good in creation and Muslims what is bad. The challenge before us is how to hold these two aspects together and balance exclusivity and inclusivity. The contextual approach seems to create space for that, but we still need to take it a step further.

The key point here is the realization of God's love. That love has a very clear identity but is, at the same time, vulnerable. God's love is – to use a variation on Karl Barth – the inner ground of both creation and recreation. God intended to establish a loving relationship with human beings and with creation. It is the same love that moved God to overhaul his creation in Christ. That love is vulnerable because it can be rejected or trampled upon. If it could be enforced, it would not be love but manipulation. That is also why the kingdom of Christ is not of this world; it gives people a free choice of who they want to follow as king. At the cross we see the ultimate vulnerability as God sacrifices his Son for his beloved creation. That is unconditional love. It is not selfish but gives of itself, no matter how its beloved responds.

---

3. Volf, *Exclusion and Embrace*.
4. Volf, 63.

The church is called to give expression to that vulnerable love, also, in the context of Islam. It needs to truly become what it is in Christ – the new community of creation. The church has received life with him and must share that life, in all vulnerability, with Muslims. It does not enforce it with power or violence. The church passes on the love of Christ, regardless of how Muslims respond to it. In this way, *vulnerable love* rises above the tension between "exclusivity" and "inclusivity." It indicates the willingness for self-sacrifice in order to share the true life. That characterizes the nature of the church.

Vulnerable love has at least five aspects. In relation to Islam, the church is (1) vulnerably fearless, (2) vulnerably devoted to mission, (3) vulnerably inclusive, (4) vulnerably prophetic, and (5) vulnerably self-critical.

10.2 Vulnerably Fearless

The church has a vulnerable position in this world. That is especially true for the church in predominantly Islamic countries. In the Middle East, for example, it has been a minority in the midst of a large community of Muslims for centuries. The question is how the church can hold its own in that situation and if it can survive at all in the long run. We know there are regions where the church disappeared after centuries of living presence: North Africa and Asia, for example. In Iraq, the church has been decimated since the fall of Saddam Hussein's regime. Because of the civil war that has waged in Syria since 2010, the situation there, too, is not hopeful. When Muslims in Europe or America gain influence, Western Christians become anxious about whether they are next. Christians elsewhere feel equally uneasy about the presence of Islam.

George Sabra describes two ways in which Christians in the Arab world are trying to deal with their vulnerable position.[5] One strategy tries to associate itself as much as possible with an Arab Islamic context. In order to live and work together with Muslims, all focus here is on the similarities and common ground shared between the two religions. This speaks of a longing for recognition and acceptance. At a minimum, it is an attempt to become estranged from Muslims as little as possible.[6] In this strategy, Christians desire Muslims to see from their behavior that they share the cultural and political values of their environment, despite possessing their own identity. In order to accomplish this, Christians seek to distance themselves as much as possible from the cultural and political

---

5. Sabra, "Two Ways," 43–53.

6. Sabra, 44.

values of the West.[7] This attitude often comes close to the synthetic approach, especially when one's Christian identity is more or less sacrificed in an attempt to associate with Muslims.

The other strategy that Sabra describes puts much more emphasis on Christian identity as something in contrast with Islamic identity and is used in an attempt to secure the (relative) freedom and independence of the Christian community. In order to achieve that, Christians try to be religiously, socially, and culturally distinct from Islam. Without denying that Christianity is part of Arab culture, they also want to focus on other cultural values. This approach is clearly more antithetical with respect to the Islamic community than the first. Sometimes, in the battle against Muslims, even explicit political and military support can be asked (and received) of the West.

Both of the approaches that Sabra describes are essentially focused on the survival of the Christian minority in the context of Islam. When both options are no longer viable – although Sabra does not go into that – the only thing left is to flee. That can mean literally leaving the Islamic environment, but it is also possible to flee in a figurative sense: Christians can opt for a "survival mode." They can fully withdraw from society into a kind of ghetto as the last protection against an advancing enemy. The only thing that is left is the faith that God will provide; only he can help when the end is near. In this way, religion almost becomes a form of opium that helps one to persevere against one's better judgement.

The situation in the West is, in many respects, incomparable to that of the Middle East. Christians are becoming more of a minority,[8] but not among a majority of Muslims; the cultural context is secular. Yet here, too, the question is raised of whether Christians will be threatened by Islam in the future and how they should arm themselves against that possibility. It would be rather presumptuous, from our place of relative comfort, to tell persecuted brothers and sisters, who fear for their existence, how they should relate to Islam. That is not the intention of my considerations here. Still, I want to put forth several key principles for the Christian church, regardless of its context, whether pressured and persecuted or not.

The continued existence of the Christian church as the new community of the creation is not determined by the context in which it lives. If the kingdom is not of this world and thus cannot be realized through power and violence, it can similarly not be destroyed by human means. With these words, John

---

7. Sabra, 46–47.

8. See, for example, Bernts and Berghuijs, *God in Nederland*.

encouraged the marginalized church that needed to survive the confrontation with both Judaism and the Roman Empire. The church would inevitably be confronted with suffering, but it would not perish because Christ has overcome the world (John 16:33). That is still true today. The new creation has been realized in Jesus Christ; death has been conquered and that cannot be undone. The church has nothing to lose, not even in suffering. Paul actually emphasizes that suffering has become a sign of the approaching glory of God. It is evidence that the new life is about to fully break through. That is guaranteed by the Spirit of God. What believers are suffering now are the final convulsions of a defeated enemy. Even death can no longer separate the believers from the love of Christ (Rom 8:35–39). It is precisely because there is nothing to lose that the church can also be vulnerable. Even if it were to lose everything in this world, its essential being is not at risk. That gives a tremendous amount of freedom and – no matter how paradoxical this may sound – a similar amount of invulnerability. Believers can be discriminated against and insulted; they can suffer and even be killed. The church can even disappear as a visible structure in a certain place and for a certain time – still, its existence is safe in the hands of the Creator. Paradoxically speaking, the church is "vulnerably invulnerable."[9]

Every attempt to guarantee the safety of the church with power and violence is not only disastrous but is also opposite to the nature of the church. Attempts like those of Bashir Gemayel (ch. 6) to guarantee the freedom of the church in Lebanon lead to military defeat and humanitarian disasters. A Christian minority can never militarily gain the upper hand. It is a misunderstanding to think that the church needs to be protected by means of power. God's new creation, the glory that will be poured out on us, cannot and does not need to be defended with power and violence. If we do try that, we no longer defend the kingdom of Christ but an earthly human power.

The church has primarily been called to be a powerful, living, new community of creation that distinguishes itself fundamentally from its context. The church cherishes the bond with the Creator. Jesus calls his followers to "remain in him" (John 15:4, 6–7, 9) in order to be fruitful. Whether a tree remains standing and bears fruit does not depend on the size of the tree, only on if it has good roots. A well-rooted tree does not easily fall and will bear much fruit (see Ps 1; Col 2:7). That is a great challenge when social pressures

---

9. In relation to this, it is fascinating that Christianity is strongly growing in the very areas where the church had earlier almost disappeared, like North Africa, Asia, and the Middle East. In the regions where Christianity was dominant after the Middle Ages, like Europe, it is now slowly disappearing into the margins.

on the church increase. Being Christian requires sacrifices; it could lead to social, economic, and legal discrimination. To remain standing in that context, it is important that the church of Christ functions as a support group. In that way the church has been able to keep its ground even in countries where no churches are allowed.

The Christian church should be aware that the situation in the West is not the norm. Free participation in society without inequality or discrimination is not the logical consequence of following Christ like some versions of prosperity theology seem to suggest. Followers of Christ should utilize periods of freedom to prepare for more difficult times, like athletes train before the contest starts.

10.3 Vulnerably Devoted to Mission

If the church of Christ is the restored community of creation, one could ideally perceive how God has meant life to be by looking at it. The church is not just one more of the world's random organizations. It demonstrates the contours of what true life is, which is what God has intended for *all* of his creation. That is why the church in this broken creation is devoted to mission. It is "sent" to present real life to the world.

The concept of "missions" or "devotion to mission" creates mixed feelings in the context of Islam. Even though the modern missionary movement of the eighteenth and nineteenth century has done a lot of good – for example in the area of education and health care – it is not regarded favorably among Muslims. It recalls memories of proselytism and those who often did not hesitate to use pressure in order to force Muslims to leave Islam. Muslims regularly associate the cross with persecution and violence in the name of the gospel. In the time of the Crusades, "missions" coincided with "armed struggle."

It is justified to ask if it is even possible to connect a devotion to mission with the vulnerability that is essential to the Christian church. Does exclusivity not always go hand in hand with superiority and dominance? If the Christian church is on the right path, are Muslims not, by definition, on the wrong path? Does that not deny in advance that they can have any truth? In this paragraph, I would like to describe what it means when the church is "vulnerably devoted to mission." That will immediately clarify how I understand the term "mission(s)" or "missional." The term "missional" has been used in many different ways throughout history, ranging from "church planting" to "evangelism." I myself would distinguish between an eschatological, an ecclesio-centric, and a prophetic approach. In the first approach, the proclamation of the gospel in relation to the coming eschaton is at the center. This approach is marked by a sense of urgency for all nations to hear the gospel and repent and follow Jesus Christ. In the pentecostal/charismatic movement, the emphasis is strongly on the work of the Holy Spirit. Second, the ecclesio-centric approach focuses on the planting of churches. In the *classical* church planting movement – that is, the Eastern Orthodox and Roman Catholic missions – the basic doctrine is that God is present in the celebration of the heavenly liturgy and the eucharist, and it is through participation in these that people would share in the new life. The *modern* church planting movement is closer to the eschatological approach and is mainly protestant/evangelical in nature and does not have a hierarchical church model. The prophetic approach, finally, puts strong emphasis on working for a just and sustainable society in which people from different religions can live peacefully together.

These models only exist theoretically. Reality is always a combination of various elements and a lot less static.

10.3.1 The Missio Dei *and Islam*

The mission of the church is happening against the backdrop of God's creative activity. When creation derailed, God's mission started, which is the restoration of his plan for creation. His mission is everything he does to realize his original purposes.[10] That mission found its climax in the sending of Jesus Christ (Heb 1:1), and it has continued along the way of the cross and resurrection in the mission of the Spirit as the new breath of life (John 20:22). This mission of the triune God, the *missio Dei*, is the source and essence of the mission of the church. The church is not only the result of God's mission but is also included in that mission. It refers, through its essence, to the ultimate purpose of God's mission, which is the reign of God in Christ over all creation.[11]

That reign is, in principle, already a reality in the church and will one day break through in fullness. The new life comprises the totality of existence, and the church witnesses to it through its very nature. The mission of the church is a *way of life*, a manner of being in which the kingdom of Jesus is becoming visible. That means that the church does not become missional only when it undertakes missional activities. It is missional by nature. Word and deed are one. That is why we cannot say that evangelization – the proclamation of the

---

10. Wright, *Mission of God's People*, 23–24. God's mission spans from the start of the curse in Genesis 3 to the end of the curse in Rev 22. Wright, 46.

11. Wright defines "mission" therefore as "all that God is doing in his great purpose for the whole creation and all that he calls us to do in cooperation with that purpose." Wright, 27.

gospel – is the heart of the mission of the church.[12] God himself is the heart of mission. That is not just a play on words. Mission is about the being of God and the acts of God. The ultimate goal is that all of creation will come to worship God. That is what everything was created for.[13] That is already realized, albeit provisionally, in the church as a new creation. Worship is the recognition that God in Jesus through the Spirit is king. That is the only witness the church has. Mission only exists because this is not yet true for all of creation.[14] Once every knee bows in the name of Jesus and every tongue confesses that Jesus Christ is Lord to the glory of God the Father (Phil 2:10–11), the mission of God – and that of the church – is accomplished. Then God will be in all and there will only be love and worship.

Once we apply these principles to "being missional" in the context of Islam, it does not mean that the church is intent upon rationally convincing Muslims of the truth of the Christian faith. In practice that almost always leads to a sort of dogmatic/apologetic fight where Christians try to convince Muslims that Jesus is the Son of God, while Muslims are trying to convince Christians of the opposite. Many Muslims learn from a young age that faith in the trinity is equal to the unforgivable sin of *shirk*. A theological conversation about that is definitely important, but as a matter for discussion in day to day interactions between people of different backgrounds, it is often not fruitful. The church of Christ is not seeking to incorporate Muslims into Christianity. They are not an object of a project of evangelism that needs to be brought to a successful end by the church. Having faith is about far more than agreeing about a few qualifications about God, Jesus, and the Spirit. It is about participating in the history of God with the world. In the witness of the church, Muslims need to be able to taste that. "Being missional" is therefore simply inviting Muslims to worship God in Jesus Christ as king. They are not asked to become "Christian" and join "Christianity" or "Christendom." The negative associations that Muslims have with those categories make the transition to "Christianity" nearly impossible. In their eyes that would mean that they would have to conform to Western cultural, social, political, and economic systems.

This description closely connects with the characterization of the Christian community as a minority (ch. 6). The church takes its place in society without

---

12. Paas, *Pilgrims*, par. 1.4., 11–15

13. Wright, *Mission of God's People*, 53, refers to the Westminster Confession: "Man's chief end is to glorify God and enjoy him forever." "To glorify God" is also the purpose of all of creation; "to enjoy him forever" is reserved for humanity.

14. See Piper, *Let the Nations*, 15; "Mission is not the ultimate goal of the church. Worship is. Mission exists because worship doesn't."

exercising power. It therefore does not impose its faith with power, money, or other means. That has been tried. The history of missions shows that the proclamation of the gospel has been consciously or subconsciously linked with health care and education. Those who converted to Christianity would get access to healthcare and education. The gospel, however, is about the self-sacrificing, unconditional love of the king. Following Jesus can only be based on a free choice; love cannot be forced.

It helps in this context to make the distinction between power and influence or authority.[15] Power is, in this definition, always connected to a certain form of pressure, violence, or manipulation which would lead to an imposed, enforced kind of obedience. Such power is effective regardless of whether people accept it or not. Authority, on the other hand, focuses on a form of influence where people retain their freedom to make their own decisions and therefore can also choose differently. The latter abides well with the kingdom of Jesus Christ. Access to that kingdom cannot be enforced. Obedience to the king is a free choice that comes from love. The message that the church carries, however, does have authority. It's the authority of the cross and resurrection. The church has the authority to speak because in Christ the new creation has been restored.[16]

That authority is connected with the power of the Spirit of God. As the first gift of God's glory, the Spirit blows new life into creation. Without the Spirit, the witness of the church becomes rigid and dogmatic. Through the Spirit, the church of Christ shares in the power of God. The followers of Jesus become witnesses of him when they receive the power of the Holy Spirit (Acts 1:8). That also means that the signs of Jesus (see ch. 3) can only become reality in the church through the Spirit. These signs point to the kingdom of Christ and require faith. They are, therefore, not signs that are unlimitedly present at will in the church. Wherever they manifest themselves, they support the witness of the church and awaken a longing for the fullness of the kingdom. In many places today, we see such signs in the Islamic world: there are testimonies of dreams, of healings, and of special guidance.[17]

The Christian church is "vulnerably devoted to mission." Success is not guaranteed and can certainly not be enforced. Those who cannot defend

---

15. Campolo, *Choose Love*, 15–19. Campolo speaks about "noncoercive influence."

16. John uses the word *parrèsia* for this kind of authority in 1 John 2:28, often translated as "confidence." It originally means the right to speak in a public hearing (see *LSJ*). John uses it for freedom or (given) rights in relationship with God.

17. See for example Garrison, *Wind in the House.*

themselves through the use of force can easily become prey to attacks, both physically as well as mentally. The church had better be prepared for that. In the world you will have tribulation, Jesus said (John 16:33 ESV). The gospel of grace and the cross is not by definition received with open arms. It irritates people and is met with resistance (Mark 6:11). If the church is truly missional, it is very vulnerable.

10.3.2 Missional Minority

What I have been talking about so far in terms of "missions" does still need further nuancing. There is of course a difference between the Christian community that does not experience (severe) oppression or is protected by the rule of law and the persecuted church. The first enjoys the protection of the government; the second often does not. That, by the way, does not automatically imply that persecuted Christians renounce power and, because of that, have a more powerful witness. As we've seen, they – for understandable reasons – are often inclined to retreat or withdraw into isolation; their only mission is to survive (10.3). Sometimes, we see that they seek support from powerful earthly rulers who can protect them.[18] That does not help the witness of the church. Whether Christians who are in a minority position can be devoted to mission at all is a question that (Western) missiology has hardly thought about. This is also not easy to consider from a majority position. Now that the church in the West is becoming more and more marginalized, we see an awareness of these questions beginning to appear.[19] I am convinced that the church in a minority position can be missional. It is especially that very situation which forces them to rely on the power of the gospel. Moreover, Christians in countries where they are the majority would do well to listen very carefully to their brothers and sisters who live in a minority position – in the world of Islam, for example. They can learn a lot from those experiences, even for the sake of being church in a privileged position.

The church as a minority is not an unknown phenomenon. On the contrary, the first church did not have huge numbers and hardly had any economic or political power but was still a powerful community within the

---

18. Christians in Syria, for example, up until the civil war in 2011, had relative freedom and security due to the regime of Assad. Additionally, Christian political parties in Lebanon sought support from Israel during their civil war (1975–1990) but quickly turned away from that after the war and with the sudden retreat of Israel. See Fisk, *Pity the Nation*.

19. Paas, *Pilgrims*, is an example of that.

Roman Empire. Their "power" was the effective influence of the kingdom of Christ: the gospel "is the power of God for salvation to everyone who believes" (Rom 1:16).[20] The very fact that the church was not a part of the earthly power system meant that it could take its place in the midst of society. They had little to lose in society and no interests to safeguard. Because of this so-called free position, they had a message for everyone in society: those in power and their subjects, victims and oppressors, lords and slaves. The impact of the Christian community is not determined by big cathedrals, rich mission organizations, or Christian organizations. The essence of the mission of the church is in the living community of those who come together in order to glorify God. Even in the direst of circumstances, this witness of the kingdom of Christ can be heard. This reveals that the core message of the Christian church is in all circumstances inviolable because it is not determined by the broken reality around it. The power of the witness of the church lies in the living presence of God in Jesus Christ and through his Spirit.[21]

10.3.3 Mission of Life

The church is missional through its existence; it does not become missional through activities. The missional character of the community members becomes visible when they "share their life." This is how being missional is right at the center of the meeting between Christians and Muslims. There is often mention of the dialogue of life or of the heart in which people try to better understand each other by living side by side and by sharing their deepest motivations.[22] Would it not be possible to talk also about a "mission of life" or a "mission of the heart" in this context? With this I mean the "missional" encounter between Christians and Muslims at the level of personal faith. In these heart-to-heart conversations both can speak freely about all aspects of life and the role that God plays in each. Who is he truly?

Such an "experience-focused" approach communicates respect for the sincere longing of Muslims to get to know God and their search for the purpose of life and the meaning of life and death. After all, faith experiences in one way or another are related to the Spirit of God (ch. 5). The Spirit critically

---

20. Fee, *God's Empowering Presence*, 8.

21. When Paas approaches the mission of the church from her minority position, it seems primarily a pragmatic decision, *Pilgrims*. The church consists, after all, of a small group of dedicated people with a larger community of followers. My interpretation considers it more essential: the church should in her nature always be qualified as a minority without power.

22. Reitsma, *Integriteit en respect*, 16.

tests which experiences are or are not doing justice to the revelation of God through the cross of Christ. The Spirit tests those experiences and reveals what is real and is not real. This "mission of life," therefore, goes further than trying to understand each other: it is about discovering who God truly is. The *dialogues* of life and the heart are an inseparable part of that process but differ from the *missions* of life and the heart in that they do not ask for the truth behind those experiences.

The "mission of life" is accomplished through vulnerability. The believers cannot hide behind systems or dogmas. What they believe needs to be more than just words; it needs to be visible as a way of life. In the end, the witness of the church comes down to integrity. Is it truly visible in and through the church that Jesus is king? How is that revealed? Are the lives of the followers of Jesus truly marked by the cross? Only when the church actually lives in line with its status as the new community of creation will its testimony have power; it won't otherwise.

10.3.4 Theological Mission

Besides the "mission of life" and "the mission of the heart," we can – analogous to the dialogue of the mind – also speak about a mission of the mind. It would be interesting to explore what that means for theology. In the academic world the trend nowadays is to exchange theology for religious studies or the humanities. The emphasis is primarily on describing and understanding what people believe, how their sources were established, and what authority these sources have in their cultural and religious context. When Muslims and Christians meet in theological exchange, the emphasis is often on understanding and getting to know each other – by exploring and comparing certain faith themes from both religions, for example. Such understanding can also be built through "scriptural reasoning": Muslims and Christians reading and reflecting on the same religious texts together. Or they may study how their religious traditions can live and work together in society. This is indispensable. We have to understand and know each other across the divide of different backgrounds. History and the media have saddled us with stereotypes that can become destructive.

The value of this approach should not be underestimated. Yet I would still like to propose we go a step further. After all, the missional character of the Christian church also presumes a form of exclusivity when it comes to Islam. The church of Christ testifies to the fact that there is no God but the Lord and that there is no Lord but Jesus Christ (1 Cor 8:6). Muslims affirm the first statement but reject the second: there is no God but Allah and Muhammad is his prophet. Despite all the diversity, the main streams of Christianity and Islam separate here. Most Christians have a hard time recognizing Muhammad as a "Christian" prophet – they would at most see him as a kind of Old Testament prophet (see ch. 1). The Qur'an might contain some godly wisdom to them, but it is not on par with the word of God, Jesus Christ. Most Muslims cannot accept Jesus as Son of God, and they see the Bible as incomplete and corrupted. What we believe has consequences. There are strings attached; there is something at stake. Many Muslims and Christians believe that their views about God are not interchangeable. The denial of our differences is just as much a form of stereotyping as is overemphasizing them. Christianity and Islam have clashed throughout history even in their most ideal form. We have to take that reality seriously in our theological reflection on Islam, otherwise theology will be done from the mindset of the "enlightened" elite. The ultimate goal of theology should be to search for ways of speaking about God that do justice to who God really is. In the end, it is about the truth of the nature of God. Here, too, that is more than just discussing dogmas. It is about thinking through who God is in the deepest sense, in light of how he has revealed himself fully in Christ in order to recreate his world. The Christian church cannot suspend its calling to mission when it is engaged in theology.

Therefore, it does not appeal to me to exchange a normative approach to theology in the academic world for the more distant objective reflection in religious studies. Islamic and Christian theologians should not recoil from engaging in missional dialogue. The greatest challenge in such a conversation is the way in which we respond to each other when we fundamentally differ from each other in terms of what we believe. This is a vulnerable discussion that requires sensitivity and respect for each other. With all this, I recognize the fact that the relationship between Islam and Christianity in the West is not on equal footing. Christian theology has a much longer history in the Western world, while Islamic theologians in Western countries are often still developing their identity as representatives of a minority who are in a relatively new situation. That makes the Islamic community vulnerable, especially in times of increasing extremism. Christian theology in this missional conversation will have to take on a humble and vulnerable attitude, if only because the church confesses that the kingdom does not expand through power and might – not even theologically.

The question is if there is room for apologetics in this theological conversation.[23] Apologetics has always been a part of the mission of the church

---

23. For a detailed account, see Reitsma, "Christelijke apologetiek," 339–347.

and – very generally speaking – focuses on the (rational) justification of the Christian faith.[24] It seeks to explain the truth of the Christian faith, to clear up misunderstandings, and in that way to increase the plausibility of the Christian faith. Sometimes it can take on the nature of an attempt to verbally contest or combat other beliefs.[25] In practice, apologetics easily becomes an instrument for retrieving what Christianity has lost: a form of power to convince Muslims of the truth of Christianity.[26] That was exactly the reason for Colin Chapman's refusal to enter into a public debate with Ahmed Deedat in the 1990s. Deedat (1918–2005) was a known and fervent apologist for Islam who would purposely seek out public debates with Christians in order to disprove Christian faith with rational arguments and promote Islam. According to Chapman, these kinds of public debates often take the form of a boxing match. That is why he was willing to enter into a conversation with Deedat in a smaller group but not in the public arena.[27]

Christian apologetics can never become a means to publicly attack and fight others. The church is not called to engage in a battle with Islam in order to conquer Muslims. That is at odds with the core of Christian faith: the self-sacrificing love of Jesus Christ. He did not come in order to defeat others but to give himself for the restoration of the whole of creation. The truth of the gospel does not stand or fall with victories in apologetic debates or scoring points in the public realm. Jesus Christ came in vulnerability, and his victory looked like a defeat. The resurrection confirms that the crucified one is the Son of God (Rom 1:4). It could very well be that the public finds the arguments of Muslims more convincing. The love of Christ who has given himself up unto death is completely illogical in the eyes of the world and has something ridiculous about it. When this message of vulnerability is shrouded in the armor of polemics, it loses its credibility.[28] Apologetics is either vulnerable or it is not Christian.

The most important function of apologetics in relation to Muslims in my view is to equip Christians to engage in religious dialogue. In order to

---

24. See for example, Bakker, Kater, and Van Vlastuin, *Verantwoord geloof*, 5–6.

25. See Accad, "Christian Attitudes," Kindle loc. 847–848. See also "What Is Apologetics?," Bible.org, https://bible.org/seriespage/2-what-apologetics#P24_7780, accessed 30-03-2020.

26. Segers and Vries, *Wat christenen geloven*. The title – "What Christians Believe and Muslims Do Not Understand" – creates the impression that Christians do understand and need to explain to Muslims what they believe. That is not the intention of the authors, but it can easily be read that way.

27. See Chapman, "Is Dialogue Going Anywhere?" Deedat did not respond to the proposal.

28. Van Gorder, *No God*, 23.

follow Christ, you do not have to turn off your brain. Apologetics helps one to recognize misunderstandings, unmask caricatures, and think the Christian faith through. As a part of theology, it is a form of worship with the mind.

10.3.5 Ten Ethical Guidelines

Christians and Muslims who regularly meet each other in Great Britain as part of the Christian-Muslim Forum have very clearly worded what mission without power and force means. They give ten directions for good practice. The introduction to their list explains why this is important:[29]

> As members of the Christian Muslim Forum we are deeply committed to our own faiths (Christianity and Islam) and we wish to bear faithful witnesses of them. As Christians and Muslims we are committed to working together for the common good. We recognize that both communities actively invite others to share their faith and acknowledge that all faiths have the same right to share their faith with others.
>
> There are diverse attitudes and approaches amongst us which can be controversial and raise questions. This paper is not a theology of Christian evangelism or mission or Da'wah (invitation to Islam); rather it offers guidelines for good practice.
>
> The Christian-Muslim Forum offers the following suggestions that we hope will equip Christians and Muslims (and others) to share their faith with integrity and compassion for those whom they meet.
>
> 1. We bear witness to and proclaim our faith not only through words but through our attitudes, actions and lifestyles.
>
> 2. We cannot convert people, only God can do that. In our language and methods, we should recognise that people's choice of faith is primarily a matter between themselves and God.
>
> 3. Sharing our faith should never be coercive; this is especially important when working with children, young people and vulnerable adults. Everyone should have the choice to accept or

---

29. Christian Muslim Forum, Ethical Guidelines: For Christian and Muslim Witness in Britain (2009), http://46.101.6.182/wp-content/uploads/2018/12/CMF-Ethical-Guidelines-for-Christian-and-Muslim-Witness-in-Britain.pdf. Used by permission.

reject the message we proclaim and we will accept people's choices without resentment.

4. Whilst we might care for people in need or who are facing personal crises, we should never manipulate these situations in order to gain a convert.

5. An invitation to convert should never be linked with financial, material or other inducements. It should be a decision of the heart and mind alone.

6. We will speak of our faith without demeaning or ridiculing the faiths of others.

7. We will speak clearly and honestly about our faith, even when that is uncomfortable or controversial.

8. We will be honest about our motivations for activities and we will inform people when events will include the sharing of faith.

9. Whilst recognising that either community will naturally rejoice with and support those who have chosen to join them, we will be sensitive to the loss that others may feel.

10. Whilst we may feel hurt when someone we know and love chooses to leave our faith, we will respect their decision and will not force them to stay or harass them afterwards.

10.4 Vulnerably Inclusive
10.4.1 Embrace

The church as the new community of creation is an inclusive community. It shows how God has intended life to be as a community with a colorful diversity of individuals. That diversity has been distorted in our broken reality and become a source of contradictions. People no longer understand each other and pit cultural, ethnic, and religious motivations against each other (see ch. 8). In the Christian church that diversity is not "wiped away, but redeemed."[30] The vulnerable love of God is relational, inclusive, and embracing. The church is called to live out its new identity in communion with the rest of creation. Despite its exclusivity, the vulnerable missional character of the church of Christ does not create adversaries but seeks out a relationship. Muslims are not fought but embraced.

---

30. See Howell and Paris, *Cultural Anthropology*, 42.

This inclusivity can be motivated in different ways: for starters, Muslims and Christians are connected on the basis of God's purposes with creation. Every human being is created in the image of God and reaches his or her destiny by serving and worshipping God. Second, Muslims and Christians both share in their rebellion against the Creator and in the resulting distortion of creation. Christians and Muslims are both completely dependent on God's grace. That is the third motive. They need God's forgiving love in the same way in order to be human according to his purposes. That love is unconditional. Christ did not come because his people asked for him but despite the fact that they did not want to receive him (John 1:11). He embraced them before they reached out to him (see Rom 5:8). That is emphasized by the work of the Holy Spirit, which is the fourth motive. God works through his Spirit in all of creation; no one is excluded. Through the Spirit of Christ, the church connects with Muslims' zeal for God and with their spiritual experiences. The Spirit tests these experiences critically in light of the presence of Christ. For these four reasons, the kingdom of Christ is inclusive, and the church of Christ is called to be present in the world as an inclusive community.

That entails that the Christian community welcomes and embraces Muslims. It builds bridges. This way Muslims can experience what the love of God in Christ means. The kingdom of Christ does not exist, like other kingdoms, at the expense of other empires. It comprises all nations and ethnicities; there is no distinction between gender or way of life. No one is *a priori* excluded by God, and no one can enter God's kingdom on the basis of personal achievements or religion. Only the sacrificial love of Christ on the cross offers entrance to this kingdom. If Christians can only share in the new life through God's grace, there is no reason why others cannot also share in it.

That sounds harmonious. Does it do enough justice to the fact that Muslims reject Jesus Christ as Savior? Isn't it necessary for them to first recognize Christ before they can be embraced by the community of Christ? Are we not justifying evil in the world and especially terror that is done in the name of Islam? Is not the persecuted church's need for support more important than the urge to embrace Muslims? Does the fight against evil not require a more antithetical approach?

10.4.2 Respecting and Accepting

Inclusivity does not exclude exclusivity. Only those who follow Jesus Christ are members of the church that is named after him. According to Paul, it is not possible to have both communion with Christ and with idols at the same time

(1 Cor 10:21). The communion with Christ makes the church one community (1 Cor 10:16–17). In this way we can also say that it is not possible to belong to Christ and at the same time reject him as the ultimate revelation of God. At the same time, the church is principally open to any newcomer: everyone is invited to participate in the new history of God. When the church is present in the world with open arms, even embracing those who reject the gospel and are themselves rejected by the world, it is a living testimony of the kingdom of God. It invites everyone to participate in the new life in Christ, and in this way shows that this life is only a reality in and through him.

It is important here to make a distinction between "respecting" and "accepting" what Muslims believe, or between "understanding" and "agreeing." Having respect for Muslims means that I am making an honest attempt to understand what Muslims believe. That does not go so far as to mean that I, as a Christian, agree that Muhammad is a prophet or that the Qur'an was dictated by God. In doing so, I would give up my own identity as a Christian, and that is no longer respect but lack of self-esteem.

In practice, this distinction is not without tension. Having respect means that I try my best to understand Islam, even when some aspects of it go against my religious convictions or norms and values. It also implies that I accept that Muslims do not recognize Christ as God's revelation, as that is at the heart of *their* identity. I need to respect that even though I am thoroughly convinced that they can only receive the fullness of the life of God in Christ. As long as they are Muslims, I do not expect them to follow Christ. As soon as they start to follow Christ, they are no longer Muslims in the traditional sense. Respect requires of me that I will try to *understand* Muslims in everything, but that does not mean that I can *agree* with all their ideas.

This requires of the Christian church that above all it truly wants to get to know Muslims. Respect for Islam means that we need to take the great variety within Islam seriously and recognize it. That is Islam as we encounter it in practice. This religious studies perspective is in every way legitimate. Respect also implies that we allow Muslims to define for themselves what they believe; Christians cannot determine who is or is not a true Muslim. Muslims who start to follow Christ do – as insiders – have an important voice in this, but theirs is not the only one.[31] Christians do not paint all Muslims with the same brush.

---

31. Christian theology will need to do justice to the conversations Muslims have with each other about that. That is also true for Muslims who have become Christians. However, their view cannot be seen as the final authority on what Islam is, just as the experience of ex-Christians cannot have the last word on what Christianity means in the deepest sense. They just reflect how they themselves have experienced Islam/Christianity.

The church of Christ should strongly distance themselves from certain populist practices. Muslims do not continuously need to answer for the violence that is perpetrated by extremists in the name of Islam. Nevertheless, respect for Islam also means that we take these excesses of Islamic faith seriously. We owe that to the victims of such extremism. Islam is neither only a religion of peace nor only of pure violence. Just like Christianity, it is a religion with many faces. After all, both democratic and non-democratic movements within Islam refer to the same sources but in very different ways.

The distinction between "understanding" and "agreeing" – or respect and acceptance – gives room for the church of Christ to not just be open to Muslims when they are ready to accept the truth of the Christian faith but also (or especially) when they are not. Just as Christ put his arms around the church even before it was willing to accept him, he asks his follower to embrace Muslims. That calling is not dependent on the response of those embraced. It has much more to do with the nature of the community of Christ. This call to embrace applies to all Muslims without distinction. The Bible does not even make an exception for extremists. Paul calls upon the church to bless those who persecute the church and to not curse them (Rom 12:14). Jesus even requires us to love our enemies and pray for those who persecute the church (Matt 5:44). That is how the children of the Father ought to behave because the Creator makes his sun rise on the evil and on the good and sends rain on the just and unjust (Matt 5:45). Even without extremism this is a vulnerable position and not without risk. There is no guarantee that the love of Christ will be received with equal warmth. True love can be rejected. It can in turn also lead to suffering. That, however, is no reason not to love.

10.4.3 Contextualization

Inclusivity implies diversity. The Christian community does not adopt one culture but is manifested in all kinds of cultures and contexts (see ch. 8). Muslims who start to follow Jesus do not need to leave their history and context behind. The gospel enters into the heart of their own culture and, in this way, transforms that context so that the new creation becomes visible. Gospel and culture are continuously interacting. Is it possible to hold on to the contextual setting without damaging the gospel? Is it feasible to let the gospel speak clearly without losing the connection to the environment? This is a highly vulnerable process. Muslims who have started to follow Jesus are trying this, but it is like walking a tightrope.

An interesting illustration of the vulnerability of this type of contextualization is an example from the practice of Bible translation. It concerns considerations related to so-called "Muslims-sensitive" Bible translations.[32] The organization SIL International was committed to a special Bible translation that would create the least amount of misunderstandings in an Islamic context. Discussion was primarily focused on the translation of the concepts of Father (for God) and Son of God (for Jesus). It is generally known that the title "Son of God" is problematic in the Islamic world.[33] Not only does the Qur'an repeatedly emphasize the fact that God does not have a son,[34] the term also raises numerous unnecessary misunderstandings. The impression can be created that Jesus has physically descended from God and that Miriam (Mary) is a partner of God.[35] Such ideas are not only blasphemous to Muslims but also to Christians. The question in this debate was whether you can express the term "Son of God" in such a way that you maintain its meaning but avoid misunderstandings. Do you translate literally with explanations in the margins? Or do you pick a term that overcomes the problem? In some Bible translations in Islamic contexts the latter option is taken by translating "Son of God" as "Messiah," "the Spiritual Son of God," or "the Beloved Son who came from the Father."

These kinds of questions are of course always asked when the Bible is translated in a new cultural context. For example, when the concept of "bread" is unknown in a certain culture, we can translate the expression that Jesus is the "bread of life" literally, and then give an explanation of what bread is, or we can translate with reference to a local food like rice that Jesus is the rice of life. Does this principle also apply to key theological concepts, such as "Father" and "Son of God"? These concepts are part of the fundamental Christian Creeds: the Apostles' Creed, accepted by all Western churches,[36] and the Nicene Creed accepted in both the Western and the Eastern churches (albeit here without the filioque). Can these terms therefore be translated at all? If we are to take the position that this is not possible, are we doing enough justice to the metaphorical nature of these terms? And does "Son of God" in

---

32. Kroneman, "Bijbelvertalen voor moslims"; Hansen, "The Son and the Crescent."

33. Brown, "Explaining the Biblical Term," 135–145.

34. For example, Surah 9:30–31 (Sūrat al-Tawba); 112:2–3 (Sūrat al-Ikhlās).

35. Surah 5:116 (Sūrat al-Mā"ida).

36. The Eastern churches do not accept the authority of the Apostles' Creed, since it has not been approved by a major ecumenical council.

English have the same sound and meaning as the Greek equivalent of the New Testament?[37]

Eventually a special commission of the World Evangelical Alliance spent time studying this matter and advised to keep "godly kinship words" in the target language and, if necessary, give an explanation if misunderstandings could arise.[38] This example shows how complex contextualization can be. In this case there are more factors at work than simply the technical aspect of translating contextually. There were dozens of sensitivities due to the Islamic context it concerned. Critics were afraid that proponents of Muslim-sensitive translations would seek to make the gospel more palatable for Muslims: weakening the sonship of Jesus would make it easier for Muslims to start following Christ. If that would have been the original intent, it would have wronged both the Bible and Christian tradition. Translating in a Muslim-sensitive way, however, is not the same as translating in a Muslim-friendly way or in a Muslim-pleasing way. In this case, the problem was also that many critics approached the matter from a dogmatic perspective without much understanding of the technical side of translating contextually.

Moreover, Muslim-sensitive translations do not necessarily show more sensitivity to their context. Many Christians in the Islamic world do not support such translations because the attempt to accommodate Muslims with a more approachable translation can also confuse them. They know very well that Christians believe in Jesus as the Son of God. What does it mean then when a concept in "the holy book" is suddenly translated differently? Is that an attempt to tempt Muslims to become Christians? Or do Christians now question the essence of their own faith? If Muslim-sensitive translations are primarily a Western idea, it could easily be a new form of colonialism, and that, too, is at odds with contextualization.

10.5 Vulnerably Prophetic

Emphasizing the inclusive nature of the church of Christ raises the question of whether it takes the reality of evil in this world seriously enough. Should the church really embrace people who are resisting Jesus Christ? Is it not primarily called to actively resist evil? The powers of the old creation still

---

37. For different arguments, see Brown, Penny, and Gray, "Muslim-Idiom Bible Translations," 87–105, and Abernathy, "Translating 'Son of God,'" 176–203.

38. See WEA Global Review Panel, *Report to World Evangelical Alliance*; see also Kroneman, "Bijbelvertalen," 20.

assert themselves in terrible ways. Isn't it also the calling of the church that is not being persecuted to stand up for Christians who are persecuted, whether it is in the name of Islam or another religion or ideology? How can the church that is "not of this world" do something about evil without renouncing its essence as a "minority"? If it does not want to choose isolation, it can hardly seek out political or military might in order to combat evil. Or does the end justify the means?

10.5.1 Understanding and Agreement

In thinking about evil that is done in the name of Islam, it helps to make the above-mentioned distinction between "understanding" and "agreement." As much as I loathe evil, as much as I reject it on a biblical basis, and no matter how much I would like to fight it, none of that releases me from the duty to first seek to *understand* it. The following two examples will illustrate what I mean. First of all, I have insurmountable difficulty with the circumcision of women. It is diametrically opposed to the purposes that I believe God has with creation. Nonetheless, I would need to try to understand why parents – often mothers – would let their daughters get circumcised. Otherwise I would not be able to fight it. For example, I need to know that this is not typically Islamic. It seems to play an important role in Islam due to the fact that female circumcision is often practiced in countries and regions where Islam is prevalent. Within the Islamic community in other parts of the world, however, it is not found. Besides that, the practice happens in non-Islamic communities in Africa as well, including Christian communities.

Another example concerns extremism that is motivated by Islamic texts. I detest what ISIS is doing and see it as a distortion of God's good creation. At the same time, I will need to understand how it is possible that ISIS has received so much support and why otherwise "reasonable" people can suddenly behave so violently. I need to understand how it is related to the battle between Sunni and Shi'a Islam as well as to opposition against the way in which the West has interfered in the region and not fulfilled its promises.[39] I need to understand how certain radical Muslims want to give their lives for the honor of God (as well as for their own honor). To make it clear: I do not in any way agree with their actions. The "understanding" is in no way a justification of evil. But it does create more space to fight it.

---

39. See, for example, Aarts and Keulen, *Islam*.

10.5.2 The Prophetic Church

The church does not resign itself to evil, but it responds to evil in a Christ-like way. It addresses evil without the use of force and violence. That is what I call prophetic. The prophets of the Old Testament reminded Israel of the Torah. They testified to the covenant of God and made Israel look at itself. They confronted the people with their brokenness and disobedience and warned against its consequences. The Torah is clear that the people of Israel were awaiting judgement if they did not keep to the agreements of the covenant. That is why prophets called the people to repentance. They regularly experienced ridicule, confinement, or persecution. They were also not exempt from the divine judgement that came over Israel.

That is what I have in mind in calling the church prophetic. It holds the world in which we live accountable in light of the eschatological reality of the new creation. It is only able to do that due to the Spirit of Christ. That Spirit is, after all, the Spirit of prophesy.[40] The Holy Spirit, as the first gift of God's glory, critiques the old life and convicts the world of sin, righteousness, and judgement (John 16:8).[41] In this way, the prophetic church, just like the prophets of the Old Testament, points to the consequences of the choices people make today. The Spirit, as the first gift of God's glory, points to the future where the powers of the old creation will definitively be dealt with.

The darkness can only be expelled by turning on a light. The church exposes evil in the world by confronting it with the goodness of the new creation. That appeals to the world for change. It is prophetic to turn the other cheek (Matt 5:38–39). When someone asks for your tunic when suing you in court, give him your cloak as well (Matt 5:40). And when a Roman soldier forces you to go one mile with him, go two (Matt 5:41). Loving your neighbor and hating your enemy is what would be relatively "normal" in a distorted creation. But loving your enemies and praying for those who persecute you (Matt 5:43–44), that is food for thought.

It is not possible to overcome evil with evil. Violence against Christians and Muslims does not disappear from this world by responding to it with violence. On the contrary, it only strengthens hatred. At best it leads to a reversal in roles. The oppressed today often become the oppressors of tomorrow. Those

---

40. Paul refers to prophecy as one of the gifts of the Spirit (1 Cor 12:10). In Judaism during the Second Temple period there was a close connection between the work of the Spirit of God and prophecy. If the Spirit would be poured out in the last days, there would also be prophets again. Reitsma, *Geest en schepping*, 79–80; cf. Notley, *Concept of the Holy Spirit*, 14.

41. There are different opinions on the meaning of prophecy in the New Testament. See for example Grudem, *Gift of Prophecy*; Aune, *Prophecy in Early Christianity*.

who topple regimes with violence are fundamentally not much better than those previously in power. Evil can only be overcome with good (Rom 12:21). That is because evil is far more than merely violence. That is, however, the first thing that comes to mind for Christians in relation to Islam when discussing evil: the attacks of extremist Muslims like ISIS, violence against Muslims who turn away from Islam, the oppression of women, or the discrimination of minorities. These are the things that Christians – understandably so – are concerned about. Who wouldn't be afraid at the threat of physical suffering, oppression, and persecution? Nevertheless, this suffering is only one aspect of the broken reality. All evil in the distorted creation is in one way or another related to rebellion against the Almighty. Where he is no longer at the center of people's worship, life derails. Evil can only be eradicated from the world when that deeper root is being addressed. Only the worship of God in Christ can bring an end to violence. Only the cross can break the cycle of hatred.

It is the task of the government, not the church, to contain violence. That is why it carries the sword (Rom 13:4). But if it fails, the church of Christ cannot take over from the government – at least, not without violating the gospel of Christ. It is for this reason that its prophetic mission is to also call political powers to account and expose any evil intentions.

In thinking of the church in the context of Islam it is valuable to explore the possibilities of nonviolent resistance and to rethink the heritage of the iconic examples of Gandhi and Martin Luther King Jr.

If the church were to choose to always do the right thing, evil would ultimately no longer have any power over it. The church can and will be confronted with suffering, but those who do evil have no authority or power over its conscience. Like one Muslim who started to follow Jesus once told me: "They can force me to go on my knees in the mosque, they can make me say the Shahada [the Islamic confession of faith] out loud, but they have no influence on who is Lord of my heart. If I say the confession while I recognize Christ as Lord in my heart, then that confession has no value from an Islamic point of view."[42]

---

42. A fascinating example of someone who has dedicated himself to nonviolent resistance is Sami Awad from Bethlehem. Together with Muslims, Jews, and Christians, he nonviolently strives for peace in the Middle East. His story is personal. His dad became a refugee at age nine and his uncle was deported by the Israelis during the first Intifada for his nonviolent resistance against the occupation. Awad, *Never Give Up*.

10.5.3 Pacifism?

We can wonder if this positive testimony of the church has any meaning in the face of extreme evil. Isn't it entirely senseless, or even absurd, to think of nonviolent resistance against groups like ISIS, Boko Haram, or oppressive regimes found in Saudi Arabia or North Korea? Does it mean that the church should be pacifist? Here we face the limits of what we can accomplish in a broken world. It is impossible to ban all evil through our resistance. We can use all means to overcome evil, as long as they do not lead us to denounce our principles. For me, this is the limit: when I can no longer do justice to the cross of Christ as self-sacrificial suffering. In that sense, the word "crusades," as a conquest of the cross, is a contradiction in terms.

The dilemma that arises here is exemplified in what Christians in Syria experienced during the civil war in the years after 2010. Some pastors chose to start militias in order to fight evil and protect their church members. Others explicitly chose nonviolent resistance. That dilemma plays an important role in the movie *The Mission*.[43] A missionary outpost run by Jesuits in the South American jungle falls into the hands of the Portuguese and needs to be evacuated. One of the leaders of the mission resists the Portuguese in a nonviolent way. Another takes up weapons and tries to save the lives of a group of children by using violence. Both die and the mission outpost is destroyed. Their opponents were too strong. Which response would have been the most Christian one? That question is impossible to answer when living in a safe environment. Christians in each specific context need to ask what response is required of them and does the most justice to the gospel. Even Bonhoeffer decided eventually to support an attack on Hitler's life, even though violence was completely against his principles. He saw no other option than to prevent worse evil in this way.

10.5.4 The Persecuted Church

The vulnerably prophetic nature of the church also reflects the contours of the way in which the church that has all kinds of freedom should relate to the persecuted church. Christian organizations or churches that stand up for the fights of persecuted Christians emphasize, with good reason, that persecution is not "normal." It is and remains a sign of the opposition of "the world" against Christ and his followers. It is inherent to the distortion of creation. But in the fight against persecution it is important that we keep remembering that

---

43. Roland Joffé, dir. *The Mission*. Written by Robert Bolt, Warner Bros., 1986.

suffering in this broken world is an inescapable part of following Jesus. Every form of resistance against suffering that attempts to create a sort of heavenly peace on earth for the church of Christ sends the wrong signal. There is the constant temptation to use suffering as an instrument to present the kingdom of Christ, by a roundabout way, as a power among other earthly powers once again. Ripken points to the fact that many Western organizations that attempt to stand up for the persecuted church create the impression that they want to stop persecution and export Western forms of democracy. Collecting money and support is done in order to save believers from persecution.[44] In a situation like this, standing up for the rights of persecuted Christians on the basis of human rights (advocacy) is easily paired with politically lobbying the European Union, the United States, or the United Nations. "Suffering" is used as a weapon in a power struggle between Christian organizations in the Western world and those in power in certain Islamic contexts. Even though it is entirely understandable from the perspective of human nature to use every means possible to end persecution, this eventually clashes with the nature of the kingdom of Christ.[45] Even in the context of suffering, the kingdom of Jesus expands only through witness. How can the church show that Jesus is crucified – is the king of a kingdom that is not of this world – if we use the powers of this world at the same time in order to escape the "cross"? It is not until the end of history that the glory of God will completely break through and there will be a definitive end to the suffering of the church. Until that time, the work of Christian support organizations should not be focused on ending or eradicating the suffering of the persecuted church. It can only be meant to support persecuted Christians in their suffering and encourage them to not give up the fight. The worldwide body of Christ, in history and today, belongs to the cloud of witnesses that encourages the believers to persevere (Heb 11; 12:1–2).

The challenge is to find the way of the kingdom of Christ between the glorification of suffering and the fighting of persecution. That is a careful balancing act. The church is not called to be passive. Everything that does justice to the character of the gospel can be used. It is possible to draw attention to the difficult situation of persecuted Christians, as awareness is the foundation of support. We can also visit Christians in difficult situations and encourage them. There is a possibility to train leaders who can show the way of Christ

---

44. "Four-fold agenda: 1. Stop the persecution; 2. Punish the persecutors; 3. Promote Western forms of government and democracy; and 4. Raise funds that will aid in the rescuing of believers from persecution." Ripken, "Recapturing the Role," 358.

45. "Biblical vision would respond in a different way." Ripken, 358.

to believers who are under pressure. We can also offer legal support to the persecuted church. There is the bond of prayer. Sometimes there is no other way to help Christians than to evacuate them to other places. Even Joseph and Mary had to flee with Jesus to Egypt in order to escape death.

One of the opportunities that the church as a minority has is to build bridges between people groups before there is any persecution. The church that is not restricted like the persecuted church in its societal freedom can assist in that process, and perhaps that is even the most fruitful way of doing something for the church in difficult situations. Therefore, when tensions increase, there would be a network of leaders who could work in their communities for understanding and respect. One example of such a project is the Interfaith Mediation Centre in Nigeria.[46] Pastor James Movel Wuye and Imam Mohammad Nurayn Ashafa have worked together there for a long time to bring reconciliation between Christians and Muslims. This is exceptional seeing that they both led opposing militias in North Africa in the 1990s. They were out to kill each other. James lost his right arm in this armed struggle and Mohammad his spiritual mentor and two family members. Today they travel the country together as brothers. Once they got to know each other, certain prejudices disappeared, and they recognized the longing for peace. The fight had amounted to little. Now they contribute to reducing the tension between differing groups of people. The relationships that are built are channels to make it possible to talk about difficulties and differences. But that dialogue also brings a form of suffering. It requires self-sacrifice and the setting aside of prejudices, bitterness, and hatred. It also requires vulnerability in relating to their own communities, which hold similar feelings and are often not ready or able to walk the path of reconciliation.[47]

Lastly, being vulnerably prophetic also means that Christian organizations need to ask themselves if it is fundamentally acceptable to only stand up for Christians. There are Christian organizations that offer assistance during disasters to non-Christians, but there are little or no Christian organizations that stand up for the rights of persecuted Muslims in, for example, Myanmar or China. It is understandable that Christians are concerned about their own brothers and sisters, but does that fit the inclusive nature of the kingdom of

---

46. See United Religions Initiative, "Interfaith Mediation Centre, Kaduna: Last Peace and Good Governance," https://uri.org/who-we-are/cooperation-circle/interfaith-mediation-centre-kaduna.

47. For the story of Wuye and Ashafa see "Voices of Dialogue," https://www.kaiciid.org/news-events/news/voices-dialogue-co-founders-nigerias-interfaith-mediation-centre-share-their-story.

Christ? Special initiatives only for Christians can create the impression that in the eyes of the church the Christians who are persecuted deserve more support than Muslims who suffer under similar circumstances. However, isn't it the case that the suffering of all God's creatures is opposite to the vision of God? And isn't anything we do for one of the least of the world something we do for Christ (Matt 25:40, 45)? Every form of suffering and evil needs to be addressed and combatted. It is ultimately not about the welfare of the church but about the honor of God. As long as his creation is distorted, he does not receive the honor that he is worthy of. Exactly because the church knows what suffering with Christ is, it should be able to identify with all of creation. Its compassion for persecuted people reflects something of God's compassion for all of his creation. Or should we exclude Muslims from that compassion because they reject the core confession of the Christian faith?

10.6 Vulnerably Self-Critical
10.6.1 Islam as a Question to the Christian Church

In 2010, filmmaker Stephen Marshall followed conservative American Christian Aaron Taylor and Islamic Jihadist Khalid Kelly for three years. It resulted in a documentary about their lives after September 11th, 2001, called *Holy Wars*.[48] Taylor, the Christian, responds to the attacks by initiating a "spiritual" battle and sharing the gospel in as many Islamic countries as possible. One of the places this quest brings him is Pakistan. Kelly, a Catholic Irishman who converted to Islam, is committed to introducing Islamic law, which also eventually brings him to Pakistan, where he feels at home among the Taliban. Halfway through the documentary, both men meet each other. They engage in a pretty one-sided conversation in which Kelly expresses his grievances about Christianity. His argumentation makes a deep impression on Taylor who, from that moment on, reflects more critically on the connection between his own conservative Christian background, crusade mentality, and American politics. As a result, he experiences a transformation. He no longer wants to seek a "holy" war, not even with words, but seeks a connection in order to share the love of Christ. He remains an evangelical Christian, but one with more social engagement. He eventually writes a book about his experiences: *Alone with a Jihadist: A Biblical Response to Holy War*.[49] Kelly becomes more and more extreme and eventually sees no other way than to join the Taliban.

---

48. *Holy Wars* documentary, https://www.imdb.com/title/tt1014799/.
49. Taylor, *Alone with a Jihadist*.

To him, they are the "true" Muslims because they want to implement Shari'a. However, Kelly does not get a residence permit in Pakistan and returns to Ireland. Marshall ends his documentary remarking that it is easy to see Aaron Taylor as the hero of the story: "But his transformation would not have been possible without Khalid Kelly and his deep dedication to the state of Muslims in the world. We do not always choose the messenger, but we can choose to listen to the message. Even an Islamist can change our view of the world."[50]

The Christian church cannot develop fully as the new creation without the encounter with Islam. According to Martin Buber, we need the other in order to fully develop our humanity.[51] In the same way, my being Christian can only fully flourish in meeting Muslims. In that respect, we need to seriously consider if the coming of Islam does not carry a message from God – not that Muhammad is his prophet but that the church must learn to live through the Holy Spirit out of the grace of Christ. We have seen that different Christians throughout history have interpreted Islam as a judgement from God on a disobedient church (see 1.3). That was already true for *Pseudo-Methodius* at the end of the seventh century, shortly after the birth of Islam.[52] Luther saw the rise of the Turks as an instrument of God that he used to "chastise" the church and, at the same time, call it to repentance and spiritual renewal.[53] That is an idea the church should at least consider. Paul, admittedly, emphasizes that for those who are in Christ there is no condemnation (κατάκριμα) anymore (Rom 8:1), but that does not exclude the fact that the judgement (κρίμα) begins with the household of God (1 Pet 4:17).

Judgement, here, is related to the guidelines of God, which are the principles of the true life as he has meant it from the beginning.[54] The judgement intends to bring the church of Christ back to the original plan. Even when we do not want to speak too easily about "judgement," we can still see Islam as a "tool" that God uses to urge his church to continuously remain focused on his purposes. Islam challenges the church about whether it truly lives as a new creation.

---

50. *Holy Wars* documentary, https://www.imdb.com/title/tt1014799//.

51. See M. Buber, *Ich und Du.*

52. *Pseudo-Methodius* XI, 5–7; See Reinink, *Die Syrische Apokalypse.* For dating details, see xii, xv–xx. Explored more thoroughly in Reitsma, *De kerk.*

53. Baumann, *Gottes Ruf,* 47.

54. מִשְׁפָּט; *krima* in the LXX; God's "judgements," prescriptions. This means the principles that give direction, as God has intended them in creation for the true life. See, for example, Deut 26:17 and other places in the Torah. When the church is judged she is reoriented to that original plan.

One of the factors that, according to Cragg, contributed to the rise of Islam was the failure of the Christian church: "a failure in love, in purity, and in fervor, a failure of the spirit."[55] The church in his view did not succeed in presenting the true image of Christ, so that Islam in fact claims "to displace what it had never effectively known."[56] According to Cragg, there is still *jāhiliyah* – ignorance – in Islam concerning Jesus.[57] *Jāhiliyah* is the term Muslims normally use to describe the period of time before the coming of Muhammad, a time of darkness and ignorance. According to Cragg that is still the case when it comes to the nature of the person of Jesus. The Qur'an, and later traditions, offer a caricatural picture of Jesus.[58] According to Cragg that is, in part, the church's fault – not only because of theological disagreements and disputes but also because it has given the wrong presentation of Christianity. The kind of Christianity that Islam was confronted with was weakened as a result of different wars. In the Byzantine Empire, faith was closely connected to the power of the emperor: cross and sword were inseparable. Christian minorities like Assyrian Christians and the Monophysites were condemned, persecuted, and sometimes had to flee for their lives. Those are most likely the kinds of Christians that Muhammad met. Theological disputes had weakened Christianity spiritually as well.[59] That is the image Muhammad had of Christianity. The Crusades and the crusader mentality, as well as the Western colonialism of the last two hundred years, have only further confirmed that image for Muslims. And even though much of today's "invisibly" exported values of secularity, cheap love, sex, abundance, and individualism do not come from the Christian tradition, they are seen by many Muslims as "Christian" because, in their eyes, there is no difference between "the West" and "Christianity."

Cragg emphasizes that the past cannot be undone in the present but that the Christian church should be conscious of the role it plays in it all. It will need to face its history and strive today to transport a veritable image of Christ. That is also why Cragg calls the presence of Islam an appeal to the Christian church today. The call to prayer from the minaret is a call for the Christian community to undo the alienation: "The objective is not, as the Crusaders

---

55. Cragg, *Call of the Minaret*, 219.
56. Cragg, 219.
57. Cragg, 220.
58. Cragg, 235–236.
59. Cragg, 236–237.

believed, the repossession of what Christendom has lost, but the restoration to Muslims of the Christ whom they have missed."[60]

To put it differently, Christians need to think through how they can avoid putting up stumbling blocks to the gospel for Muslims. Paul was prepared to renounce eating meat and become weak to the weak and strong to the strong, and he wanted to take care of his own income. All of that in order to not be a hindrance to the gospel (1 Cor 8–10). But how can the church of Christ, without denying its own identity, renounce all that can form an impediment to Muslims in getting to know the true Christ? Here we can think of different aspects we have discussed before, like power, influence, prosperity, our attitude towards the state of Israel, and our way of life. Other things can easily be added to this list. Paul went very far in this regard and was ready to commit his life entirely to the gospel in order to save at least some of his fellow Jews (Rom 11:14). It did eventually cost him his life. If the church reflects on its own position it is thus extremely vulnerable.

10.6.2 Merciful Humility

If the church needs to characterize itself, it would start with the recognition that it lives through grace. Christianity is, just like Islam, a human response to the revelation of God that is judged by the measure in which it reflects the gospel and conveys a true picture of Christ. That is where we experience tension. The church is a new creation, and at the same time, it is also continuously critiqued in light of the new creation. Christians should, no less than Muslims, give an account of whether they have done justice to the nature of God and if they truly have demonstrated the new life. Christianity, too, is under the critical eye of the gospel, just like every other form of religiosity.

As the first expression of the new creation, the church of Christ has a high calling. The recognition that it fails in answering that calling can have a crippling effect. It can lead to a legalistic posture in which we can try to purify the church from all kinds of heresy and ethical misconduct. It can also lead to a defensive posture in which we try to excuse all kinds of false steps the church has taken. It is, however, not about the truth of Christendom or Christianity but about who Christ is. The Christian church could be more generous towards

---

60. Cragg, 220. Cragg calls this "retrieval," which indicates the bringing back of what was lost. In an IT context, it refers to bringing back lost data, the reinstallation of information and systems. See also Baumann, *Gottes Ruf*, 87–93.

Muslims in its recognition of its own shortcomings in history.[61] It suits the church more to confess and ask for forgiveness than to justify what has gone wrong.[62] Being a Christian is to witness to what God has done in Christ, not to Christian excellence and superiority. It is a life of forgiveness.

That is why Christians need to be humble in their judgement of Muslims. Judgement belongs to God. Whether Muslims are good or not, whether they are outside of God's grace or not, that is not for the church to decide. "Judge not, and you will not be judged" (Luke 6:37). Whoever judges another has called a judgement on themselves, "for with the judgment you pronounce you will be judged, and with the measure you use it will be measured to you" (Matt 7:2). It is easier to see the speck in someone else's eye and miss the log in your own eyes (Matt 7:3).

That is why the controversy that Christians sometimes have with Muslims about which religion is better and more peaceful is completely irrelevant. In these types of discussions, Christians often refer to the fact that Muhammad was a statesman who did not shrink back from using the sword. Islam supposedly has often spread over the world through violence. Christ, on the other hand, came into Jerusalem on a donkey to die on a cross. He did not enforce his kingdom with violence. Apart from the fact that we should not compare Muhammad to Christ,[63] this reasoning does not explain how it is possible that during the course of history, Christianity has also spread through violence and cruelty.[64] If the church indeed believes that Jesus is different from Muhammad, it will need to explain why it has shown a face so different from Jesus Christ on so many pages in history. I do not ignore the many good things that the Christian tradition has brought, but we do need to note that Christians have often compromised the gospel and dishonored God. The church has enough on its plate with its own heritage. Christians should be more worried about that than about a theoretical discussion on whether Muhammad has been more violent than Jesus Christ.

Theology plays an important role in Christianity's continuous critical self-reflection. Which texts have given rise to connecting the cross with power and

---

61. See for example the response of Yale Divinity School's Center for Faith and Culture in a page-wide advertisement in the New York Times that was signed by many Christians in December 2007 titled "Loving God and Neighbor Together."

62. For this reason, in March of 1996, at the initiative of Youth with a Mission, a reconciliation march was held in which Christians traveled from Cologne via Istanbul to Israel. See for example Poorta, "De eerste holocaust," 13.

63. See 4.3.

64. See Armstrong, *Fields of Blood.*

violence? How do we interpret them? And why do those biblical texts have a different value than similar texts in the Islamic tradition? How, for example, is the suicide attack of Samson (Judg 16:30) different from modern suicide terrorists?[65] How does Jehu's beheading of the seventy sons of Ahab relate to the cruelty of ISIS in the Middle East? How do we read the laws that require the death penalty for those who leave the faith (Deut 17:2–7) in light of the honor killings faced by Muslims when they start to follow Jesus? What do we think of the rule that those who commit adultery must be stoned (Deut 22:22)? Is that comparable to similar laws in strict Islamic countries?

Only if we are prepared to be self-critical, in a modest, humble way, can we question Muslims critically about their tradition. For example, what is the place of Christians as a minority in an Islamic society? Why are Christians put under pressure in a growing number of Muslim-majority countries? Is it specific to the sources in Islam that Christians in the Islamic world are often seen as second-class citizens? Islam has not only stood against a violent Christianity, but it has, at times, itself perpetuated violence. Is that only a derailment we call extremism or is it also inherent to classical Islam? What does it mean for understanding God? These questions need to be honestly brought to the table but require mutual humility and respect.

In this context, in my inaugural address at Vrije Universiteit, I questioned Christian politics.[66] It seems to be an outdated discussion in light of growing populism. Nevertheless, it remains a point of discussion in light of international developments. My main objection to it is the link between Christian faith and political pressure. Every political party, whether Christian or secular, wants to realize its ideals as much as possible. Whenever a party carries governing responsibilities, it also imposes these ideals on people who might not agree with it. That is why, in politics, we need to compromise. In extreme cases, a government will enforce these ideals or compromises with violence. When a Christian political party develops a policy based on Christian principles, it intends for it to become implemented and therefore is willing to impose it even on people who do not follow Christ. That is opposite to the freedom of the gospel. God does not force anyone to live life according to the principles of his kingdom. If Christ was willing to sacrifice himself and his own interests in service of others, how can a Christian (with weapons if necessary) fight for a kingdom that is marked by this world? Not only that: Christian politics creates the impression that a party's policies are in line with the principles of

---

65. See Reitsma, "Divinely Approved?," 853–866.
66. Reitsma, "De kerk," 21.

the kingdom of Christ. In reality, a great variety of different policies are possible on the basis of the same Christian principles. Christians can adhere to different political parties, which relativizes the "Christian character" of Christian politics. An important point of difference between the various Christian views on politics is the extent to which people are willing to justify their compromise as legitimate in relation to the gospel. Compromising could weaken the Christian character on certain kinds of politics. Without compromises and bipartisanship, however, doing politics is virtually impossible.

Should Christians, for the above-mentioned reasons, ignore politics? Should they avoid voting and never run for office? Not in the least. But their political involvement would need to be characterized by humility and restraint. Christians in politics need to watch for the temptation to think that they can restore our broken reality. The purpose cannot be to promote a more "Christian" society. I bring up this topic of politics with Islam in mind. Whoever strives to (re)Christianize a country – and thus give less space to Muslims – will sooner rather than later try to make the kingdom of God coincide with their own principles. If Christians take an active role in political rule, it would always need to be focused primarily on containing evil and striving for rights and justice. Politics, too, is characterized by the limitations of our existence.

10.6.3 Parting with Crusader Theology

Many Muslims still see Christians as crusaders: expansionists who purely care about the conquest of territory. Ever since Constantine, cross and sword have been closely linked. This was the case during the Crusades, it was typical of the colonial period, and it is still seen in the meddling of many Western countries in the Islamic world. And the West, as mentioned before, is wrongly considered "Christian." Throughout history, Islam has often encountered the kind of Christianity that has attempted to defend itself or expand itself with weapons. The founding of the state of Israel, the two Gulf wars in 1991 and 2003, and the great political and economic pressure placed on many Islamic countries have continuously been seen by Muslims as writing on the wall. Radical Muslims view this "meddling" as a justification to commit attacks or take up arms against the West in general and Christians in particular.

When we recall the "characteristics" of the kingdom of Christ, we can only conclude with shame that the "fall of Christianity" has led to disruptions in these matters. The church should never again take on a "crusader mentality." The cross is not compatible with the sword. The nature of the church of

Christ contradicts any attempt to realize or protect the kingdom of God or the Christian church with the sword.

An often raised counterargument is that Europe would have been Islamic today if Charles Martel, in AD 732, had not used the sword in the battle at Poitiers or if the Austrians many centuries later hadn't entered into the fight with the Ottomans.[67] Christianity could then possibly have vanished from Europe completely. I can understand that kind of reasoning from a practical point of view. This is often how it works in the world, and earthly powers can quickly – or slowly – make religions disappear through political force and social pressure. However, we also need to face the question of whether the disappearance of Christianity – in Asia and North Africa, for example – was really caused by the coming of Islam. Jenkins has shown that there were countless other reasons for this disappearance. The church was divided and not really rooted in society.[68] The demise of the Byzantine Empire is certainly also due to all kinds of internal and external conflicts. If the gospel can only be protected with weapons, it is not worth living for, let alone dying for. Would it, in that case, really be the power of God (Rom 1:16)? I am convinced that the essence of the Christian faith is untouchable in the end, no matter what situation the church finds itself in. And I also definitely do not want to downplay that terror and domination can make people utterly vulnerable. How long can a community endure severe subordination and discrimination or even persecution? No matter how much it is true that the gates of hell cannot prevail against the church (Matt 16:18), if Christians are expelled or killed in massive numbers, the church does disappear in a certain region. This is what seems to be happening in Syria and Iraq in the second decade of the twenty-first century. At the same time, we need to question whether military intervention can prevent the church from disappearing. When Bashir Gemayel declared that he refused to live in *dhimmitude*, he added that Christians needed to conquer all of Lebanon to ensure that their church bells could ring out joys and sorrows whenever they wished and Christians would be able to live in freedom.[69] The consequence of an approach like this would certainly be that Muslims, Druze, and other groups in Lebanon would be reduced to their own kind of *dhimmi*-status, although now under Christian domination. Such a nation might be

---

67. Chapman, *Cross and Crescent*, 12–13.

68. See Jenkins, *Lost History of Christianity*. Jenkins shows that the shrinking of the churches in the Middle East was not primarily due to violence or persecution that came from Islam in the seventh and eighth centuries but to a much slower assimilation of culture and society.

69. Cited in Ye'or, *Dhimmi*, 403–405.

called "Christian," but it does not promote freedom of religion or equality for all citizens. Gemayel was killed in an attack for which his followers took revenge by killing two to three thousand women, children, and older men in the Palestinian camps of Sabra and Chatila in Southern Beirut.[70] They did so with repulsive cruelty that can easily be compared to the violence of groups like ISIS in Iraq and Syria and Boko Haram in Nigeria. It poignantly demonstrates that those who want complete freedom to ring church bells whenever they wish can only accomplish that goal without violence if the majority will agree to it. The fact that the Christian faith is also slowly eroding and disappearing in the West without the threat of other powers somehow proves the same thing. "Power" and "majority" are no guarantees for a flourishing Christian community.

To be sure to avoid misunderstandings: evil powers, like that of militant and extremist Muslims, need to be curbed. We need to distinguish here explicitly between the Christian church and the government. According to Paul, the (non-Christian) government has the task of curbing evil. It carries the sword in order to give those who do evil and spread terror their deserved punishment (Rom 13:4). That principle, in my view, seems to apply also to leaders of the EU, the UN, or the Arab League when it comes to conflicts that transcend national or regional borders. That, however, is something quite different from guaranteeing the existence of the church, enforcing kingdom principles, and implementing democracy and human rights through violence if necessary. It is for that reason that Luther did not see the defense of Vienna in 1529 as the calling of the Pope but of the emperor. The church was, according to him, called to humility, penance, and prayer. The battle of the church is fought kneeling.

10.6.4 The Persecuted Church as a Mirror

The suffering of the persecuted church is, as we have seen earlier, complex. Besides religious motives, many other factors play a role, such as ethnicity and historical, political, and economic developments. Nevertheless, the persecuted church holds up a mirror to Christianity as a whole.

The persecuted church and suffering

The nature of the church in a distorted creation is characterized by suffering. As the new community of creation, it is the opposite, in many respects, of the old life. That is true both in relation to suffering as a result of the brokenness

---

70. Estimations vary from 800 (UN) to 3,500 (Hout, *Sabra and Shatila*, 296). See Reitsma, *God of My Enemy*, 13 fn22.

of creation as well as the age-old rebellion against God and his work in Christ. Suffering is not a denial of the new creation, but until its fulness arrives, it is a part of reality.

The persecuted church shows that suffering in every form belongs to the DNA of the church if it wants to be connected to Christ (see ch. 9). It shares God's pain over a broken creation.[71] There is something fundamentally wrong when the church no longer suffers due to the brokenness of the world. A church that is not bothered by the fact that God is not honored in the way he deserves has lost its soul. Whoever can remain indifferent to the loss of God's intention with creation misses communion with the heart of the Creator. If the church of Christ can carelessly ignore the persecution of brothers and sisters by Muslims, then it has lost the connection with the suffering Christ. That involvement is not limited to the "body of Christ" alone. If the church does not care about the fact that many others besides its fellow believers are oppressed, the question is if it is still the church of Christ. If we see the situation of the church in the West as normal and not as an exception, we have explicitly or implicitly embraced the prosperity gospel.

In this way the persecuted church is a great support to the church that does not know persecution. Just as the latter urges the persecuted church to keep going in the midst of suffering, the persecuted church urges the former to resist the temptation to exchange the cross for a gospel of property and happiness. The persecuted church forces Christianity to think differently about suffering and to continuously be aware that we are strangers on earth, pilgrims on our way to glory. In that way, the persecuted church encourages Christians in the West who suffer because of the brokenness of creation to not give up. The persecuted church cannot give up when there is opposition or persecution, and in the same way, other Christians should also not give up when suffering comes. The promise that Christ is with them always to the end of the age is meant for both of them (Matt 28:20).

The church will always know both joy and sadness in the present – in between – time. Joy over the new life in Christ and the glory that is about to break through, and pain over the powers of the old *aeon*: "through honor and dishonor, through slander and praise," we are treated "as dying, and behold,

---

71. That is true no matter what the context is. Dawn emphasizes that the characteristic of the church as a worshipping community is the very thing that connects her to God's pain. She argues that much of the modern worship in churches trivializes that pain from God over a broken world. Dawn, *Royal Waste of Time*, 237.

we live . . . as sorrowful, yet always rejoicing; as poor, yet making many rich; as having nothing, yet possessing everything" (2 Cor 6:8–10 ESV).

The persecuted church and dedication to Christ

The persecuted church holds up a mirror for us in yet another way. Those who want to follow Jesus in the free West can participate in society without restrictions. It has hardly any consequences for finding a job or getting access to education or health care. For many Christians in the context of Islam this is not true. Either they follow Jesus and are not fully worthy in society or they are fully respected members of society by compromising their dedication to Christ. There are no other options. In this way the essence of the persecuted church is an admonition to Christians that believing requires a total dedication of all areas of life to Christ. It is all or nothing. Love cannot be compartmentalized. Parents who have multiple children do not split up that love, they multiply it.

That is also important when looking at Christian witness in the context of Islam. Muslims seem to think at times that Christianity is primarily about a vertical relationship with God. This notion is enforced by certain Christian circles' strong emphasis on life after death. That is, however, only one part of the gospel. In Christ, it is ultimately about the complete renewal of all of creation. Therefore, that the church is a new creation has to be visible in all areas of life.

10.7 Vulnerably Just?

In non-Western cultures it is common to tell stories. If I want to criticize someone, I would not say this bluntly and straightforwardly, but I would tell a story in which the other can recognize themselves very clearly. Sometimes bystanders will also get the point; sometimes they will not. In either case, it ensures that the person I'm addressing will not be called to account publicly and lose their honor. This is probably also why Jesus told parables. By using stories from everyday life, he spoke to the people of his time. One such parable strongly speaks to the relationship between the church and Islam.

10.7.1 The Pharisee and the Tax Collector[72]

It is the parable of the pharisee and the tax collector (Luke 18:9–14).[73] Jesus tells the story with an eye on so-called people "who trusted in themselves that

---

72. This appeared in another form in Reitsma, *Adembenemend*, 73–81.
73. See also in Bailey, *Poet and Peasant*, 142–156.

they were righteous, and treated others with contempt" (18:9). It is, however, a question whether they are also righteous "in the eyes of God" (18:14).

A pharisee and a tax collector are going to the temple to pray. It is probable that this is about a public prayer during one of the prayer times. This explains why both enter the temple. Apparently, lots of people are praying at this point in time, otherwise it would not mean much that the tax collector is standing "at a distance" (18:13).[74]

The pharisee is one of the spiritual leaders of Israel, he knows the law and closely follows all 613 laws and commands. Because of his religious commitment, he is most likely held in high regard by the common folk. You could say that he is a faithful covenant partner, the prototype of a righteous person. The tax collector, on the other hand, is a traitor: he collects (too much) tax for the enemies who occupy God's land. He is scorned by his own people. Religiously and politically, he is an outcast, and from an economic point of view, a thief. He is therefore the prototype of an unrighteous person who has broken the covenant with God.[75]

The pharisee

The pharisee is very deliberately standing apart from all other people. The text has some variances but that does not make much difference to its meaning.[76] Either "he is standing by himself and prays these things" or "he stands and prays these things by himself." In both cases, he has purposely separated himself from people. He wants to keep away from sinners because he considers himself above them. That is apparent from his prayer. It is not God who is central, but he himself. "*I* thank you, that *I* am not like other men" and "*I* fast twice a week; *I* give tithes of all that *I* get." He considers himself spiritually superior. All sinners in the temple are in sharp contrast to his own perception of himself (18:11–12).[77] He is the prototype of those who consider *themselves* righteous and scorn others (18:9).

Being righteous has to do with life as God has intended. The Torah describes the contours of that life. Those who live according to the decrees of God live in accordance with God's purpose for creation. That is, therefore, a life of worship: God is at the center. God is the righteous one. He has taken the initiative for the covenant and remains faithful to his promises to Israel

---

74. See Bailey, 145.

75. Nolland, *Luke II*, 875.

76. Some manuscripts place ταῦτα after πρὸς ἑαυτόν (A, W, 063, f 13, M), others before (P75, a2, B, (L), T, Q, Y).

77. Bailey, *Poet and Peasant*, 149.

and the world (Ps 145[LXX 144]:17). Human beings are dependent on his goodness and grace. The righteous live by the love of God and respond to it.

That is exactly where the problem lies with this pharisee. His prayer in the temple shows that not God but he himself is at the center. He worships himself instead of the Creator, and that means he is breaking the covenant. Instead of having a humble awareness of dependence, he boasts about the covenant. He has started to see it as a privilege. It is evidence to him that he *himself* is very special. That is why he is applauding *himself*. He seems to be congratulating God for having such a wonderful covenant partner: "Look at me in comparison to those sinners over there, thieves, people who are unrighteous or idolatrous or even this tax collector" (see 18:11). The scorn for others is overtly present when he is subtly pointing out to God that he is far better than a regular partner in the covenant. He is actually doing more than God is expecting him according to the Torah. He fasts *twice a week* even though the Torah only requires fasting on the Day of Atonement and other festival and remembrance days (Lev 23:32; Num 39:7 CEV).[78] He is giving a tenth of everything, even though a tenth is only requested of the harvest (Lev 27:30; Num 18:27; Deut 12:17).[79] That is why he – almost literally – makes a sharp distinction between himself and others. He scorns them (18:9) and casts a judgement that only belongs to God: "They are unclean and I am clean; they are outside and I am inside." While the scent of the offering is most likely still hanging in the temple and you can almost smell the atonement,[80] this man thinks he does not need it.

The tax collector

The tax collector is, in one way, not distinguished from the pharisee: he, too, is standing apart from the other people. But he picks that spot because he does not feel good enough. He knows that he actually does not belong in the temple because he has broken the covenant with God. His body language expresses timidity. He cannot look God and people in the eye, that is why he does not dare to lift up his eyes. He is beating himself on the chest out of embarrassment. It is an exceptional gesture because, in the time of Jesus, that was mostly done by women who would beat themselves on the chest out of grief and sadness. He realizes how very lost he is and is ashamed to death. As he calls out to God, he deeply realizes that he has nothing to go on. He needs atonement and is calling out for mercy (18:13). The word that is used here (ἱλάσκομαι)

---

78. In these passages "afflicting yourselves" is interpreted as including fasting.
79. Bailey, *Poet and Peasant*, 152.
80. Bailey, 147.

is associated with an offering for atonement. In the New Testament, it is only used for Jesus's atonement offering – propitiation for sin (Rom 3:25; cf. Heb 2:17). The tax collector is asking God for reconciliation in order to be able to share in the new life. He is, in a way, connecting himself with the sacrifice that has been made that day in the temple.

Righteous

The outcome of the parable cannot be a surprise to an attentive listener. It is not the pious pharisee that goes home justified but the tax collector. When they arrived at the temple, the pharisee walked ahead; now that they are going home, the roles are reversed (Luke 18:14).[81] The tax collector knows he is in need of God's grace; God is at the center for him. The pharisee thinks he can manage without that grace and shows himself, in this way, to be an unfaithful covenant partner. The problem is not so much what he said about the tax collector. That was correct. The tax collector would entirely agree: he is a sinner and a traitor. The problem lies in what the pharisee said *about himself.* He did not realize that just like the tax collector he was only able to share in the covenant of God through grace. Because he thought he did not need that grace, he honored himself and thus broke the relationship with God. He elevated himself and consequently went home humiliated (18:14).

The tax collector, therefore, does not go home justified because he was so desperate. He acknowledged that he needed God and could only live through grace. That is the sign of the covenant; the relationship with God exists only because of atonement. He humbled himself and completely recognized his dependence on God. That is why he was exalted. He could look God in the eyes again.[82]

Righteousness and justification only exist because of grace and reconciliation with God. That is why Jesus, with this parable, points indirectly to himself. In God's eyes, he is the righteous one par excellence. All others who are made righteous can only be that way due to the atonement offering of Jesus. He has "humbled himself by becoming obedient to the point of death, even death on a cross. Therefore God has highly exalted him and bestowed on him the name that is above every name, so that at the name of Jesus every knee

---

81. Bailey, 144.

82. Whoever wants to enter the kingdom has to become like a child (Luke 18:17). A child, here, is not the sign of an innocent faith but of dependence. Every child knows that without the care of parents and caretakers it cannot survive. A child must live from what others give and from – as one might say – grace.

should bow, in heaven and on earth and under the earth, and every tongue confess that Jesus Christ is Lord, to the glory of God the Father" (Phil 2:8–11).

10.7.2 The Tax Collector, the Pharisee, the Christian Church, and Islam

With these parables, Jesus addresses the Jewish leaders of his day. The story can also be interpreted as a profound message for the church in relation to Islam. The church is continuously faced with the temptation to walk in the way of the Pharisee and consider itself superior to Muslims. Christians can be condescending about Muslims: "Thankfully we are not as bad as those Muslims"; "Muslims are the ones who are committing attacks and fighting holy wars. Christians don't do that." If the church is really aware of its own nature, it realizes that it can only really bear fruit thanks to the grace of God. Without the grace of God, it is nowhere. In that sense, it is no different from Muslims.

Those who, like the tax collector, realize that they can only exist because of God's grace will recognize themselves in others. Whoever knows Christ will look at Muslims with different eyes. Only when the church of Christ realizes that it owes everything to God's grace can it share its life with Muslims. Only then is it possible to talk about Jesus, about God, and about how he has meant for this life to be. Only when we realize that Christianity is not much better than Islam can we convey to Muslims who Jesus Christ is.

Looking at it from this perspective, the parable is also an appeal to Muslims. Whoever wants to enter the kingdom and wants to share in the real life will have to realize that they cannot make any contributions to it. It is only through the grace and self-sacrificing love of Christ that Muslims can participate in the history of God and human beings. That grace is not the same as the mercy that almost every Surah uses when talking about God. Namely, that "mercy" does not automatically imply that God loves sinners.

The equivalent of the humility of the tax collector is self-sacrificing, vulnerable love. He leaves all self-righteousness behind. He is standing next to the Pharisee empty handed; he is losing out to the Pharisee's list of accomplishments and achievements. That is not much different for Christians in relation to Islam. The Christian church cannot maintain it is better than Islam. It does not have to justify itself; its righteousness is in Christ. He is walking with the church in order for it to continuously discover who he wants to be for the world today. In a robust humility, Christians invite Muslims to walk with them to get to know the greatness of Christ's grace. That grace enables the followers of Jesus to continue to love despite ridicule and opposition. That is the power of vulnerable love.

Bibliography

Aarts, P., and J. Keulen, eds. *Islam, de woede en het Westen*. Amsterdam: Bulaaq, 2001.

Abernathy, D. "Translating 'Son of God' in Missionary Bible Translation: A Critique of 'Muslim-Idiom Bible Translations: Claims and Facts.'" *St Francis Magazine* 6, no. 1 (February 2010): 176–203.

Accad, F. E. *Building Bridges: Christianity and Islam*. Colorado Springs: NavPress, 2001.

Accad, M. "Christian Attitudes toward Islam and Muslims: A Kerygmatic Approach." In *Toward Respectful Understanding and Witness among Muslims: Essays in Honor of J. Dudley Woodberry*, edited by J. Dudley Woodberry, Evelyne A. Reisacher, Joseph L. Cumming, Dean S. Gilliland, and Charles E. van Engen, Kindle location 672–1165. Pasadena: William Carey Library, 2011.

———. *Sacred Misinterpretation: Reaching across the Christian-Muslim Divide*. Grand Rapids: Eerdmans, 2019.

Akthar, S. *Islam as Political Religion: The Future of an Imperial Faith*. London: Routledge, 2011.

Alexander, R. "Are There Really 100,000 New Christian Martyrs Every Year?" News Magazine. BBC, 12 November 2013. http://www.bbc.com/news/magazine-24864587.

Al-Faruqi, I. R. "Islam and Zionism." In *Voices of Resurgent Islam*, edited by J. L. Esposito, 261–267. Oxford: Oxford University Press, 1983.

Al Hout, B. N. *Sabra and Shatila: September 1982*. London: Pluto Press, 2004.

Anderson, A. *An Introduction to Pentecostalism*. Cambridge: Cambridge University Press, 2004.

Armstrong, K. *Fields of Blood: Religion and the History of Violence*. New York: Anchor Books, 2015.

Ashton, J. *Understanding the Fourth Gospel*. Oxford: Oxford University Press, 1991.

Aune, D. E. *Prophecy in Early Christianity and the Ancient Mediterranean World*. Grand Rapids: Eerdmans, 1991.

Awad, Sami. "The Palestinian Exodus." Blog: Never Give Up: Trust in the Power of Nonviolence to Heal the World. Accessed 1 March 2020. https://samiawad.wordpress.com.

Ayoub, M. "*Dhimmah* in the Qur'an and the Hadith." In *A Muslim View of Christianity: Essays on Dialogue by Mahmoud Ayoub*, edited by I. A. Omar, 98–107. Maryknoll: Orbis Books, 2007.

———. "Muslim Views of Christianity." In *A Muslim View of Christianity: Essays on Dialogue by Mahmoud Ayoub*, edited by I. A. Omar, 212–245. Maryknoll: Orbis Books, 2007.

————. "Nearest in Amity: Christians in the Qur'an and Contemporary Exegetical Tradition." In *A Muslim View of Christianity: Essays on Dialogue by Mahmoud Ayoub*, edited by I. A. Omar, 187–211. Maryknoll: Orbis Books, 2007.

Badawi, Z. "Jerusalem and Islam." In *Jerusalem Today: What Future for the Peace Process?*, edited by G. Karmi, 137–143. Reading: Garnet Publishing, 1997.

Bailey, K. E. *Poet and Peasant and Through Peasant Eyes: A Literary-Cultural Approach to the Parables in Luke*. Combined edition. Grand Rapids: Eerdmans, 1996.

Bakker, H. A., M. J. Kater, and W. van Vlastuin, eds. *Verantwoord geloof. Handboek christelijke apologetiek*. Kampen: Brevier, 2014.

Barth, K. *Die Kirchliche Dogmatik*. Vol. 3. Zürich: Evangelischer Verlag, 1945.

Bat Ye'or. *The Dhimmi: Jews and Christians under Islam*. London: Associated University Press, 1985.

Bauckham, R. *God Crucified: Monotheism and Christology in the New Testament*. Grand Rapids: Eerdmans, 1998.

————. *The Testimony of the Beloved Disciple: Narrative, History, and Theology in the Gospel of John*. Grand Rapid: Baker Academic, 2007.

Baumann, A. *Der Islam: Gottes Ruf zur Umkehr? Eine vernachlässigte Deutung aus christlicher Sicht*. Basel und Gießen: Brunnen Verlag, 2003.

BBC. "Arab Leaders Relaunch Peace Plan." BBC News, 28 March 2007. http://news.bbc.co.uk/2/hi/middle_east/6501573.stm.

Bennett, C. *Understanding Christian-Muslim Relations*. London: Continuum, 2008.

Berger, M. *Klassieke sharia en vernieuwing*. Amsterdam: WRR/Amsterdam University Press, 2006.

Berkhof, H. *Christian Faith: An Introduction to the Study of the Faith*. Rev. ed. Grand Rapids: Eerdmans, 1990.

Bernard, J. H., and A. H. McNeile. *A Critical and Exegetical Commentary on the Gospel According to St. John*. Vol. 1. International Critical Commentary. Edinburgh: T&T Clark, 1942.

Bernts, T., and J. Berghuijs. *God in Nederland 1966–2015*. Utrecht: Ten Have, 2016.

Bevans, S. B. *Models of Contextual Theology*. Revised edition. Faith and Culture Series. Maryknoll: Orbis, 2012.

Bijlefeld, W. A. *De islam als na-christelijke religie*. Den Haag: Van Keulen, 1959.

Blaß, F., A. Debrunner, and F. Rehkopf. *Grammatik des neutestamentlichen Griechisch*. Göttingen: Vandenhoeck & Ruprecht, 1990.

Blomberg, C. *The Historical Reliability of John's Gospel: Issues and Commentary*. Leicester: Inter-Varsity Press, 2001.

Boer, M. C. de. *Johannine Perspectives on the Death of Jesus*. Contributions to Biblical Exegesis and Theology 17. Leuven: Peeters, 1996.

Bosch, D. J. *Transforming Mission: Paradigm Shifts in Theology of Mission*. 13th edition. Maryknoll: Orbis, 1998.

Bowie, F. *The Anthropology of Religion: An Introduction*. 2nd edition. Oxford: Blackwell Publishing, 2006.

Boyd-MacMillan, R. *Faith That Endures: The Essential Guide to the Persecuted Church.* Ellel: Sovereign World, 2006.

Brown, D. W. *A New Introduction to Islam.* 3rd edition. Oxford: J. Wiley & Sons, 2017.

Brown, F., S. R. Driver, and C. A. Briggs. *Hebrew-Aramaic and English Lexicon of the Old Testament.* BibleWorks 8. Ontario: Online Bible Foundation, 1997.

Brown, R. "Explaining the Biblical Term 'Son(s) of God' in Muslim Contexts." *International Journal of Frontier Missions* 22, no. 3 (2005): 91–96; 22, no. 4 (2005): 135–145.

Brown, R. E. *The Gospel According to John, XII–XXI: Introduction, Translation and Notes.* Anchor Bible Commentary 29A. New York: Doubleday, 1966.

Brown, R. E., J. Penny, and L. Gray. "Muslim-Idiom Bible Translations: Claims and Facts." *St Francis Magazine* 5, no. 6 (December 2009): 87–105.

Bruce, F. F. *The Gospel of John: Introduction, Exposition and Notes.* Grand Rapids: Eerdmans, 1983.

Brunson, A. C. *Psalm 118 in the Gospel of John: An Intertextual Study on the New Exodus Pattern in the Theology of John.* WUNT 158, 2nd volume. Tübingen: Mohr Siebeck, 2003.

Buber, M. *Ich und Du.* 17th edition. Gütersloh: Lambert Schneider/Gütersloher Verlagshaus, 2017.

Bultmann, R. "Alētheia (ἀλήθεια)." In *TWNT*, vol. 1, edited by Gerhard Kittel and Gerhard Friedrich, 239–251. Stuttgart: Kohlhammer, 1932–1979.

Burge, G. *Whose Land? Whose Promise? What Christians Are Not Being Told about Israel and the Palestinians.* Carlisle: Paternoster Press, 2003.

Cahen, Cl. "Dhimma." In *Encyclopaedia of Islam*, 2nd ed., edited by P. Bearman, Th. Bianquis, C. E. Bosworth, E. van Donzel, and W. P. Heinrichs. Leiden: Brill, 2000. Accessed 1 March 2020. DOI: http://dx.doi.org/10.1163/1573-3912_islam_SIM_1823.

Carson, D. A. *The Gospel According to John.* The Pillar New Testament Commentary. Grand Rapids: Eerdmans, 1991.

Cassidy, R. J. *John's Gospel in New Perspective: Christology and the Realities of Roman Power.* Maryknoll: Orbis, 1992.

Castelli, A. "Praying for the Persecuted Church: US Christian Activism in the Global Arena." *Journal of Human Rights* 4, no. 3 (2005): 321–351.

Chapman, C. *Cross and Crescent: Responding to the Challenges of Islam.* Revised edition. Leicester: Inter-Varsity Press, 2007.

———. "Evangelicals, Islam and the Israeli-Palestinian Conflict." *Muslim-Christian Encounter: Torch Trinity Centre for Islamic Studies Journal* 5, no. 1 (2012): 137–152.

———. "Is Dialogue Going Anywhere? Reflections on a Century of Christian-Muslim Relations." Lecture, Centre for Muslim-Christian Studies, Oxford, 28 February 2012. http://www.cmcsoxford.org.uk/downloadlibrary/C.%20Chapman%20paper.pdf.

Chehata, C. "Dhimma." In *Encyclopaedia of Islam*, 2nd ed., edited by P. Bearman, Th. Bianquis, C. E. Bosworth, E. van Donzel, and W. P. Heinrichs. Leiden: Brill, 2000. Accessed 1 March 2020. DOI: http://dx.doi.org/10.1163/1573-3912_islam_SIM_1824.

Christian Muslim Forum. *Ethical Guidelines for Christian and Muslim Witness in Britain*. http://46.101.6.182/wp-content/uploads/2018/12/CMF-Ethical-Guidelines-for-Christian-and-Muslim-Witness-in-Britain.pdf.

Christoffersson, O. *The Earnest Expectation of the Creature: The Flood-Tradition as Matrix of Romans 8:18–27*. Coniectanea Biblica New Testament Series 23. Stockholm: Almqvist & Wiksell, 1990.

Cimino, R. "'No God in Common': American Evangelical Discourse on Islam after 9/11." *Review of Religious Research*, 47, no. 2 (2005): 162–174.

Coe, S. "Contextualizing Theology." In *Mission Trends, No 3: Third World Theologies*, edited by G. Anderson, T. Stransky, 19–24. New York: Paulist Press, 1976.

Conn, H., "Contextualization: A New Dimension for Cross-Cultural Hermeneutics." *Evangelical Missions Quarterly* 14, no. 1 (January 1978): 44–45.

Costa, R. O., ed. *One Faith, Many Cultures: Inculturation, Indigenization, and Contextualization*. Boston Theological Institute Annual Series 2. Cambridge: Boston Theological Institute, 1988.

Cragg, K. *The Call of the Minaret*. Oxford: Oneworld, 2000.

———. *Muhammad and the Christian: A Question of Response*. Oxford: Oneworld, 1992.

Damascenus, Johannes, and Theodorus Abū Qurra. *De eerste christelijke polemiek met de islam*. Vertaald en toegelicht door Michiel Op de Coul en Marcel Poorthuis. Zoetermeer: Meinema, 2011.

Davies, W. D. "Reflections on Aspects of the Jewish Background of the Gospel of John." In *Exploring the Gospel of John: In Honor of D. Moody Smith*, edited by R. A. Culpepper and C. C. Black, 43–64. Louisville: Westminster John Knox Press, 1996.

Dawes, G. W. "The Danger of Idolatry: First Corinthians 8:7–13." *The Catholic Biblical Quarterly* 58 (1996): 82–98.

Dawn, M. J. *A Royal Waste of Time: The Splendor of Worshiping God and Being Church for the World*. Grand Rapids: Eerdmans, 1999.

DeSilva, A. *Honor, Patronage, Kinship and Purity. Unlocking New Testament Culture*. Downers Grove: IVP Academic, 2000.

Diebold-Scheuermann, C. *Jesus vor Pilatus: Eine exegetische Untersuchung zum Verhöhr durch Pilatus (Joh. 18, 28–19, 16a)*. SBB 32. Stuttgart: Katholisches Bibelwerk, 1996.

Doi, A. R. I. *Sharīʿah: The Islamic Law*. London: Ta-ha Publishers, 1984.

Dunn, J. D. G. *Romans 1–8*. Word Biblical Commentary 38A. Dallas: Word Books, 2002. CD-ROM.

Elias, N., and J. L. Scotson. *The Established and the Outsiders: A Sociological Enquiry into Community Problems*. London: Frank Cass & Co., 1965.

Ellethy, Y. *Islam, Context, Pluralism and Democracy: Classical and Modern Interpretations*. London: Routledge, 2015.

Encyclopedia of Christianity. Vol. 4. Grand Rapids: Eerdmans, 2005.

Esposito, J. L. *Islam: The Straight Path*. Revised 3rd·edition. Oxford: Oxford University Press, 2005.

Fee, G. D. *The First Epistle to the Corinthians*. NICNT. Grand Rapids: Eerdmans, 1987.

————. *God's Empowering Presence: The Holy Spirit in the Letters of Paul*. Peabody: Hendrickson, 1994.

Fisk, R. *Pity the Nation: Lebanon at War*. 3rd edition. Oxford: Oxford University Press, 2001.

Fitzmyer, J. A. *First Corinthians: A New Translation with Introduction and Commentary*. AB. New Haven: Yale University Press, 2008.

————. *Romans*. AB. New York: Doubleday, 2003.

Fotopoulos, J. "Arguments Concerning Food Offered to Idols: Corinthian Quotations and Pauline Refutations in a Rhetorical *Partitio* (1 Corinthians 8:1–9)." *The Catholic Biblical Quarterly* 67 (2005): 611–631.

————. "The Rhetorical Situation, Arrangement, and Argumentation of 1 Corinthians 8:1–13: Insights into Paul's Instructions on Idol-Food in Greco-Roman Context." *Greek Orthodox Theological Review* 47, no. 1–4 (2002): 165–198.

Francisco, A. S. *Martin Luther and Islam: A Study in Sixteenth-Century Polemics and Apologetics*. Leiden: Brill, 2007.

Gardner, P. D. *The Gifts of God and the Authentication of a Christian: An Exegetical Study of 1 Corinthians 8–11:1*. New York: University Press of America, 1994.

Garland, D. E. "The Dispute Over Food Sacrificed to Idols (1 Cor 8:1–11:1)." *Perspectives in Religious Studies* 30, no. 2 (2003): 173–197.

Garrison, D. *A Wind in the House of Islam: How God Is Drawing Muslims around the World to Faith in Jesus Christ*. Monument: WIGtake, 2014.

Glaser, I. "Thinking Biblically about Islam." In *Between Naivety and Hostility: Uncovering the Best Christian Responses to Islam in Britain*, edited by S. Bell and C. Chapman, 14–34. Milton Keynes: Authentic, 2011.

Goldsmith, M. "Immanuel – Immanu-Allah: The Name of the Creator Deity and the Name of God." *St. Francis Magazine* 3, no. 3 (Dec. 2007): 1–5.

Goldziher, I., J. Schacht, and J. Schacht. "Fiḳh." In *Encyclopaedia of Islam*, 2nd ed., edited by P. Bearman, Th. Bianquis, C. E. Bosworth, E. van Donzel, and W. P. Heinrichs. Leiden: Brill, 2000. Accessed 1 March 2020. DOI: http://dx.doi.org/10.1163/1573-3912_islam_SIM_2364.

Gooch, P. D. *Dangerous Food: 1 Corinthians 8–10 in Its Context*. Studies in Christianity and Judaism 5. Waterloo: Wilfrid Laurier University Press, 1993.

Gort, J. D. "De vis en het water. Enkele inleidende notities inzake contextualiteit." In *Veelkleurig christendom. Contextualisatie in Noord, Zuid, Oost en West*, edited by C. van der Burg, J. Gort, R. Kranenborg, L. Minnema, and H. Vroom, 13–31. Zoetermeer: Meinema, 2003.

Green, J. G., S. McKnight, and I. H. Marshall, eds. *Dictionary of Jesus and the Gospels*. Downers Grove: InterVarsity Press, 1998. CD-ROM.

Green, L. C. "New Study: Pastors Grow More Polarized on Islam." *Newsroom* (blog). Lifeway, 22 October 2015. Accessed 1 March 2020. https://blog.lifeway.com/newsroom/2015/10/22/new-study-pastors-grow-more-polarized-on-islam/.

Grudem, W. *The Gift of Prophecy in the New Testament and Today.* 5th ed. Eastbourne: Kingsway, 2001.

Hansen, C. "The Son and the Crescent." *Christianity Today*, February 4, 2011. Accessed 1 March 2020. https://www.christianitytoday.com/ct/2011/february/soncrescent.html.

Heering, G. J. *De zondeval van het christendom. Een studie over christendom, staat en oorlog.* Arnhem: Van Loghum Slaterus' Uitg. Maatschappij, 1928.

Heschel, A. J. *The Sabbath: Its Meaning for Modern Man.* New York: Noonday Press, 1951.

Hesselgrave, D. J., and E. Rommen. *Contextualization: Meaning, Methods and Models.* Grand Rapids: Baker Book House, 1989.

Hick, J. *A Christian Theology of Religions: The Rainbow of Faiths.* Louisville: Westminster Press, 1995.

———. *God Has Many Names.* Philadelphia: Westminster Press, 1982.

Hick, J., and P. Knitter, eds. *The Myth of Christian Uniqueness: Toward a Pluralistic Theology of Religions.* Maryknoll: Orbis Books, 1987.

Hill, J. *The History of Christianity.* Oxford: Lion Hudson, 2007.

Hitchcock, M. *The Coming Islamic Invasion of Israel.* Sisters, OR: Multnomah, 2002.

Hofstede, G. *Cultures and Organizations: Software of the Mind, Intercultural Cooperation and Its Importance for Survival.* Maidenhead: McGraw-Hill, 1991.

Hofstede, G. J., P. B. Pedersen, and G. Hofstede. *Exploring Culture: Exercises, Stories and Synthetic Cultures.* London: Nicholas Brealey Publishing, 2002. Kindle.

Howarth, T. "Taqiyya (Dissimulation) and Integrity." In *Between Naivity and Hostility: Uncovering the Best Christian Responses to Islam in Britain*, edited by S. Bell and C. Chapman, 218–236. Milton Keynes: Authentic, 2011.

Howell, B. M., and J. W. Paris. *Introducing Cultural Anthropology: A Christian Perspective.* Grand Rapids: Baker Academic, 2011.

Ignatius. "The Epistle of Ignatius to the Smyrnaeans," chapter IV. Accessed 1 March 2020. http://www.newadvent.org/fathers/0109.htm.

Jansen, H. *Christelijke theologie na Auschwitz. De geschiedenis van 2000 jaar kerkelijk antisemitisme.* Dl. 1, 2, 3. 's-Gravenhage: Boekencentrum, 1981–1985.

———. *Van jodenhaat naar zelfmoordterrorisme. Islamisering van het Europees antisemitisme in het Midden Oosten.* Heerenveen: Groen, 2006.

Jeffrey, G. *War on Terror: Unfolding Bible Prophecy.* Toronto: Frontier Research, 2002.

Jenkins, P. *The Lost History of Christianity: The Thousand-Year Golden Age of the Church in the Middle East, Africa, and Asia – and How It Died.* New York: HarperOne, 2008.

———. *The Next Christendom: The Coming of Global Christianity.* Oxford: Oxford University Press, 2002.

Johnson, T. M., G. A. Zurlo, A. W. Hickman, and P. F. Crossing. "Christianity 2016: Latin America and Projecting Religions to 2050." *IBMR* 40, no. 1 (2016): 22–29.

Jones, E. Stanley. *Christ and Human Suffering*. London: Hodder & Stoughton, 1933.

———. *Christus en het Menschelijk Lijden*. Amsterdam: Paris, 1934.

Juynboll, G. H. A., and D. W. Brown. "Sunna." In *Encyclopaedia of Islam*, 2nd ed., edited by P. Bearman, Th. Bianquis, C. E. Bosworth, E. van Donzel, and W. P. Heinrichs. Leiden: Brill, 2000. Accessed 1 March 2020. DOI: http://dx.doi.org/10.1163/1573-3912_islam_COM_1123.

Kärkkäinen, V. M. *An Introduction to the Theology of Religions*. Downers Grove: IVP Academic, 2003.

Keck, L. E. "Derivation as Destiny." In *Exploring the Gospel of John*, edited by R. A. Culpepper and C. C. Black, 274–288. Louisville: Westminster John Knox Press, 1996.

Keener, C. S. *The Gospel of John: A Commentary*. Vol. 1. Grand Rapids: Baker Academic, 2003.

Kennedy, J., and M. Valenta. "Religious Pluralism and the Dutch State: Reflections on the Future of Article 23." In *Geloven in het publieke domein. Verkenningen van een dubbele transformative*, edited by W. B. H. J. van de Donk, A. P. Jonkers, G. J. Kronjee, and R. J. J. M. Plum, 337–351. Amsterdam: Amsterdam University Press, 2006.

Kerkorde Protestantse Kerk in de Nederlands, art. I-7 (Church Order of the Protestant Church in the Netherlands).

Kierspel, L. *The Jews and the World in the Fourth Gospel*. WUNT 220, 2nd volume. Tübingen: Mohr Siebeck, 2006.

Kirk, J. A. *What Is Mission? Theological Explorations*. London: Darton Longman & Todd, 1999.

Knitter, P. *No Other Name? A Critical Survey of Christian Attitudes Toward the World Religions*. Maryknoll, NY: Orbis Books, 1985.

Koester, C. R. *Symbolism in the Fourth Gospel: Meaning, Mystery, Community*. Minneapolis: Augsburg Fortress, 1995.

Koffeman, L. J., and B. J. G. Reitsma, eds. *Vervolgnota Integriteit en Respect: Reacties en Aandachtspunten*, April 2013. Accessed 1 March 2020. https://www.protestantsekerk.nl/download1654/Vervolgnota-Integriteit-en-RespectMDO%2013-01.

Kraemer, H. *De islam als godsdienstig en als zendingsprobleem*. 's Gravenhage: Boekencentrum, 1938.

Kroneman, D. "Bijbelvertalen voor moslims: uitdaging en oplossing." In *Tussenruimte* no. 7/4 (2014): 17–21.

Krooneman, H. *Een ongemakkelijke waarheid. SGP-beleidsnotitie over geloofsvervolging vandaag*. Den Haag: SGP, 2014.

Kümmel, W. G. *Einleitung in das Neuen Testament*. Heidelberg: Quelle & Meyer, 1983.

Lewis, R. D. *When Cultures Collide: Leading Across Cultures.* Revised edition. Boston: Nicholas Brealey Publishing, 2006. Kindle.

Liddell, H. G., and R. Scott. *A Greek-English Lexicon: With a Revised Supplement.* 9th ed. Edited by H. S. Jones and R. McKenzie. BibleWorks 8. Oxford: Clarendon, 1996.

Lindars, B. *The Gospel of John.* NCB. London: Oliphants, 1972.

Lindsey, H. *The Everlasting Hatred: The Roots of Jihad.* Murrieta, CA: Oracle House, 2003.

Love, R. *Muslims, Magic and the Kingdom of God.* Pasadena: William Carey Library, 2000.

Lowry, Lindy. "Understanding the 2018 World Watch List." Open Doors, 12 January 2018. Accessed 21 January 2019. https://www.opendoorsusa.org/christian-persecution/stories/understanding-2018-world-watch-list/.

Madelung, W. "Shī'a." In *Encyclopaedia of Islam*, 2nd ed., edited by P. Bearman, Th. Bianquis, C. E. Bosworth, E. van Donzel, and W. P. Heinrichs. Leiden: Brill, 2000. Accessed 1 March 2020. DOI: http://dx.doi.org/10.1163/1573-3912_islam_SIM_6920.

Mallouhi, C. A. *Waging Peace on Islam.* London: Monarch Books, 2000.

Marrakesh Declaration: Executive Summary of the Marrakesh Declaration on the Rights of Religious Minorities in Predominantly Muslim Majority Communities. January 2016. Accessed 1 March 2020. http://www.marrakeshdeclaration.org/marrakesh-declaration.html.

Marshall, P. "Persecution of Christians in the Contemporary World." *International Bulletin of Missionary Research* 22, no. 1 (1998): 2–8.

———. *Their Blood Cries Out: The Worldwide Tragedy of Modern Christians Who Are Dying for Their Faith.* With L. Gilbert. Dallas: Word, 1997.

Massington, L., B. Radtke, W. C. Chittick, F. de Jong, L. Lewisohn, Th. Zarcone, C. Ernst, Françoise Aubin, and J. O. Hunwick. "Taṣawwuf." In *Encyclopaedia of Islam*, 2nd ed., edited by P. Bearman, Th. Bianquis, C. E. Bosworth, E. van Donzel, and W. P. Heinrichs. Leiden: Brill, 2000. Accessed 1 March 2020. DOI: http://dx.doi.org/10.1163/1573-3912_islam_COM_1188.

McAuliffe, J. D. *Qur'ānic Christians: An Analysis of Classical and Modern Exegesis.* Cambridge: Cambridge University Press, 2007.

McCarthy, M. "Spirituality in a Postmodern Era." In *The Blackwell Reader in Pastoral and Practical Theology*, edited by J. Woodward and S. Pattison, 224–233. Oxford: Wiley-Blackwell, 2000.

Meral, Z. *No Place to Call Home: Experiences of Apostates from Islam and Failures of International Community.* London: Christian Solidarity Worldwide, 2008.

Middle East Council of Churches. *What Is Western Fundamentalist Christian Zionism?* Cyprus: Working Group on Christian Zionism, 1988.

Moltmann, J. *Gott in der Schöpfung. Ökologische Schöpfungslehre.* München: Chr. Kaiser Verlag, 1987.

Morris, L. *The Gospel According to John.* NICNT. Grand Rapids: Eerdmans, 1995.

Motyer, S. *Israel in the Plan of God: Light on Today's Debate*. Leicester: Inter-Varsity Press, 1989.

Moucarry, C. *Faith to Faith: Christianity and Islam in Dialogue*. Leicester: Inter-Varsity Press, 2001.

Mulder, E., and T. Milo. *De omstreden bronnen van de islam*. Zoetermeer: Meinema, 2009.

Nasr, V. *The Shia Revival*. New York: W. W. Norton & Company, 2006.

Newbigin, L. *The Gospel in a Pluralist Society*. Grand Rapids: Eerdmans, 1989.

Nolland, J. *Luke*. Vol. 2. Word Biblical Commentary 35B. Dallas: Word, 2002.

Noordmans, O. *Verzamelde Werken*. Vol. 2. Kampen: Kok, 1979.

Notley, R. S. *The Concept of the Holy Spirit in Jewish Literature of the Second Temple Period and "Pre-Pauline" Christianity*. Jerusalem: Published by author, 1991.

Open Doors. *Open Doors Analytical*. http://www.opendoorsanalytical.org/. Password: freedom.

———. *Complete World Watch List Methodology*. World Watch Research, October 2019. http://opendoorsanalytical.org/wp-content/uploads/2019/10/Complete-WWL-methodology-October-2019-FINAL.pdf.

———. *Country Dossiers*. http://opendoorsanalytical.org/country-dossiers/.

———. *World Watch List Documentation*. http://opendoorsanalytical.org/world-watch-list-documentation/.

———. *WWL 2020. Compilation of All Main Documents*. 15 January 2020. http://opendoorsanalytical.org/wp-content/uploads/2020/01/WWL-2020-Compilation-of-main-documents.pdf.

"Open Letter to Dr Ibrahim Awwad Al-Badri, Alias 'Abu Bakr Al-Baghdadi,' and to the Fighters and Followers of the Self-Declared 'Islamic State.'" 24 Dhul-Qi'da 1435 AH/19 September 2014 CE. http://www.lettertobaghdadi.com/pdf/Booklet-Combined.pdf.

Otis, G., Jr. *The Last of the Giants: Lifting the Veil on Islam and the End Times*. Grand Rapids: Chosen Books, 1991.

Paas, S. *Pilgrims and Priests. Christian Mission in a Post-Christian Society*. Norwich: SCM Press, 2019.

Panikkar, R. *The Intra-Religious Dialogue*. New York: Paulis, 1978.

———. *The Unknown Christ of Hinduism*. Revised edition. London: Darton Longman & Todd, 1981.

Pappe, I. *The Ethnic Cleansing of Palestine*. Oxford: Oneworld, 2007.

Penner, G. M. *In the Shadow of the Cross: A Biblical Theology of Persecution*. Bartlesville: Living Sacrifice Books, 2004.

The Pew Forum on Religion and Public Life. "The Future of the Global Muslim Population: Projections for 2010–2030." Pew Research Center, 27 January 2011. Accessed 1 March 2020. https://www.pewforum.org/2011/01/27/the-future-of-the-global-muslim-population/.

———. "Mapping the Global Muslim Population: A Report on the Size and Distribution of the World's Muslim Population." Pew Research Center, 7 October 2009. Accessed 1 March 2020. https://www.pewforum.org/2009/10/07/mapping-the-global-muslim-population/.

———. "New Pew Forum Report Analyzes Religious Restrictions around the World: Three-Year Study Finds One-Third of Global Population Experiences an Increase." Pew Research Center, 9 August 2011. Accessed 1 March 2020. https://www.pewforum.org/2011/08/09/new-pew-forum-report-analyzes-religious-restrictions-around-the-world/.

———. "Trends in Global Restrictions on Religion: Overall Decline in Religious Restrictions and Hostilities Despite Continued Rise in Religion-Related Terrorism." Pew Research Center, 23 June 2016. Accessed 1 March 2020. https://www.pewforum.org/2016/06/23/trends-in-global-restrictions-on-religion/.

Philo. *De Opificio Mundi*. In *Philo*, vol. 1, translated by F. H. Colson and G. H. Whitaker. Loeb Classical Library. Cambridge: Harvard University Press, 1981.

Piper, J. *Let the Nations Be Glad: The Supremacy of God in Missions*. 3rd ed. Grand Rapids: Baker Academics, 2010.

Poorta, S. "De eerste holocaust: Verzoeningsmars in het spoor van de eerste kruistochten." In *Reformatorisch Dagblad*, 10 May 1996.

Poorthuis, B. M., and T. Salemink. *Van Harem tot Fitna. Beeldvorming over de islam in Nederland 1848–2010*. Nijmegen: Valkhof Pers, 2008.

Protestantse Kerk in Nederland. *Het Israëlisch-Palestijns conflict in de context van de Arabische wereld van het Midden-Oosten: Bijdrage tot de meningsvorming in de Protestantse Kerk in Nederland*. 11 April 2008.

Prior, D. *1 Corinthians*. The Bible Speaks Today. Downers Grove: InterVarsity Press, 1985.

Quell, G. "Alētheia (Ἀλήθεια)." In *TWNT*, vol. 1, edited by Gerhard Kittel and Gerhard Friedrich, 233–237. Stuttgart: Kohlhammer, 1932–1979.

Rabkin, Y. M. *In naam van de Thora: De geschiedenis van de antizionistische joden*. Antwerpen/Amsterdam: Houtekiet, 2006.

Ramadan, T. *Western Muslims and the Future of Islam*. Oxford: Oxford University Press, 2004.

Ravitzky, Aviezer. "Zionism and Orthodox Judaism." In *Encyclopaedia of Judaism*. Accessed 1 March 2020. DOI: http://dx.doi.org/10.1163/1872-9029_EJ_COM_0199.

Reinink, G. J. *Die Syrische Apokalypse des Pseudo-Methodius*. Corpus Scriptorum Christianorum Orientalium 541. Scriptores Syri Tomus 221. Lovanii, 1993.

Reitsma, B. J. G. "Christelijke apologetiek in de context van de islam." In *Verantwoord geloof, handboek christelijke apologetiek*, edited by H. A. Bakker, M. J. Kater, and W. van Vlastuin, 339–347. Kampen: Brevier, 2014.

———. "De kerk in de context van de islam: macht of minderheid? Over de betekenis van Joh. 18:36 voor de houding van de kerk ten opzichte van de islam." Inaugural lecture, Vrije Universiteit, Amsterdam, 2008.

———. "Divinely Approved Suicide-Terrorism? A Christian Critique of the Death of Samson." In *Strangers and Pilgrims on Earth: Essays in Honour of Abraham van de Beek*, edited by E. van der Borght and P. van Geest, 653–866. Leiden: Brill, 2012.

———. *Geest en Schepping. Een bijbels-theologische bijdrage aan de systematische doordenking van de verhouding van de Geest van God en de geschapen werkelijkheid.* Zoetermeer: Boekencentrum, 1997.

———. *The God of My Enemy. The Middle East and the Nature of God.* Oxford: Regnum Books International, 2014.

———. "Health, Wealth and Prosperity: A Biblical-Theological Reflection." In *Evangelical Theology in Transition: Essays under the Auspices of the Center of Evangelical and Reformation Theology*, edited by C. van der Kooi, E. van Staalduine-Sulman, and A. W. Zwiep, 164–181. CERT. Amsterdam: VU University Press, 2012.

———. *Integrity and Respect Islam Memorandum.* Translation of *Integriteit en respect: Islam Memorandum Protestantse Kerk*, 9 March 2011. Accessed 1 March 2020. https://www.protestantsekerk.nl/download621/Integrity-and-Respect-Islammemorandum-20110309.

———. "The Power of the Spirit: Parameters of an Ecumencial Pneumatology in the 21st Century." *Theological Review* 23, no. 1 (2002): 3–26.

———. "Strangers in the Light: The Challenges of Being a (Christian) Minority in an Islamic Context." *Journal of Reformed Theology* 2, no. 3 (2008): 211–227.

Riley, G. J. "Demon Δαίμων." In *Dictionary of Deities and Demons in the Bible Online*, edited by Karel van der Toorn, Bob Becking, and Pieter W. van der Horst. Accessed 1 March 2020. DOI: http://dx.doi.org/10.1163/2589-7802_DDDO_DDDO_Demon.

Rippin, A. *Muslims: Their Religious Beliefs and Practices.* 3rd ed. London: Routledge, 2005.

Sabra, G. F. "Two Ways of Being a Christian in the Muslim Context of the Middle East." *Islam and Christian-Muslim Relations* 17, no. 1 (2006): 43–52.

Schirrmacher, T. "Falschmeldungen zur Christenverfolgung." Accessed 1 March 2020. https://www.thomasschirrmacher.info/blog/falschmeldungen-zur-christenverfolgung/, blog 13 Dec 2014.

Schnackenburg, R. *Das Johannesevangelium.* Vol. 1. HThKNT 4.1. Freiburg: Herder, 1965.

Schrage, W. *De erste Brief an die Korinther.* EKKNT bd. 7. Solothurn, Düsseldorf: Neukirchen-Vluyn: Benziger/Neukirchener Verlag,1995.

Segers, G. J., and M. de Vries. *Wat christenen geloven en moslims niet begrijpen. Licht over leer en leven.* Zoetermeer: Boekencentrum, 2012.

Shah-Kazemi, R. "Do Muslims and Christians Believe in the Same God." In *Do We Worship the Same God? Jews, Christians and Muslims in Dialogue*, edited by M. Volf, 76–147. Grand Rapids: Eerdmans, 2012.

Shinar, P., and W. Ende. "Salafiyya." In *Encyclopaedia of Islam*, 2nd ed., edited by P. Bearman, Th. Bianquis, C. E. Bosworth, E. van Donzel, and W. P. Heinrichs. Leiden: Brill, 2000. Accessed 1 March 2020. DOI: http://dx.doi.org/10.1163/1573-3912_islam_COM_0982.

Sleeman, M. "The Origins, Development and Future of the C5/Insider Movement Debate." *St Francis Magazine* 8, no. 4 (August 2012).

Smith, D. M. *The Theology of the Gospel of John*. 5th ed. Cambridge: Cambridge University Press, 2001.

Sookhdeo, P. *Islam: The Challenge to the Church*. Pewey: Isaac Publishing, 2006.

Stackhouse, M. L. "Contextualization, Contextuality, and Contextualism." In *One Faith, Many Cultures. Inculturation, Indigenization and Contextualization*, edited by R. O. Costa, 3–13. The Boston Theological Institute Annual Series 2. Cambridge: Boston Theological Institute, 1988.

Steenbrink, K. *De Jezusverzen in de Koran*. Zoetermeer: Meinema, 2006.

Still, E. C., III. "Paul's Aims Regarding ΕΙΔΩΛΟΘΥΤΑ: A New Proposal for Interpreting 1 Corinthians 8:1–11:1." *Novum Testamentum* 44, no. 4 (2002): 343–336.

Strengholt, J. "Contextualisatie: Een trialoog die tot transformatie leidt." *Soteria* 24, no. 3 (2007): 32–42.

———. *Gospel in the Air: 50 Years of Christian Witness Through Radio in the Arab World*. Zoetermeer: Boekencentrum, 2008.

Strothmann, R., and Moktar Djebli. "Taḳiyya." In *Encyclopaedia of Islam*, 2nd ed., edited by P. Bearman, Th. Bianquis, C. E. Bosworth, E. van Donzel, and W. P. Heinrichs. Leiden: Brill, 2000. Accessed 1 March 2020. DOI: http://dx.doi.org/10.1163/1573-3912_islam_SIM_7341.

Taylor, A. *Alone with a Jihadist: A Biblical Response to Holy War*. Manchester, CT: Foghorn Publishers, 2009.

Tennent, T. C. *Invitation to World Missions: A Trinitarian Missiology for the Twenty-First Century*. Invitation to Theological Studies Series. Grand Rapids: Kregel, 2010.

Thayer, J. *A Greek-English Lexicon of the New Testament*. Abridged and Revised Thayer Lexicon. BibleWorks 8. Ontario: Online Bible Foundation, 1997.

*The Israeli-Palestinian Conflict in the Context of the Arab World of the Middle East: A Contribution to Opinion Formation in the Protestant Church in the Netherland*s. General Synod, 11 April 2008.

Thiselton, A. C. *The First Epistle to the Corinthians*. NIGTC. Grand Rapids: Eerdmans, 2000.

Tieszen, C. L. "Towards Redefining Persecution." In *Suffering, Persecution and Martyrdom: Theological Reflections*, edited by C. Sauer and R. Howell, 159–172. Religious Freedom Series 2. Johannesburg: AcadSA Publishing, 2010.

Tolan, J. V., ed. *Medieval Christian Perceptions of Islam*. New York: Routledge, 2000.

Torah Jews. "Anti-Semitism and Anti-Zionism Are Unrelated." Accessed 1 March 2020. http://www.truetorahjews.org/anti-semitism-and-anti-zionism-are-unrelated.

Towner, W. S. "Clones of God: Genesis 1:26–28 and the Image of God in the Hebrew Bible." *Interpretation* 59, no. 4 (October 2005): 341–356.

Travis, J. J. "The C1 to C6 Spectrum: A Practical Tool for Defining Six Types of Christ-Centered Communities (C) Found in the Muslim Context." *EMQ* 34, no. 4 (October 1998): 407–408.

———. "The C1–C6 Spectrum after Fifteen Years." *EMQ* 51, no. 4 (2015): 358–365.

Turner, D. "Christians, Muslims, and the Name of God: Who Owns It, and How Would We Know?" In *Do We Worship the Same God? Jews, Christians and Muslims in Dialogue*, edited by M. Volf, 18–26. Grand Rapids: Eerdmans, 2012.

United Religions Initiative. "Interfaith Mediation Centre, Kaduna." Accessed 1 March 2020. https://uri.org/who-we-are/cooperation-circle/interfaith-mediation-centre-kaduna.

Vajda, G. "Ahl al-Kitāb." In *Encyclopaedia of Islam*, 2nd ed., edited by P. Bearman, Th. Bianquis, C. E. Bosworth, E. van Donzel, and W. P. Heinrichs. Leiden: Brill, 2000. Accessed 1 March 2020. DOI: http://dx.doi.org/10.1163/1573-3912_islam_SIM_0383.

Van den Toren, B. "Interculturele theologie als driegesprek." Inaugural lecture, Protestantse Theologische Universiteit te Groningen, 11 November 2014.

Van der Poll, E. W. *Sacred Times for Chosen People: Development, Analysis and Missiological Significance of Messianic Jewish Holiday Practice*. Zoetermeer: Boekencentrum, 2008.

Van Gorder, A. C. *No God but God: A Path to Muslim-Christian Dialogue on God's Nature*. Maryknoll: Orbis Books, 2003.

Van Koningsveld, P. S. *Revisionisme en Moderne Islamitische Theologie*. Leiden: Universiteit van Leiden, 2010.

Van Wolde, E. *Terug naar het begin*. Nijmegen: Radboud Universiteit Nijmegen, 2009.

Van Wonderen, R., and W. Wagenaar. *Antisemitisme onder jongeren in Nederland: oorzaken en triggerfactoren*. With F. Hermens and T. Nijs. Utrecht: Verwey-Jonker Instituut, 2015.

———. *Nader onderzoek beelden van islamitische jongeren over zionisten en Joden*. With A. Stremmelaar. Utrecht: Verwey-Jonker Instituut i.s.m. Anne Frank Stichting, 2015.

Verkuyl, J. J. *Inleiding in de nieuwere zendingswetenschap*. Kampen: Kok, 1975.

———. *Met moslims in gesprek over het Evangelie*. Kampen: Kok, 1994.

———. *Zijn alle godsiensten gelijk*. Kampen: Kok, 1964.

"Voices of Dialogue: Co-founders of Nigeria's Interfaith Mediation Centre Share Their Story from Conflict and Violence to Reconciliation and Dialogue." Accessed 1

March 2020. https://www.kaiciid.org/news-events/news/voices-dialogue-co-founders-nigerias-interfaith-mediation-centre-share-their-story.

Volf, M. *Exclusion and Embrace: A Theological Exploration of Identity, Otherness, and Reconciliation*. Nashville: Abingdon Press, 1996.

Volkskrant. "Wilders: Schrap artikel 1 van de Grondwet," 21 March 2006. Accessed 1 March 2020. http://www.volkskrant.nl/binnenland/wilders-schrap-artikel-1-van-de-grondwet~a814600/.

Vriezen, T. C. *Hoofdlijnen der theologie van het Oude Testament*. Wageningen: Veenman en Zn, 1987.

Wansink, H. "Fortuyns Kruistocht." In *De Volkskrant*, 22 December 2001. Accessed 1 March 2020. https://www.volkskrant.nl/nieuws-achtergrond/fortuyns-kruistocht~bbea6496/.

Waardenburg, J., ed. *Islam. Norm, ideaal en werkelijkheid*. Houten: Fibula, 2000.

WEA Global Review Panel. *Report to World Evangelical Alliance for Conveyance to Wycliffe and SIL International*. 15 April 2013 (finalized 26 April 2013). http://www.worldevangelicals.org/resources/rfiles/res3_697_link_1368968559.pdf.

Wengst, K. *Das Johannesevangelium*. Vol. 1. THKNT. Stuttgart: Kohlhammer, 2000.

Wenham, G. J. *Genesis 1–5*. Word Biblical Commentary 1. Dallas: Word Books, 2002. CD-ROM.

Wessels, A. *De moslimse naaste. Op weg naar een theologie van de islam*. Kampen: Kok, 1978.

———. *Thora, Evangelie en Koran: 3 boeken, 2 steden, 1 verhaal*. Kampen: Kok, 2010.

Westermann, C. *Genesis*. Bd I/1, BKAT. Neukirchen-Vluyn: Neukirchener Verlag, 1976.

Wever, R. de. "Christenvervolging. Wordt de christen echt vaker vervolgd?" Robin de Wever. http://www.robindewever.nl/w/christenvervolging-wordt-de-christen-echt-vaker-vervolgd/.

"What Is Apologetics?" Bible.org. Accessed 1 March 2020. https://bible.org/seriespage/2-what-apologetics#P24_7780.

Wildberger, H. "מֵאֵן, *'mn*." In *THAT*, vol. 1, edited by Ernst Jenni with assistance from Claus Westermann, 202–209. Munich: Chr. Kaiser Verlag; Zürich: Theologischer Verlag, 1971–1976.

Willis, W. "1 Corinthians 8–10: A Retrospective after Twenty-Five Years." *Restoration Quarterly* (2007): 103–112.

Witherington, B., III. *Conflict and Community in Corinth: Socio-Rhetorical Commentary on 1 and 2 Corinthians*. Grand Rapids: Eerdmans, 1995. Kindle.

Woodberry, J. D. "To the Muslim I Became a Muslim? The Jerusalem Council Applied." *International Journal of Frontier Missiology* 24, no. 1 (2007): 23–28.

Wright, C. J. H. *The Mission of God's People: A Biblical Theology of the Church's Mission*. Grand Rapids: Zondervan, 2010.

Wright, N. T. *The Climax of the Covenant: Christ and the Law in Pauline Theology*. London: T&T Clark, 1991.

————. *Jesus and the Victory of God.* Christian Origins and the Question of God 2. London: SPCK, 1996.

————. "Jesus, Israel, and the Cross." Lecture, C. S. Lewis Institute Seminar, "Finding and Following the True Jesus," 2002.

————. *Justification: God's Plan and Paul's Vision.* London: SPCK, 2009.

————. *The New Testament and the People of God.* Christian Origins and the Question of God 1. London: SPCK, 1996.

————. "The New Testament and the 'State.'" *Themelios* 16, no. 1 (1990): 11–17.

————. "One God, One Lord, One People. Incarnational Christology for a Church in a Pagan Environment." *Ex Auditu* (1991): 45–56.

————. *Paul and the Faithfulness of God.* Christian Origins and the Question of God. London: SPCK, 2013.

————. *Paul for Everyone: 1 Corinthians.* London: SPCK, 2004.

Zebiri, K. *Muslims and Christians Face to Face.* 2nd ed. Oxford: One World, 2003.

Index

NEW TESTAMENT

APOCRYPHA

QUR'AN

 **Langham** PARTNERSHIP

Langham Literature and its imprints are a ministry of Langham Partnership.

Langham Partnership is a global fellowship working in pursuit of the vision God entrusted to its founder John Stott –

> *to facilitate the growth of the church in maturity and Christ-likeness through raising the standards of biblical preaching and teaching.*

Our vision is to see churches in the Majority World equipped for mission and growing to maturity in Christ through the ministry of pastors and leaders who believe, teach and live by the word of God.

Our mission is to strengthen the ministry of the word of God through:
- nurturing national movements for biblical preaching
- fostering the creation and distribution of evangelical literature
- enhancing evangelical theological education

especially in countries where churches are under-resourced.

Our ministry

Langham Preaching partners with national leaders to nurture indigenous biblical preaching movements for pastors and lay preachers all around the world. With the support of a team of trainers from many countries, a multi-level programme of seminars provides practical training, and is followed by a programme for training local facilitators. Local preachers' groups and national and regional networks ensure continuity and ongoing development, seeking to build vigorous movements committed to Bible exposition.

Langham Literature provides Majority World preachers, scholars and seminary libraries with evangelical books and electronic resources through publishing and distribution, grants and discounts. The programme also fosters the creation of indigenous evangelical books in many languages, through writer's grants, strengthening local evangelical publishing houses, and investment in major regional literature projects, such as one volume Bible commentaries like *The Africa Bible Commentary* and *The South Asia Bible Commentary*.

Langham Scholars provides financial support for evangelical doctoral students from the Majority World so that, when they return home, they may train pastors and other Christian leaders with sound, biblical and theological teaching. This programme equips those who equip others. Langham Scholars also works in partnership with Majority World seminaries in strengthening evangelical theological education. A growing number of Langham Scholars study in high quality doctoral programmes in the Majority World itself. As well as teaching the next generation of pastors, graduated Langham Scholars exercise significant influence through their writing and leadership.

To learn more about Langham Partnership and the work we do visit **langham.org**

Lightning Source UK Ltd.
Milton Keynes UK
UKHW020652091020
371292UK00007B/378